# A LIFE DIVIDED

## A PSYCHOLOGIST'S MEMOIR
## ABOUT
## THE DOUBLE LIFE
## AND MURDER OF HER HUSBAND –
## AND HER ROAD TO RECOVERY

JAN CANTY, PH.D.

*There are things known and things unknown
and in between are the doors of perception.*

——*Aldous Huxley*

# TABLE OF CONTENTS

PART ONE: The Scandal

1.  **Tipping Point**: Bad news from Inspector Gil Hill, DPD, Homicide Division .......................................... 29
2.  **Launched**: First impressions of my work setting and future husband ........................................ 37
3.  **Outbreak**: History of John Carl "Lucky" Fry ........ 45
4.  **What's Age Got to Do With It?**: Marriage and in-laws ........................................................ 54
5.  **The Dawn of Dawn**: History of Dawn Marie Spens ........................................................ 62
6.  **Terms of Engagement**: Glimpses of trouble ahead. ........................................................ 69
7.  **The Newest in the Oldest Profession**: Spens turns to prostitution. ........................................ 80
8.  **Strange Bedfellows**: Al hooks up with Spens ....... 96
9.  **Desert Slumber**: Mono recuperation in Arizona 104
10. **What Might Have Been**: Miscarriage .................. 111
11. **Snow Job:** Fry and Spens travel south; brother commits suicide ........................................ 118
12. **Lies, Good-Byes and Alibis**: Spens and Fry attract law enforcement ........................................ 123
13. **Incantations, Secrets and Shoes**: Al's psychotic break and hospitalization .......................... 135
14. **Discharged, Recharged**: Al's hospitalization discharge raises tension ................................ 149
15. **Reaching for the Bottom**: Al's deeper involvement brings friction ........................................ 162
16. **I'll Huff and I'll Puff and I'll Break Into Your House**: Warning signs .............................. 172
17. **Farewell**: Al is missing ................................ 182
18. **Bloodbath**: Al's homicide ............................ 186

19. **Standing By:** Waiting in vain for Al to return home
.................................................................................. 195
20. **Disaster Control:** Fry and Spens flee Detroit ...... 207
21. **Circling the Wagons:** Monitoring the news, making a safety plan.......................................................... 218

PART TWO: The Domino Effect
22. **The Me Before:** My backstory ............................. 226
23. **Street Cleaning:** Fry and Spens arrested ............. 236
24. **The Tomb:** Escorted to the morgue ..................... 249
25. **The Buzz:** The media circus begins ..................... 260
26. **Busted Play:** Fry and Spens meet Inspector Gil Hill and his detectives................................................... 265
27. **The Memorial Circus:** Al's funeral becomes a media circus........................................................... 270
28. **Taking a Stand:** My appearance at the Preliminary Examination..................................................... 279
29. **Untangling the Web:** Excerpt from evidentiary hearing............................................................... 284
30. **The Mourning After:** Al's formal burial ............. 289
31. **Boil Down:** Pause after preliminary exam; transitioning to being alone................................ 291
32. **Facing Facts:** Finally facing what the media spewed
.................................................................................. 299
33. **Life Downstream:** Fear of AIDS........................ 307
34. **The Beautiful Prison:** The first winter alone ...... 312
35. **Exit Strategies:** Fry's attempted jail break .......... 323
36. **Waiting for Truth:** Nightmares, questions and ruminations persist............................................... 326
37. **From the Frying Pan to the Fire:** Fry's jury trial. 328
38. **Darkness Greets Dawn:** Spens' bench trial........ 341
39. **Judgment Day:** Guilty as charged – now for the penalties ........................................................... 349
40. **No Daybreak:** The long winter with financial woes, anger, insomnia.................................................. 354
41. **Boomerang:** Contact from Cauffiel who wants to write a book ...................................................... 360

42. **Unlatched**: Cauffiel fills in the blanks ............ 365
43. **Al's Rearview**: Delayed understanding of Al's background ............................................. 372

PART THREE: Recovery
44. **Connecting the Dots**: Psychological autopsy of what happened ...................................... 382
45. **Red Zone**: Getting my rhythm back .................... 392
46. **Lights! Action! Camera!** Fry interviewed while in solitaire confinement .............................. 410
47. **Crossroads**: Leaving home for good .................... 417
48. **Renewal**: Adoption and re-connecting with Detroit ........................................................ 432
49. **Resuscitation**: Life – rediscovered ...................... 436
50. **Appendix**: Where are the people in this book today? ........................................................ 441
51. **Epilogue**: Life Delivers a One-Two Punch .......... 445

# ENDORSEMENTS

- **Mark Bando**, Retired Detroit Police Officer, author of several military history books including *101st Airborne: The Screaming Eagles at Normandy* (MBI Pub, 2001), *101st Airborne: The Screaming Eagles in WWII* (Zenith Press, 2009), *Avenging Eagles: Forbidden Tales of the 101st Airborne Division WWII* (Motorbooks, 1994)

  *"Highly knowledgeable, fascinating and difficult to stop reading. Dr. Canty is a bona fide in her field of expertise."*

- **Lowell Cauffiel** a Detroit-born American true crime author, screenwriter, television producer and musician. He initially wrote for *Rolling Stone, Creem* and *Guitar Player*. His books have been on the New York Times bestseller list. His screenwriting included projects with Billy Crystal, David Schwimmer, Michael Medavoy (TriStar Pictures), Keifer Sutherland, Kathryn Morris, and Michael Douglas, among others. His non-fiction publications include *Masquerade; a true story of seduction, compulsion, and murder* (Doubleday, 1988), *Forever and Five Days* (Kensington Pub, 1992), *The Bobbitt Case – You Decide* (under pseudonym Peter Kane) (Pinnacle Books, 1992), *Eye of the beholder* (Kensington Publishers, 1994), *House of Secrets* (Kensington Publishers, 1998). Cauffiel's novels include *Dark Rage* (Kensington Publishers, 1997), *Marker* (St. Martin's Press, 1997) and *Toss* with **Boomer Esiason** (Dutton Press, 1998). Also, he made a directing debut with *Primary Purpose, Men in A Box* starring Kurtwood Smith.

*"A stunning look at the internal life of someone who was victimized by a crime. It is extremely well written and offers insights from a victim and trained psychologist. Compelling."*

- <u>Darren Drake</u>, D-AMDI, CI, CCI, accredited medicolegal death investigator and ACFEI certified criminal investigator of 30 years. He is an educator, conference speaker, and a podcast-media producer. He has a self-published book entitled *Autoerotic Fatalities: An Investigator's Guidebook (2015)* and a paper for professionals in law enforcement entitled *Interview and Interrogation – Getting Information You Want.*

  *"Very interesting story. Offers rare insights from the perspective of a victim which is useful for first responders and death investigators."*

- <u>Bruce Eather</u>, Ph.D. licensed psychologist in Washington State who is in independent practice in Tacoma, Washington and a consultant to the Federal Government/SSA.

  *"Psychiatrists and psychologists are often called upon to perform a 'psychological autopsy' on individuals whose behavior is puzzling. Dr. Canty is in the unique, dual position as the spouse of the subject as well as a psychologist. She explains her husband's behavior, and that of his accomplices, masterfully and takes the reader on her painful yet ultimately enlightening and empowering personal journey. It is a page turner."*

- <u>George Hunter</u> Detroit News crime reporter of twenty years. He is a published author of *The Sadist the Hitman and the Murder of Jane Bashara* (McFarland Press, 2016) and *Limb from Limb* (Kensington Publishing/Pinnacle true Crime, 2015). His national television appearances include CNN's Nancy Grace, Fox News' Greta Van Susteren, and MSNBC News.

*"As a longtime Detroit News crime reporter, I've seen the devastation of a high-profile tragedy can cause, long after the media has moved on. The 1985 murder of Dr. Alan Canty made headlines but all crime stories, no matter how big, eventually fade away. For survivors, the pain never leaves. After years of silence Dr. Jan Canty is telling her story and gives insight into the whirlwind she was suddenly thrown into..."*

- <u>Steve Miller</u> Michigan born journalist and true crime author whose books include: *Murder in Grosse Pointe Park: Privilege, Adultery and the Killing of Jane Bashara* (Penguin/Berkley, 2015), *Juggalo: Insane Clown Posse, Their Fans, and the World They Made* (DaCapo Press, 2016), *Detroit Rock City: The Uncensored History of Rock 'n Roll in America's Loudest City* (DaCapo Press, 2016), *Nobody's Women: The Crimes and Victims of Anthony Sowell, the Cleveland Serial Killer* (Penguin Books, 2013), co-author of *A Slaying in the Suburbs: The Tara Grant Murder* (Berkley Books, 2008) and *Girl Wanted: The Chase for Sarah Pender (Berkley Press, 2011)* which earned his place as an Edgar Award finalist.. The <u>New York Times</u> nominated him for a Pulitzer Prize in 2001.

*"Even in the murder capital of the world, Detroiters were jarred by the macabre killing and dismemberment of esteemed psychologist Alan Canty...a deep, dark true crime memoir with gripping humanity and insights that only a survivor can provide."*

- <u>Marie Osborne</u> reporter and anchor for WJR Radio

Detroit and has been named one of the most influential women in Detroit radio for her local and international stories. She is a three-time winner of the national Edward R. Murrow award and Headliner Award. Michigan Association of Broadcasters and Associated Press have honored her multiple times.

*"An incredible story that will have people riveted."*

• <u>Kathy Ryan</u> journalist with a long career writing for the Grosse Pointe News, Michigan. She has recently added stand-up comedy to her resume.

*"The murder of Alan Canty...was the lead story for weeks in newspapers and on television. His widow, Jan Canty, was as much a victim of her husband's duplicity as he was. After 30 years she comes out of the shadows to write about her life with Alan that began with love and devotion that spiraled into lies and betrayal. Jan tells the story of a survivor, a story few can tell."*

• <u>Jonathan Stanley</u> Detroit-born actor, screenwriter, and producer who was in a supporting role to Robert DeNiro in *Stone,* performed in a lead role in *Misled* with Matt Lockwood (also Detroit-born), as a lead in *This Narrow Place,* in the TV series *From G's to Gents* (as "Stan"), as an FBI agent in *Last Man Standing, Batman v Superman: Dawn of Justice* (as a Silo Officer), directed *Badges* (for which he won an award), and has several TV episodes in post-production or active filming.

*"Jan Canty's memoir about surviving a highly publicized, grisly murder of her spouse is one of the most moving non-fictional pieces I have ever read. I was pulled in and moved...could not put it down from the minute I began reading.*

*Cathartic and thrilling, this is a must read!"*

- <u>Lt. Doug Topolski</u>, Retired Dearborn Police Lieutenant, Dearborn, MI

*"Insightful, detailed, frank account of a double life, inevitable murder and the author's journey to recover from multi-faceted betrayal and most grisly homicide (even by Detroit standards). What makes her book unique are her insights as a psychologist into what was more bizarre than the other side of Alice's looking glass. The backdrop for her memoir is the notorious Cass Corridor of the 1970s -1980s intermixed with affluent Grosse Pointe Park."*

# FOREWARD

The first time I saw Jan Canty she was barely able to speak, let alone write a book.

Her appearance came only days after stunning headlines about her husband, Dr. Alan Canty, had sprawled across Detroit's morning and evening newspapers:

PSYCHOLOGIST DISAPPEARS

POLICE THINK THEY HAVE CANTY'S BODY

BODY PARTS FOUND ON I-75

TORSO FOUND MAY BE PSYCHOLOGIST

At the time I was writing for the *Detroit News Sunday Magazine.* I also was searching for the perfect story to turn into my first true crime book, a genre which was exploding in popularity in the early 1980s. As details emerged, it became clear that the murdered psychologist, had met his demise while living a double life. In Detroit's prestigious Fisher Building he was Dr. Canty, an effective Grosse Pointe psychotherapist with an upscale clientele culled from the self-improvement fervor of the Me Decade. But for more than a year in the drug-and-prostitute-ridden streets of Detroit's Cass Corridor, Al went by Dr. Al Miller, M.D., a false persona created to enable a long relationship with a young, heroin-addicted street hooker.

In Dr. Canty's murder I knew I had found my story -- a real life hybrid of *Pygmalion* and *The Strange Case of Dr. Jekyll and Mr. Hyde.* What I didn't realize at the time was a much deeper tale would need to be told, one of determination and survival in the face of potential life-crushing betrayal.

That narrative would emerge from Jan. My first sighting of her came at the preliminary examination of the prostitute and pimp who were charged with murder and dismemberment of her husband. We, a dozen reporters and trial artists, were jammed into the jury box, waiting for the first witness, when the main door of the courtroom swung open and she marched to the stand. Her testimony was brief and mostly one-word answers. Yes, she knew the murder victim. They were married eleven years. The last she heard from him he was on his way home from the office. No, she hadn't given anybody permission to dissect his body.

That was it. And she was gone, leaving us with only a brief glimpse of yet another living victim so common in homicides. Not the victim who dies. But the one who must live on engulfed in tragedy and loss.

After securing a book contract with Doubleday I knew much work lay ahead. There were dozens of people connected to the sordid story to interview, including the killer and prostitute, and several-thousand pages of police reports, trial transcripts and other documents to study. I trusted only primary sources. I didn't rely on daily TV and newspaper stories. Not only can they contain inaccuracies, they often lack context and miss the bigger picture.

I instinctively knew from that first day in court the most important interview to secure was Jan Canty. She was young, attractive and also a practicing psychologist and marriage counselor. Yet, she had been caught totally unaware of her husband's double life until she was informed of it by homicide detectives.

My first attempt to talk to Jan was a complete

disaster. Though she had not been interviewed by anyone, I suspected the local news media had traumatized her. In fact, later she would reveal that when she emerged from the morgue after identifying her husband's body parts she thought the news cameras mounted on tripods outside looked like machine guns.

I typically presented myself as a writer with empathy and no interest in sensationalism. But, flush with the knowledge of how a hardcover book can change a writer's life, I simply blew it on my introductory phone call. When Jan said she wasn't interested in being interviewed, I said, "But Dr. Canty, this is the most important project of my life."

"Your life?" she said, appalled. "Do you have any idea what has become of mine?"

She was dead on. And she hung up.

I spent the next six months investigating the other aspects of the murder case, hoping time would heal the impact of my insensitivity on that first phone call. I also wrote an in-depth magazine piece on the case. Though it would be read by more than a half million people, I was only interested in one reader: Jan. I was hoping she would see that my approach was in-depth, sensitive and nothing like the early news coverage.

I remember trembling when I finally called her to make another attempt at an interview. I was somewhat surprised when she agreed, but only to one session. Our first interview in her Fisher Building office was supposed to last only an hour.

We would talk much longer than that.

Thirty minutes into the appointment, we were experiencing a role reversal. Rather than me asking the questions, she was posing them. She knew her husband had betrayed their marriage. But she had no idea of the extent of his duplicity and his activities in the Cass Corridor. After months of research, I had some of the answers. Her hand repeatedly reached for a box of tissues as tears flowed and the conversation transitioned from Al to the trauma she was still experiencing.

When it was over she said, "I feel like I've been the patient here."

That intense meeting was the beginning of a long collaboration and ultimately a wonderful friendship. We met weekly for months. She revealed details about her life with Al, how he'd managed to deceive her. Often to her dismay, I revealed new material I learned about Al, not only from his actions in the Corridor, but his life before their marriage as well.

At one point she said, "You've come to know Al better than I ever did. You never even met him. And I lived with the man."

As our discussions continued, I sensed Jan was beginning the process of healing herself. And for me, learning about the horrible impact of dishonesty on loved ones became a cautionary tale that imparted lessons that remain with me today.

By the time I began writing *Masquerade: A True Story of Seduction, Compulsion and Murder,* Jan Canty was transforming from victim to victor -- not only as a character in my book, but as an example of the human spirit's resilience and ability to overcome incredible adversity.

You will get glimpses of that in *Masquerade.*

However, in reading her memoir *A Life Divided,* it's

clear that I was only scratching the surface. In *A Life Divided* Jan has written a story of survival and enlightenment propelled forward by the psychological machinations of loss, betrayal and trauma. Jan brings not only her skills as a psychologist, her writing benefits from the insights that only time and reflection can bring. She digs deep. Most importantly, she has the courage to bare her soul without fear of embarrassment or humiliation. The result is a work of rigorous self-honesty and renewal.

Jan's revelations in her memoir present a stunning contrast to the trauma she experienced testifying that day in a Detroit courtroom. And there's a lesson there for survivors of homicides, for the family members and loved ones of the deceased. **There is a recovery available for those who choose to seek it.**

*A Life Divided* has the quality many accomplished authors strive for but often find difficult to achieve. It's called *heart*.

With Jan Canty, it's the heart of a hero.

— Lowell Cauffiel
April 2020

# PREFACE

When I made the tentative decision to leave my redacted life and set pen to paper, the book you hold in your hands was intended to be a straightforward memoir - the personal story behind the murder of my spouse. But, like a kite on a string, the writing periodically pulled me where <u>it</u> wanted to go. Although the project was never free of its tether, I yielded to the flow from time to time.

I see now that the first direction it tugged me toward was to my admittedly subjective and brief account of the history of the Cass Corridor of Detroit. Most of the true-life events described in the following pages unraveled there. It was an area I knew well. I'd been born nearby and moved back in 1971 to attend college and reside in the northern edge of the Corridor. I rented a three-story efficiency walk-up built in 1928 which cost $85 a month (a week's wages). I was 21. My grandparents' familiar boarding house was only a mile away. My apartment building has since been torn down to make way for the New Center Building.

But as Detroit withered, so did the Corridor. It had been on the decline for a while. One of the most popular bars, Old Miami, was next to a machine shop where prostitutes turned tricks on mattresses laid out on the floor back in the late 1960s. Rents in the area were then $25 a month. The only two grocery stores were torched and never rebuilt. Trash piled up. At one time the city shut off power due to "scrapping" (stealing of copper wires) and all the streetlights went out.

When I took up residence there I placed my mattress on the floor away from the large windows for safety. It was not unusual to overhear automatic weapons throughout the night. Nightfall also brought more rats and loitering. The number of official (known) homicides inched upwards during the time I lived there from 550 to 693 per year.* The number of missing was impossible to tally. You will hear from Detroit Police Officer Mark Bando in future chapters describe the many challenges law enforcement faced in solving homicides, not the least of which was the sheer number of them.

During my attendance at nearby Wayne State University I'd tiptoe around unconscious men in stairwells and sometimes sat near drifters in darkened lecture halls who sought refuge from bitter winters. The 297 blue light emergency phones (which connected directly to police on campus simply by picking up the receiver) were installed to reduce campus rapes, arson, stalking and thefts. The downtown area also had the highest pedestrian-vehicle fatality rate in the country. The only thriving businesses were drug sales and prostitution. At the time of my husband's murder, there were about 1300 prostitutes working the Corridor day and night; some as young as twelve. Gangs proliferated. Businesses withered, finally closed, were boarded up and set afire.

But the Corridor had its own celebrities and flavor. Jim Chatelain, Brenda Goodman, Robert Sestok, Nancy Mitchnick, Michael Luchs and Gordon Newton were budding local artists. Bud Spangler, Wendell Harrison were notable musicians along with poet and songstress Jonie Mitchell who wrote "Both Sides Now" while living in "The Verona" early in her career. She described the area as "internally decaying." Gilda Radner and Janis Joplin also called it home at one time. Hitsville USA (nearby but not on Cass Avenue) produced a string of 110 top hits between 1961-1971 for Motown, including the likes of the Supremes, the Four Tops, Jackson 5 and other artists on competing labels. There was Indian Joe, Femm Noir, One-Armed Bob Bagley, Mr. Universe, Limey Dave, Pat "The Rat" Halley and Electric Louie added a flourish and uniqueness found nowhere else on earth. (To get an idea of what it was like and see some of the structures mentioned in this book, take a peek at the series *Low Winter Sun* that was filmed there. Many of the structures have since been torn down.)

Today the Corridor is known as "Midtown" to disentangle it from its colorful past. It's been gentrified and sanitized with an unusual mix of stylish wrought iron fences and functional cyclone ones. Rents have skyrocketed. Crime has declined. I hardly recognize the place that offered a chance to earn a graduate degree and work anywhere around the world as well as a toxin called "mixed jive" which was readily available in darkened alleys and bars by people you'd likely cross the street to avoid. The Cass Corridor had something for everyone.

The second trajectory this writing project pulled me toward was another 'then versus now' having to do with the experience of so-called "homicide survivors." In a nutshell, before WWII the person bringing legal charges against someone usually served as their own attorney. But the criminal justice system matured and in time the plaintiff's presence in the courtroom was viewed as redundant, since the prosecutor was a stand-in for the accuser. By the 1950's it was even frowned upon to have plaintiffs in the courtroom in criminal cases. No one wanted to deal with the tearful mother, the frightened wife, angry husband or forlorn child sitting near the jury box or weeping in open court. Journalists had more rights in the courtroom than the family of the deceased.

Back in 1985, when much of this book takes place, formal support for homicide survivors was unknown inside (and outside) of courtrooms. I'm speaking specifically of victim advocates, victim impact statements, notice of hearings, participation in probation hearings and freedom from victimization from the defendant's family. We were an afterthought at best, an inconvenience at worst. The prevailing sentiment was that our presence threatened the rights of the accused. (Some still hold this opinion today.) Consequently, the accused took center stage while eschewing homicide survivors to the shadows. This is reflected in books, movies, podcasts, academic research and television to this day. Not only is the public led to believe that the verdict or memorial service signals the end of the story, but it's as if the deceased lived in a vacuum. The parents and spouses and children of the deceased remain remote - rarely heard or seen, let alone their grief journey understood. How much do we know about Fred Goldman's reactions to the murder of his son, Ron Goldman, who was stabbed to death outside Nichole Brown's Brentwood California home over 26 years ago? Or Cindy Anthony, grandmother of Caylee Anthony who reported her granddaughter missing to the police in 2008? What has been the fallout on the homicide survivors connected with Sandy Hook eight years ago, or the repercussions on the family of Travis Alexander who was murdered by Jodi Arias?

If you're like most people you draw a blank. Hence this book (and my podcast, *Domino Effect of Murder*). Both aim to provide the real-life repercussions of violent death that can only be told by someone who has traveled the path. The secret known to every homicide survivor is that the narrative doesn't end after a conviction or burial. In many ways that is where it starts.

So, what began as a personal history became intertwined with the record of the Corridor and the Homicide Survivor movement. But, it's no surprise that we are made by history.

*source: https://www.clickondetroit.com/features/2017/02/22/from-the-vault-1975-special-on-murder-in-detroit/

# ACKNOWLEDGEMENTS

*Cover design 2020 by Fjmoraga, fiverr*

*Illustrations 2020 by my twin, Jeanne*

*Formatting 2020 by Chelly Peeler, Inkitout*

*Author photography 2019 by Sabrina Joella*

*Special thanks to (in no particular order)* Mark Bando, Marlanna Landeros, Barbara Smeenge Mckay, Heather Campese, Paula Gerstman, Ray Danford, Jr., Darren Drake, Jim Saros, Rachel Caudill, Rick Breitenbecher, Cheryl Naborczyk McCarty, Sara Harvey Newell, Vickie Lynn Pace, Jayne Taormina, L. Marie Cook, Kathy Ryan, Dawn Evoe-Danowski, Ann Gilpin, Robert Majkowski, Bruce Eather, Ph.D., Linda Violet, Thom Seling, Doug Topolski, Shelby Leigh Toner, Marie Osborne, Alejandra Stamper, Edward Kowalczyk, Donna Conway, Vickie Evans Fuller, Jon White, Alastaire Monopoly, Lisa Black, Kay Sanborn, Laura Nicole Barlow, Sheree Martin, Julie Kiori, Tayna Jewell, my family and my faithful mascot, Gretta, who slept by my side patiently–more or less–through the numerous late-night edits.

# PART ONE

# THE SCANDAL

# PROLOGUE

Fog slowed my progression and wrapped my car in murkiness on an evening I needed to be home on time. The premature darkness that bound itself with foul weather deepened as I passed a mom-and-pop charter boat business that looked like it had no business.

One more mile.

Triangular patches of streetlight glow guided me, but only on my left. To my right was a rusty breakwater containing Fox Creek Canal. Atop the metal barrier was a forlorn, long chain-link fence, which served as an unofficial "keep out!" message to Detroiters who wished to enter "The Pointes." That was one of the quirks of Wayne County, Michigan — its patchwork of historically affluent mini-mansions and majestic buildings, which shared uneasy borders with burned-out storefronts, rentals, foreclosures and residents who lived paycheck to paycheck. To say it was a line of disunity, of controversy, minimized the uneasy truce between these islands of inequity.

Even though this was a shortcut, it was foolish to choose Alter Road on a night like this. I knew better. Fox Creek Canal, south of Jefferson Avenue, was eerily quiet on the best of nights. It always seemed cryptic, which may have been one reason it served as a primary entry for booze from Canada during prohibition. The barely-two-lane road without shoulders gave off a claustrophobic tension, especially when bordered by the rolling grey mist.

Rain dotted my windshield. I turned off the radio to

reduce distractions, yet a creepy sensation in my neck redirected my attention to my rearview. A quick check confirmed my fears. I had company. Headlights too close, too determined to be nothing. The pursuer mirrored my speed changes. For the next two blocks, I tried in vain to glimpse details of the vehicle and driver.

My side street appeared, and I hastily turned left onto Essex, hoping to prove myself wrong. Who was behind me? What did they want? There was a dip near the bend in the road ahead and I hoped, when combined with the night haze, it would conceal my taillights long enough to lose him.

I nearly careened off Essex onto our brick driveway, making another sharp left onto the lawn, and took cover behind our tall, thick hedge. The ignition was extinguished. I waited. Listened. Watched. The night silence contrasted with the tambourine in my chest.

My husband, Al, was late getting home, again.

I remained motionless for what felt like an eternity and watched the dreamy mist drift slowly over silhouetted streetlights. I resisted the temptation to dash into the house as I didn't want the dome light to signal my location.

The same headlights emerged through the gloom. It was an old car with at least two occupants that paused at each driveway, clearly looking for someone. Their rough muffler confirmed it was the same vehicle. I was glad my car did not have much reflective chrome. They glided by slowly, presumably without seeing me. The glow of their red taillights soon faded. The mist swallowed the threat.

I exhaled.

This wasn't the first unnerving event in recent weeks. There had been drunk dials around midnight in the past two weeks by a man who asked for some woman. He spoke in a slow, southern accent, refusing to give his name. His words were slurred, his mood irritated. His breathing audible, as if half-awake. Why did he call repeatedly? Then there was the stranger out front who stopped to ask, "Is this where Dr. Alan Canty lives?" while I was gardening a few days earlier. The driver seemed friendly enough. And the last thing I recalled was finding three dry cigarette butts under our kitchen window after days of rain. Whose were they? When these experiences were viewed as one it appeared something ominous, something far-reaching was coming. Al, on the other hand, was dismissive of these worries, which only compounded mine.

# ONE

# TIPPING POINT

I'd been summoned to the Detroit Police Headquarters by Inspector Gil Hill early Sunday. My parents and I arrived at 1300 Beaubien and were greeted by Detective Marylss Landeros. We rode the jarring, dimly-lit elevator in silence, as most strangers do. She knew the drill, the customs of the police department, the locations in this foreign landscape, the dark language of death. She understood the criminal justice system, the point people, the "way things were done." Moreover, Landeros paced her questions and knew when to stop talking altogether. For this and other abilities, she easily generated my trust and cooperation.

We exchanged minimal interaction while moving down a long, starkly-lit hall, where voices and footsteps echoed, to a dark wood door with an old window and thick, hand-painted block letters on it that spelled a word I dared not speak. We halted. The warm hallway smelled of body odor, bleach, and oldness. Tall windows emitted razor-sharp light, adding to the harshness of that unwelcoming space.

The four of us entered and sat on a wooden bench that looked as worn out as us, then faced an office concealed behind rippled glass. Booms of profanity from an irritated male voice inside were overheard while a silhouette slammed the phone. It ramped up our collective tension. I sat closer to Dad. We wanted to be anywhere but there. Notices of wanted criminals on a large bulletin board created rows of menacing onlookers. They glared at us defiantly. Below them, equally disturbing, were photos of missing children, some of whom had been long gone. How had we descended into such depravity?

The unadorned entry abruptly opened and Detective Landeros stood to usher me in. That was no ordinary Sunday. Each person who crossed the worn perimeter left their "me before" outside and emerged the "me after." It was a tipping point, a razor wire, a fault line. There was no in-between. No do-overs, no second takes.

Inspector Gil Hill waited behind his obsolete, no-nonsense wood desk that rested at an imposing angle in front of the three linemen who'd interviewed me earlier in the week. Mismatched, five-drawer file cabinets lined the opposite wall, no doubt housing a catalog of horror. The men stood stiffly with backs against the tall partition, broad shoulders nearly touching. *Did they ever sit down?*

One man spoke. "You might remember me. I'm Detective Bernard Brantley." He was observant, a bit unsettled and reserved.

Inspector Hill motioned for me to sit while he briefly stood with hands on hips.

Hill had a renegade tuft of grey hair near his right temple that contrasted with the rest of his thick, black, coiled hair. Somehow, his razor-thin mustache remained curiously still when he spoke. His fingers were long and steady. The deep grooves of his broad forehead were etched by years of misery. One particularly deep line spanned the bridge of his nose, adding intensity to his gaze. Hill's tenor voice clipped his words, which he used sparingly.

Gil Hill, born in 1931, hailed from Birmingham, Alabama and was raised by a devoted mother without a silver spoon or child support. He longed to attend Howard University. Thurgood Marshall inspired him. So did Joe Louis. He faced "Whites Only" signs literally and figuratively. Hill enlisted in the Air Force in 1950, to become a pilot and was stationed at Detroit's Selfridge Air Force Base. After passing the aviation test, he was denied because he "didn't have enough teeth." He channeled the inequity into grit and wit and joined the Detroit Police Department in 1959 when there were no people of color in positions of authority. The precinct urinal's sign proclaimed, "NAACP Blood Bank." He never forgot it. Along the way, Hill honed a reputation for being streetwise, foul-mouthed and getting suspects to talk. Five years before, he consulted with the Atlanta Police Department where he helped solve a series of ghastly child murders.

Detroit Homicide Inspector Gil Hill (Credit: Marco Mancinelli)

The lean inspector, then in his early fifties, was in the prime of his career. He directed phone calls to be held then motioned again for me to sit. He paused.

The stiff, oak chair that faced him was uncomfortable and worn, like its surroundings. My feet did not reach the floor.

Detective Landeros stood to the side.

All eyes were on me.

Hill tapped his right hand once on a closed, tan folder laying on his tired green blotter. There was no desk clutter. No frills. An old ceiling fan softly clattered above. *What had it overheard? Confessions? Lies? Threats?* I could only wait and imagine what was coming.

Meanwhile, my parents waited impatiently outside Hill's office. Mom focused on thoughts of safety and knew enough to speculate Al had associated with what she called "mixed up, bad people." Dad sat rigidly in stony silence, feeling powerless to fix the powerful chaos that

32

entangled his family. He'd always been protective, steady, and reliable, but it was insufficient to shield our family that day. This was a disfigured side of Detroit that Dad had never seen, despite having lived inside the city limits most of his life.

Everything felt chilling. What did that conspicuous, thin file have to do with me, my life, my missing husband, the future? Hill would soon discharge secrets beneath his palm while I braced in preparation for words I'd never be ready to hear.

Hill cleared his throat once, looked up and reported, "We found your husband's name and address in an alley house on Casper Street."

Before I could digest the significance of that, Detective Brantley compounded the news. "We're interviewing neighbors as we speak." More declarations followed.

My thoughts felt shoved through a paper shredder as he continued. "...airs in order?"

"What? Could you repeat that?" I asked.

"Are your financial affairs in order? Are you suspicious of money problems?"

"Yes, yes," I quietly stammered. "He won't talk about it. He's evasive. When he was hospitalized, I found unpaid bills. I've tried many times to..." My throat felt suddenly dry. "Why do you ask? What does money have to do with Al not coming home?"

Hill paused and chose his next words carefully.

I felt a tsunami thundering ashore.

"Can my parents come in?" I interrupted.

He nodded, and I stood to fetch them, but he gestured to remain seated while one lineman broke formation. The three of us were as comfortable as taxpayers summoned for an audit.

Dodging the question, Hill probed our last conversation. "Al called around 3:00 and said he'd be home around 7:00. We talked about the storm, but our conversation didn't last long."

Hill waited for more.

"Well, the last thing I said was 'be safe.' That's it. He sounded the same as always."

Hill briefly reflected on my statement, shifted his seat and inquired, "Have you recently felt followed, like in the last few weeks?"

The question elevated my discomfort, my confusion, which I'd been trying to contain. I studied Hill's face, still rummaging for answers. "Why do you ask? How can that be connect...?"

"I take that as a yes?" he interrupted.

I nervously nodded. "Well, okay. Actually, *twice*. Once for sure, but the first time I wasn't positive."

"What details can you recall?"

My sense of dread climbed along with agitation. Mom looked alarmed.

"Well, it was dark, so I mainly saw headlights. The first time I turned left onto Mack Avenue and so did they. I slowed, hoping they'd pass, but they didn't. The headlights stayed with me until I reached my street, so I didn't go home."

"What do you mean?"

"I mean I drove to a brightly-lit store, but they passed by. I didn't see them anymore."

"I understand. And the time you *were* sure?"

"It was three weeks ago and, again, it was dark and

pretty foggy. It had started to rain. The driver behind me was aggressive. They got close to my bumper then backed off. It was weird. Then I remembered this bend in the road ahead where they wouldn't see me for a few seconds. It kind of dips, too. Anyway, I got there, sped up, turned off my lights and rushed home. But, instead of parking in the driveway, I turned sharp left onto the lawn and hid behind our big hedge with my car off." I gestured with my hand to clarify my words. "I locked my doors and waited."

"What next?"

"Well, headlights moved past the hedge coming slowly. They paused at our neighbors' driveways and then ours but drove on."

"And the car?"

"It wasn't really big, not a van or station wagon. I can't name the color. It looked like two or three people inside. The rain and the hedge blocked a good view. Oh, and it made a noise like a bad muffler."

Inspector Hill nodded while Brantley jotted notes.

I asked again, "What does this have to do with my husband?"

Inspector Hill's next words punched their way in. He paused, knowing he had our attention. Looking straight at us, he declared, "I feel in my gut your husband is dead due to circumstantial evidence, but we don't have his body yet."

Mom squeezed my hand.

I hung my head, held my breath and felt my heart pulsating in my temples. *This can't be,* I thought again. Without looking at Dad, I knew he was upset and frantic, trying to fix the unfixable. Hill's words faded in and out.

I stared at the old floor, trying to steady myself in

this new reality. My heart felt suddenly swollen. I doubted my legs could lift me.

*Freefall.*

What next? What can a person do in this situation?

# TWO

# LAUNCHED

The meandering path to my future husband started with a suggestion from an old high school friend who knew I needed additional income.

"Dr. Canty is a psychologist downtown in the Fisher Building and needs a typist," he informed me.

The location was a bonus, as it was near Wayne State University in south-central Detroit where I'd just been accepted as a sophomore. The priceless, unbelievable acceptance letter was an open-ended ticket to anywhere *if* I could stockpile tuition and outlast the academic demands. Enrollment was fast approaching, and I didn't want to postpone registration.

It was the spring of 1972 when I first spoke by phone with Dr. W. Alan Canty. His office was in the prestigious "golden tower of the Fisher Building" on West Grand Boulevard near the Lodge Freeway. This was just north of the netherworld known as the Cass Corridor.

Community college had been gratifying, but my eyes were on the uncertain horizon. I really needed that job.

It didn't take long to get into a jam the evening of my interview. "Paid parking!" I lamented aloud. The two-dollars and fifty-cents could not be amassed after frantically searching my old VW for spare change, so I reluctantly parked at the shadowy curb. As I turned off my headlights a disheveled, frantic, wide-eyed man with wiry grey hair rapped urgently on the passenger side, demanding money. The wind stirred his long, frazzled hair, making him appear feral but he disappeared as suddenly as he loomed. I hastily pulled into the sanctuary of the paid lot knowing full well I'd need a small loan from a man who had not yet agreed to be my employer.

The heavy, revolving brass door released me into a majestic, vintage skyscraper. I was in *awe...* The massive arched windows framed the navy-blue light of dusk, which, in turn, reflected subtly against the enormous bronze chandeliers suspended from what looked like a mosaic ceiling. Glossy inlaid marble floors reflected the softly-lit arches of intricate frescoes in gold leaf and a palate of color resembling a peacock. The central, vaulted arcade, with multiple balconies, was three stories tall and radiated a soft yellow hue. I felt dwarfed by this luxurious space, this jewel of a building, which seemed like a spacious, echoing cathedral.

In today's dollars, the Fisher Brothers paid roughly half a billion dollars for its construction in 1928. It soared twenty-five stories and boasted five-hundred-thousand square feet of luxury office space. Nearly one-quarter ton of gold embellished the ceiling in the central six-hundred-foot-high arcade. Gold was also used on the large spire atop the structure but was removed during World War II for fear it could become a target. Several fifty-foot Tiffany chandeliers graced the massive arched entry, which brought a soft radiance to the polished colonnade morning and night. The interior was trimmed with four-hundred-thirty tons of bronze with more than forty types of marble, from all over the world, pieced together in art deco patterns. Even the nine-story attached parking garage had brass banisters and tiled restrooms. Detroiters dubbed it the city's "largest art object."

Other pedestrians, tenants perhaps, were well-dressed, self-assured and hurried. Some carried heavy briefcases, a few scanned documents and one jarred me on his way to use the ATM. Two well-dressed women discussed the Fisher Theater performance as I walked past. I was way out of range. I could not even afford to park there!

The "Golden Tower" of the Fisher Building and central arcade
(Credit: Crain's Detroit Business)

I rode the carpeted, quiet elevator alone, checked my reflection in the brass door and spit my gum into its wrapper. My favorite clothes now seemed hopelessly plain and cheap. *Hold your head up and don't bite your lip.*

It was eerily quiet at that time of night, after work hours, on floor eight. I gingerly stepped off the elevator and paused. Few lights were on. Dr. Canty's office was halfway down the polished, windowless corridor to the right. The only sounds were my echoed footsteps and elevator chime.

The psychologist and his domain were the opposite of my expectations—and the lobby's opulence. I'd assumed "shrinks" were stuffy men in tweedy vests, with pocket watches, bushy beards, and scowls who spoke five-syllable words with a foreign accent behind a fragrant pipe. His shelves of books should have been leather-bound and groan under the weight of titles like *Quantum Reactivated und die Ursprune,* along with a drawing of Freud and intimate lighting. That was not what I found. Instead, everything was just…flavorless. The entire office was homogenous beige, punctuated with harshly-framed car "art" and certificates in cheap frames. The minimalist furniture sat under harsh fluorescent lights. The floor, economic linoleum, was the color of cardboard. Everything needed dusting and smelled of stale cigarettes.

The man who greeted me was not exactly dignified. "Oh, hello! Glad you made it! Come in!" he said warmly. He had an awkward smile. "Any problems getting here?"

His question reminded me I needed a loan, but I set that aside for now.

"Nice to meet you, Doctor. I had no trouble finding it at all because my grandfather's boarding house used to be over on Pallister. As a kid, this building reminded me of a castle when we drove by, but this is the first time I've been inside. It's so well maintained. The lobby looks like an old cathedral."

I had mixed impressions of my future employer once inside his spiritless, five-room office suite. The sandy-haired psychologist who shook my hand was refreshingly easygoing, animated, bright and patient but bungling and hesitant to maintain eye contact. His "style"—dare I use that word?—was casual. He wore dated, black-rimmed bifocals, a tedious golf shirt, shapeless khaki pants with practical shoes and an old wristwatch. Dr. Canty's cadence was reminiscent of Charlie Chaplin. He smoked heavily and was forever dusting cigarette ashes from his middle-aged middle. Sometimes his grin seemed ill-timed. Anyone could see he wasn't organized. He was probably in his forties.

Within twenty minutes, the job was mine after which I felt a little lost and a little found.

"Can you start Monday?"

Relieved, I accepted the offer and was about to depart when I suddenly remembered my quandary. Now I was the one who struggled with eye contact. With red-faced embarrassment, I described the need for a loan. He burst out laughing, seeming eager to assist, and handed me three dollars out of a large roll of cash. He assured me it was the right decision. In turn, I assured him he could deduct it from my first paycheck.

Within weeks, Dr. Canty asked me to complete his typing in the office, rather than home, thereby acting as his receptionist. I jumped at the chance, as it came with a needed raise.

Al at the time we met. This was on the back cover of the paperback I was hired to type for him around 1971.

One of dozens of brass panels on elevator doors in the Fisher Building, all of which depict arts and industry.

My employer was the first to show genuine enthusiasm in my academic goals. "Of *course,* you can do it! One semester at a time!" He was fond of saying, "It's ninety-percent persistence and ten-percent grey matter!" — referring to the anatomy of the brain. It always made me laugh.

"If you're stuck, review a high school textbook, then try again. Take your hardest classes in the summer by themselves. You'll get there!"

In time I learned Dr. Canty was divorced. He spoke highly of his former wife. Al, as he encouraged me to call him, admired her intelligence and clear-headedness. Al's lack of bitterness, sunny disposition, bashfulness, interest in my goals and unpretentiousness had me looking forward to work.

Al's office on the 8th Floor of the Fisher Building. Al saw patients to the left. Straight ahead is reception area where I sat.

It's odd how much of my life centered close to the Cass Corridor. My grandfather's boarding house was three blocks north, though both my grandparents had passed away. I'd been born in Florence Crittenon Hospital five miles away—which was fortunate since their old, leaky incubators did not threaten blindness, like their newer counterparts. Then there was the majestic Detroit Institute of Arts (DIA) where I would escape between classes, typically to gaze at *The Wreck* by Eugene Louis Gabriel Isabey (c 1907). Wistful memories of twilight doubleheaders at Tiger Stadium not too far away comforted me, as did the music from early Motown performers. Hitsville USA—the forerunner to Motown— was nearly visible from my apartment. I was fortunate, as a teen, to babysit for a friend of Barry Gordy and heard stories behind the various successes of early Motown performers.

Neglected high rise buildings in
the Cass Corridor

Cass Ave had something
for everyone

The Cass Corridor led a double life. It was capable of transporting occupants to a professional degree and high-rise offices of multinational corporations, or to dark shooting dens, prison, and a chance to meet their maker in shadowy, perilous alleys. The direction chosen meant life or death, being confined or having options. But sometimes those paths were not mutually exclusive.

# THREE

# OUTBREAK

East of campus was a man whose path should never have intersected mine. He was someone even men crossed the street to avoid. John Carl Fry originated from a three-bedroom mobile on the northwest Tennessee-Kentucky border in a dusty patch called Fulton near the Mississippi River, an hour and a half north of Memphis. He made his appearance August 31, 1946. He was impatient. Corrosive. Arrogant. Aggressive. And quite controlling. He became the boogieman personified.

John sprouted from a troubled family that struggled to make ends meet. His father worked steadily driving big rigs of Tennessee crude but work as an asphalt cowboy didn't provide enough time away since he periodically separated from his family. In that vacuum John became the de-facto man of the house, helping with his younger brothers, which, to his credit, he did faithfully. When Johnnie Fry's father wasn't commanding sixty feet of chrome and steel, he was overheard pounding John. And not just with fists. Pete Fry drummed rage and self-preservation into his oldest with handles of axes and punishing words. John's mother, Nell, did not intervene. The brutality embedded a lifelong disrespect for authority, tutored John in the "art" of savagery and laid the groundwork for the angry thug he'd become. Predictably, Fry ripened into an unstable, supercell updraft of temporarily harnessed energy. To compensate for his father's cruelty, John's grandmother doted on him, which riled his father more, and around they went. Regardless of whether Johnnie Carl was born flawed or damaged by cruel and inconsistent treatment he predictably grew into a reward-driven survival machine, poised and ready to victimize the world beyond his roots, sometimes for the sheer pleasure of it.

Johnnie Fry began consuming drugs at thirteen. Before he had a reason to shave, John routinely consumed a six-pack and smoked bud. By twenty-one, he graduated to heroin ("H"), although incarceration interrupted his habit periodically. John's toxins of choice became H, cocaine and "mixed jive." He'd do anything to keep the pipeline open. *Anything.* At some point he unknowingly, yet predictably, contracted Hepatitis C from carelessness and complacency. It would wait patiently to carry out its ruination.

John's basic assumption, the tenet upon which his life would revolve, was he saw nothing wrong with his actions or thoughts. Subjectively, it was logical. He didn't look back with regret, let alone guilt, think twice about his behavior, nor look forward with unease. He developed a frighteningly high watermark for disgust, which opened the gate to do disgusting things with ease, even amusement. People were little more than inconvenient two-dimensional moving objects, like ducks at a carnival game, with mysterious and bothersome concerns. Fry obtained what he wanted through extortion, intimidation, theft, and deceit. He learned early when caught in a lie or challenged with facts, he could skate on through if he'd just tweak his story—even if blatantly contradictory. The confused listener may think him crazy, but that merely puzzled John. As he saw it, deception was the logical thing to do. He'd lie about important things like his legal record, and less important things, like what he said to whom. He lied about his name, who he knew and where he'd been. He *specialized* in disinformation. He professed to be on the side of the underdog, the underappreciated, the downtrodden, yet that, too, was a lie.

John used prolonged eye contact, the kind that drilled into others, which effortlessly rankled his listener. Many experienced this as a "predatory stare." He rarely felt anxiety or embarrassment so was incapable of understanding those emotions in others—if he even noticed. He was indifferent to their uncertainty, their *humanness*. What mattered were his needs and wants. Fry faced the world with a tight-fitting mask that concealed the gaping nothingness, the hollowness, beneath. He viewed himself as a superior person in a flawed world where others were just a means to an end. The tools of his trade were to manipulate, intimidate and repudiate. He was drawn to a parasitic lifestyle. To *hell* with the host!

It was an open secret that Pete Fry favored Johnny's younger brother, Jim Dale Fry, nicknamed Six Pack. "Six" was on a par with John when it came to drugs, despite being younger. His preferred poisons were alcohol and angel dust, known as "T" or "hog." It made Six unpredictably wild, paranoid, and even suicidal. Perhaps because of his father's favoritism, Johnnie and Six developed a love-hate relationship, but never lost contact, despite periods of "radio silence."

John Fry dropped out of school. He resented being told what to do, though he was bright enough to do the work. Teachers were no match for his defiance. The curriculum was no match for his boredom. Fellow students gladly gave him passage. He didn't adjust any better to Army life, where he was court-martialed twice. When his mother died, he was sentenced for desertion at Fort Carson in 1967 and washed out altogether with a dishonorable discharge.

John perfected a shuffle and bloated ego before he could legally buy liquor. His rap sheet grew proportionate to his size, which he arrogantly treated as his resume. He'd be the first to point out he was no mere misdemeanant. In 1969 he joined the other five-thousand inmates at Jackson Prison where he refined his escape skills—no small feat considering the concrete enclosure had a thirty-three-foot-tall barrier with twelve watchtowers. Fry called the Indiana Federal Penitentiary home in 1971, a facility where federal death sentences were carried out—including future inmate Timothy McVeigh's. Fry's next stop was the Minnesota Federal Penitentiary where he was housed simultaneously with actor Tim Allen in 1978. He also served time at Marquette Penitentiary in upper Michigan, a place so tough that Warden Catlin and Deputy Warden Menhennett were both stabbed to death by prisoners in December of 1921. Fry boasted about his ten years in state and federal lockups across three states for bad checks, conspiracy, larceny, counterfeiting, assault, and breaking and entering. Fry completed high school behind bars with ease. He adapted well inside, as social chameleons do. He was responsible for assigning work details as a clerk, gave homegrown advice as a drug counselor and even enrolled in a couple of college-level social science classes. He strutted with a shotgun shine.

John could make people feel comfortable, even at ease, when it served his needs. He just determined what they wanted then exploited it. Fry was an opportunist, a snake charmer who lusted for power and money, the very qualities he claimed he despised in others.

John Fry from the Kentucky-Tennessee border grew into a crude man of five feet ten inches tall with a barrel chest, narrowly-spaced snake eyes, thinning hair, reddish beard, and unkempt mustache. He vaguely resembled an irritable Hulk Hogan minus the careful hygiene. Predictably, life in the fast lane and chronic pain from abscesses and injuries contributed to going prematurely gray.

In the early 1980s, Fry joined a motorcycle club, which failed to hone his rough edges. John earned the dubious name "Lucky" the hard way. It came from surviving a vicious assault meted out by rival bikers in 1983. As if to refine the stereotype, he shaved his head and acquired seventeen tattoos over the years, some while in prison. The ink on the back of his arms boasted "White Power," broadcasting a sense of superiority without a rational basis. Another, "FTW" (*Fuck the World*) summed up his attitude toward everyone on the planet. Two others seemed an unlikely pair: a Tweety Bird next to skull and crossbones predicting, "As you are I was. As I am you will be." Over time, the gallery of ink grew blurry and resembled the skin condition known as port-wine.

I've always viewed tattoos as a kind of Morse code for personality dynamics. Fry exhibited one, "LBT" (*Living on Borrowed Time*) after the hammering that nearly claimed his life, which seemed particularly prophetic. Indeed, he was LBT.

The middle-aged biker spoke in a soft, slow, southern accent using simple, coarse language, seizing opportunities to obtain easy money while circumventing the law. He felt entitled, exceptional and accountable to no one. Laws were mere barricades to toy with, pathetic tests of his obvious superiority. He believed rules and limits applied to less enlightened, less entitled people. Rise and grind jobs were beneath him. He surged ahead toward self-destruction. Full throttle. He had swagger but was no John Gotti. He never mastered how to channel his anger, use finesse or develop patience. The resentment and beatings from youth eroded his soul, instilling self-preservation and a lifelong quest for retaliation. *Someone* was going to pay. All it took to unleash his fury, to get onto his radar, was being defied, pushed, or abusing a child. John was, so to speak, without an emergency brake. Earlier a girlfriend found out the hard way when she laid a hand on him in anger. He grabbed a bat, clubbed her innocent furniture to smithereens, then drummed potholes deep in her drywall before three men subdued him.

He confessed, "My old man hit me with anything he could get his hands on. Ever since I just go *out* when any motherfucker lays a hand on me!"

By adulthood, his bite was worse than his bark and

unleashed without much warning. The apple did not drop far from that family tree.

The menacing man from the south married and divorced three times, acknowledging (and denying) he'd produced at least five children, none of whom he financially supported. Fatherhood disinterested him, which was fine with their mothers. Lucky would do *whatever* it took to acquire what he wanted - even pimping girlfriends. Fry nursed grudges, took offense easily and never let personal feelings interfere. He held mock executions to keep people in line, and for his own enjoyment, which put an entirely new spin on "paying it forward." Fry never developed a conscience, genuine remorse nor humility. He had the empathy of an avalanche. He was savvy at telling others what they wanted to hear, wrapped in pseudo-sincerity and quasi-philosophy. John was large and in charge.

Fry swaggered into the sediment of the southern Cass Corridor area of south-central Detroit after his brush with death, less than two miles from Wayne State University where he pitched his services as pimp/protector to the vulnerable young women walking the perilous streets. Lucky had no trouble finding work. His scruffy appearance and reputation alone dissuaded assaults on the young hookers, which fortified his bloated ego. One of "his girls" dared use his works after which he reflexively put her in the hospital for six weeks with broken ribs and ruptured spleen suffered behind the greasy White Grove Diner on Second Avenue. Yet, through it all, Fry saw himself as a protector of women, a businessman, an entrepreneur. And, occasionally, he actually was, as he sporadically brokered peace among

51

quarreling dope dealers and prevented tricks from skipping on debts owed to him and others. His illegal employment brought idle time, allowed him to lay back, "get baked" and wait for hand-delivered cash. John "Lucky" Carl Fry was a walking, talking wrecking ball, and proud of it.

John "Lucky" Carl Fry around 1983
(Credit: Mark Bando)

Fry resembled other pimps. Most didn't complete high school on time, if ever. He, like others, witnessed domestic violence and alcoholism growing up. He had a long criminal record before sending his first escort to the streets and, like most, began his flesh-peddling in his mid-twenties. He knew the chance of being prosecuted was small if he intimidated enough witnesses. Besides, the penalties were light compared to the money to be made.

Like most pimps, John minimized, justified, and often glorified the abuse he directed toward "his girls." He could be congenial and glib *until confronted* and, like his cohorts, capable of sudden retaliation without hesitation. He was exceptionally territorial and easily bored. He claimed the streets and the streets claimed him.

# FOUR

# WHAT'S AGE GOT TO DO WITH IT?

"I want a double major of Psychology and English with an emphasis in art history," I explained over lunch to attentive eyes, "so I can write children's books and understand kids better. Maybe art therapy would be interesting."

Al smiled encouragingly, as he often did.

My future was assured—albeit fuzzy—and time was on my side.

Although it meant little then, Al introduced me to a tenant in the elevator. The dignified, grey-haired man in the expensive, black wool overcoat and bowler-style hat complimented me for hauling heavy textbooks around month after month, no matter the weather. Al smiled broadly, leaned against the handrail, cocked his head, and responded, "Yup. A real diamond in the rough, she is."

I took this to mean I had potential but lacked polish

and experience. It pinched.

Over dinner the following week, Al again asked about school. "It's going well. I'm learning about the cognitive development of preschoolers and approaching this as kind of like a foreign correspondent on assignment."

He chuckled and shared my enthusiasm. We began to see one another socially. Gradually he became the peace in my dreams.

The time came to introduce Al to my parents. They noticed our eighteen-year age difference but didn't see it as insurmountable. What concerned them more was his tendency to bluff, first evident when Dad tried to discuss car restoration. It didn't matter that Al wasn't an expert at the craft. They were more worried when I didn't see his hyperbole which they discreetly pointed out but fell on deaf ears. My friends, likewise, lacked enthusiasm. They could not see how Al inspired me to reach for goals. He believed a college degree was not only possible, but inevitable. He was a gentleman, had a sense of humor and eyes only for me.

We decided I should meet his parents, but this grew oddly complicated despite Al's careful consideration for when and how to accomplish this seemingly complex matter. We agreed on a time, but, en route, he changed his mind, offering an anemic explanation— "it wasn't a good time."

When we tried again, he introduced me as "someone who works for him." He left it there, dangling like conspicuous flypaper. This brought hurt feelings and unasked questions.

We next met at his parents' modest home, near

Chandler Park Drive and Moross Rd. near St. John's Hospital, where they directed me to a witness stand cleverly disguised as a Wedgewood blue, antique upholstered armchair. The interrogation began.

"Do you plan on graduate school?" "What do your parents think?" "Do you appreciate your age difference?" "What does your father do for a living?" and on and *on*. It was taxing, one-sided and invasive. Between questions they sighed or tapped their fingers as if reloading.

Al churned in his seat, biting a hangnail and said little. His parents seemed out of control with doubt, curiosity, and discomfort. It was a relief to leave.

Al and me later reminisced about dinner table conversations growing up. In my childhood, too many discussions were devoted to my brother's football coach and '32 Ford. "Should it be competitive on the salt or the strip?" I reluctantly learned about hash marks, field goals, *Hemmings Motor News* and blue dot taillights.

Al countered he and his mother listened to graphic accounts of sexual psychopathic cases over dinner.

"What do you mean?" I asked.

"You know… Homicide. Rape. Pedophiles. Blood. Guts. Yeah. Dad liked a captive audience. Someone to listen to him pontificate."

We attended the annual Belle Isle Grand Prix and strolled summer evenings in Hart Plaza alongside the huge fountain near the Detroit River. Al drove us to the imposing Dodge mansion where I was flabbergasted to learn the impressive 1920 ivy-covered stone residence with leaded windows, circular drive, lavish landscaping, and turrets was just the *gatehouse*.

We adopted *Lelli's* on Woodward near East Grand

Boulevard as "our" restaurant. It was a nondescript, dark green trim and brick old house, a former "blind pig" (illegal saloon and gambling establishment during prohibition). Curb appeal was absent. It purposely appeared abandoned with boarded-up windows and a dull exterior. The only flicker of life from Woodward Avenue was an insignificant, electric, green and yellow sign that said "*Lelli's.*" But, once through the narrow, dark alley, guests were greeted with tuxedoed valets and an extraordinary aroma of fresh Italian cuisine. Violinists threaded through tiny, secluded dining rooms while soft white Christmas lights reflected the heavy stucco year 'round. The candles lent a festive ambiance to each private table. There were numerous original oil paintings, most from the Barbizon School or French Impressionist eras, and beautiful table linens. Never had I set foot in such elegance, which seemed to delight Al.

Another special place became *Dominique's Joint* in Grosse Pointe on Mack Avenue. It was intimate and enticing. The large stained-glass front window depicted a scowling fifty-fiveish man in a vintage tuxedo with thick, dark hair, caterpillar-like eyebrows, and ominous expression. As we dined, the candles brightened up Al's smiling face, occasionally reflected in his eyeglasses. At a distance, we overheard the owner's opinion that Jimmy Hoffa "will be found if they *want* him found" since he "was buried under 696" — a freeway then under construction.

This was unquestionably a remarkable time in the Motor City, and I felt fully alive, confident and lucky. I had direction. My date was supportive, well-educated and attentive. Never had I felt so understood, so validated. Our future was promising, not the dark cloud my neighbor foretold over coffee grounds. Life wasn't just good. It was *great!*

Al eventually hinted at commitment. He saw me as capable in ways I had not.

"Graduate school? *Me?* That's quite a goal. *Really?*"

He nodded and replied, "Look how far you've already come."

He never showed resentment when scheduling conflicts arose between school and us. In fact, he'd never directed an unkind word in my direction despite opportunities to do so—like the time I typed "youth in Asia" for "euthanasia" in a report for him. He said I "livened things up." Then there was his bashful smile. It never ceased to endear him to me. He was happy, no doubt about it.

This Doctor Canty, *my* Doctor Canty, invited me to New York City during his enrollment at the Edgar Alanson White Institute of Psychoanalysis. It was an astonishing opportunity for an undergraduate and, moreover, the first time I'd flown! Our reservations waited at the regal Plaza Hotel in Manhattan where he'd booked us adjacent rooms on the ninth floor. A uniformed man graciously welcomed our taxi, then motioned us toward the middle set of tall hotel doors, which framed a lobby suitable for a castle. I stopped and gazed upward, trying to soak it in, savoring and memorizing this moment.

My suite resembled a movie set with its elevated ceilings hoisted with crown molding, four silk lampshades, thick carpet, original oil paintings from the "Luminism" genre, white marble mosaic in the bathroom with inlaid vines of brass, a thick robe, fresh fruit, one beautiful chandelier and something called "turn down service." The walls were a pleasant gray punctuated with tall windows that faced Central Park, just on the cusp of autumn.

Al suggested room service while he was in his meetings and nudged me to shop in the hotel's stores.

"Just put it on the tab. You know, give them your room number. I'll get it. Have fun! You're in the Big Apple!"

So, the following afternoon I gingerly explored a clothing store on the Mezzanine and examined a sturdy, chocolate brown leather purse with odd symbols, reminiscent of cattle brands.

The lavishly perfumed, bejeweled salesclerk with black, patent leather hair swooped in and purred, "*Eeeexcellent* choice!" as if it was our secret. "That Louis Vuitton is a new item! It runs two hundred-seventy-nine-dollars plus shipping." (Approximately six hundred dollars today.) "Where might I send it?"

"Well, does it come without the designs?"

She was incredulous. "*Noooo!* This is a *Vuitton!* That is the *trademark,* you see?"

I didn't see. I was out of range again and returned to my private corner of New York where I later studied room service options at an impressive antique desk with fresh flowers in a fluted vase. The alcohol menu was leather-bound. Hunger rumbled. What the heck was "Orecchietta with Escarole and Cavolifiore?" The price, alone, turned me off and some items had no price listed! I felt as out of place there as the day I first stepped into the Fisher Building.

The next evening, we attended an early dinner where Al introduced me to the elderly Richard Sterba,

M.D., a Viennese psychoanalyst who knew Doctor Sigmund Freud and his daughter, Doctor Anna Freud. Dr. Sterba invited me to ask a question, perhaps because I'd been quiet.

"Well, why was Freud's desktop so full of archeological finds?"

He chuckled and exclaimed, through his heavy German accent, "Well, of *course*, it is because Freud loved to dig up the past!"

Afterward, Al and I rode in a horse-drawn carriage around Central Park as long shadows merged into one. It was magical. The complete Manhattan experience made my head spin. If Al was trying to impress, it was working.

A few months later, we returned to New York for a symposium at the Institute for Rational Living to meet the founder Albert Ellis, Ph.D., and his longtime partner, Janet. As we stood in the foyer of the brownstone, I whispered, "I can't believe I'm *here*, Al! I've read about him in class, but I'm actually *in* his institute!"

Al smiled and gave me a cryptic hug. I took a longer look at my companion. He was generous, funny and quite an optimist. We were happy. I had found my grounding force.

Life had opened to me.

Our age difference gave me pause. I was twenty-two. He was forty. Although I was aware age similarity was one factor in successful marriages, guys I'd known not only lacked direction, they didn't have a compass. I'd aimed at finding someone with a strong work ethic, intelligence and integrity, a loyal partner who had a sense of humor. I begrudgingly accepted the probability I'd be a widow in my sixties. Realistically we'd have at least thirty or so years together. In the end, I proposed to him over breakfast.

Al grinned like a schoolboy, held my hand, and asked, "When?"

I took out a paper calendar and blindly stabbed a fork onto a Saturday in autumn. *Green light.*

He promised, "If you think I'll be good to you, you're right."

What could go wrong?

Our wedding day

# FIVE

# THE DAWN OF DAWN

Attractive. Unyielding. Opportunistic. Dawn Marie Spens, first daughter of Roy, Jr. and Henrietta "Sandy" Spens, was born January 11, 1965. She blossomed into an intelligent, angry, alluring teen with a younger, asthmatic sister who secured her share of the meager emotional resources in the household.

Spens grew up in a bungalow on Elkhart Street in Harper Woods, Michigan. Her parents, married in 1964, had a troubled relationship that didn't improve with time. Her father, a machinist, was a revolving door, creating a constant stirring of insecurity and tension. However, Dawn's mother was seldom home at all, leaving her daughters with excessive idle time. The house, like its inhabitants, was in disarray with echoes of unkind words ricocheting down the short hallway, clothes strewn about, overflowing ashtrays and undertow of strain.

Dawn attended Tyrone Elementary where she experimented with stolen cigarettes. It escalated into chain-smoking Marlboros. Inevitably, Dawn grew bored, stubborn, savvy, depressed and unruly as elementary school ended. She experimented with marijuana and mescaline the summer preceding junior high and progressed to Valium, Tylenol-4s and Black Beauties—and the boys who supplied the venom. Spens took a willful pride in being expelled for drugs early in the school year and once boldly smoked during class, setting her schoolwork on fire. Incredibly, her consequences were mild, which reinforced a mindset of impunity. It would not be her last slap on the wrist. Dawn learned early how to deflect remorse and culpability, a handy skill in her future career downtown.

Although Spens was tight-lipped about her home life, peers knew Roy Spens controlled her use of the phone. Friends were concerned but shut out. Dawn did have one solid, clear-headed friend in Dee Cusmano. They'd meet up at Memorial Park, across from Harper Woods High, sometimes because they were briskly ushered out of Dawn's house by her father for unknown reasons, no matter the weather.

Dawn's anger and depression were palpable by age twelve when she made a suicide attempt using her mother's medications. She was held for six weeks in a psychiatric hospital. Once discharged, Dawn again faced turbulence at home. During one fracas her father threatened to kill her mother, validating his warning with a gash to her head requiring fourteen stitches to close. Roy Spens developed an alcohol problem. Predictably, her parents divorced, yet cohabitated briefly. Roy won permanent custody of his daughters. Sandy Spens had a new man, rearranged her life in nearby Windsor, Canada and, for reasons understood only by her, encouraged

Dawn to correspond with a lonely prison inmate. It was Dawn's friend, Dee, who wisely advised her to break it off.

The capable teen managed the school bookstore and attended pep rallies. No one ever considered Dawn slow. She earned solid grades despite a brackish home life, idle time and jaded outlook. Perhaps academics were her escape, or how she delivered peace to her stressed family. Or maybe Dawn realized that those in authority sometimes provided high achievers, particularly attractive ones, with preferential treatment, a "get-out-of-jail-free card" from the Community Chest.

Dawn Marie Spens naturally aroused the attention of male students. She possessed a waterfall of glossy brownish-red hair parted in the middle, a pouty lower lip, flawless skin and large doe eyes framed with dense lashes. Her gaze displayed a curious mixture of sadness and confidence, vigilance and defiance, but rarely vulnerability or fear. At an alarmingly young age, she cultivated a shrugging indifference to life, bitterness, and learned how to turn on the charm when useful. Childhood innocence withered before it fully bloomed.

Drugs were as plentiful as the boys who furnished them. Dee tried again to intervene by encouraging Dawn to examine her choices. One guy, Donnie Scott Carlton, was on Dee's radar.

Dee asked, "What do you see in someone like that?"

"Well, he's nice to me. He takes me places and pays attention to me."

But Dawn would not heed the warnings from the one person who had her best interests at heart, a peer perceptive enough to see through the haze of adolescence. Dawn was never taught her life would be a summation of her decisions.

Spens worked at Little Caesar's at Eastland Mall during her senior year and likely planned her exit from all she knew. She was accelerating onto the adolescent Autobahn without a seatbelt, map or braking power. She cut class, but on days she attended she sometimes displayed a vacant, twenty-thousand-mile stare. Dee knew her friend was directed straight for a cliff, swept along by drugs, guys, bitterness, and obstinacy.

Using her savings, Dawn purchased an old Plymouth Duster. Even the mistreatment of it by Donnie failed to open her eyes. This promising adolescent, a teen who'd succeeded academically despite her home life, veered away from a favorable future and perceptive friend two months shy of her 1982 graduation, though she'd been selected valedictorian.

The defiant teenager from Elkhart Street believed she would outrun her frustrations by moving past the Detroit City Limits sign. She stubbornly swapped Harper Woods for a downtown slum, a high school schedule for idle time and the presence of her irritable father for an irritable dropout boyfriend. She was untethered to home and safety.

Dawn Spens,
freshman year
1979-80
Credit: Harper Woods Yearbook

Sophomore year
1980-81

Eastbound I-94 to Lodge Fwy

Donnie Carlton, who bore a passing resemblance to a young Sean Penn, said, "There were a lot of problems going down with her dad. He'd beat her and didn't let her talk on the phone. He'd hang up while she was talkin' to me and smack her. She finally got sick of it and got out."

Unfortunately, Dawn settled into the hazardous Cass Corridor, with cheap rents, plentiful drugs and trouble everywhere. Dawn emulated the tumultuous relationship she witnessed at home. Donnie introduced her to skid row, poverty, partner abuse and worse.

The exchange of working-class suburbs for historic Detroit's Cass Corridor blight was akin to relocating to Beirut. The Corridor, situated between I-75 and the Lodge Freeway south of I-94, occupied three square miles. A portion was later reinvented as Midtown. Wayne State University bordered the "more respectable" northern tip, as did the World Headquarters for General Motors and the Fisher Building. The large blue Motown building, before its hasty exodus to Los Angeles in 1972, was nearby. The further south, the more hazard, drugs and desperation.

*Oh, I think I see the bottom.*
*Yes, I'm sure I see the bottom.*
*I shall hit the bottom,*
*hit it very hard, and oh, how it will hurt!*
*— Lewis Carroll*

Governor Cass's peaceful ribbon farm of the 1850s became Body Bag City. Homicides hovered at ten a week, triple that of Chicago and New York, and many went unreported. One-third of Michigan's budget was directed to the Department of Corrections. Forty-percent of the city stumbled to low income.

Dawn had chosen squalor replete with theft, vandalism and a brash displays of weapon sales in broad daylight. Corruption spread like an oil slick, contributing to the city's eventual economic collapse. Charles Beckham, former city water and sewerage director, was convicted of bribery for a sludge-handling contract in 1984. Detroit Police Chief Hart — appointed in 1976 — was found guilty of embezzling over two-million-dollars over seven years from cash captured from drug dealers and set aside for undercover drug operations. Hart's actions left the undercover drug program so strapped for cash that narcotic officers paid for street-level buys of drugs out of their own pockets. There were pockets of the city that became deaf to 911 calls.

Detroit in general, and the Corridor in particular, imploded. Its inner scaffolding had rusted and crumbled and was no longer a magnet for hope and inspiration. City Hall was governed by corrupt administrators, organized crime, drugs, and cynicism. Some once-dignified blocks of three-story Victorian homes were razed and eventually returned to tracts of urban prairie complete with pheasants and weedy streets. Detroit's creditors, unions and pension boards all wanted their due. Like the ill-fated Northwest Flight 255 which crashed shortly after takeoff from Detroit Metro in 1987, the city disintegrated because of poor judgment, neglect and confusion. Both went down in flames dooming its occupants.

In this setting Dawn was surrounded by the like-minded, the similarly adrift. She stumbled into a sinister rabbit hole where trust, loyalty, and empathy were exploited and imitated.

Deserted multi-family home
830 Peterboro – Detroit

Deserted mansions
3113 Cass – Detroit
(Credit: Steve Neavling)

*SIX*

# TERMS OF ENGAGEMENT

Our marriage certificate, signed in front of a handful of guests on a beautiful, warm fall afternoon, must have contained exceedingly fine print, a clause that escaped my notice. Most likely it read, *"I will be your faithful husband as long as you remain admiring and unseasoned."*

We had a modest ceremony, a private beginning of a marriage that would end in public mockery. I believed my mother's classic satin wedding dress would bring us luck. Our chariot was a convertible, burgundy 1932 Ford. We had no time for a honeymoon. "Someday," we promised, "we'll fly off to a sunny beach. Maybe after grad school." However, it was postponed repeatedly. We drifted into routines dominated by work, school, and care of a house big enough for a multi-generation family.

My siblings had moved west, and my parents retired in Arizona, which made it an even greater disappointment I could not connect with my in-laws. Having missed the closeness of my family, I'd hoped they would welcome a daughter, but the Canty family was apparently limited to an enrollment of three.

My mother-in-law, Gladys, was a petite, outgoing, intelligent woman in her seventies with a habit of holding her hard-working hands up wide near her face, stiff, palms out, as she spoke. Sometimes she gasped as she did, suggesting an undercurrent of nervousness. The wispy tips of her reddish-grey hair were perpetually disobedient, despite efforts to corral them into a grandmotherly topknot. Hand-drawn, red eyebrows framed her bright blue eyes, her face lined by the decades. Gladys Foster Canty, always pale, never mentioned feeling tired, let alone sick. She was perpetually chilly, preferring light cardigans even in summer. No one had seen her in pants or shorts, *ever*, and Gladys was rarely without her apron. Never did she utter a profane word. She was unendingly polite and prim and proper. Gladys bore a passing resemblance to Maggie Smith's Violet Crawley in the British television series *Downton Abbey*, though Gladys was considerably smaller.

Mrs. Canty chose the name "Jannie" for me, which grated my nerves. Even worse, she occasionally addressed me as "*Little* Jannie." It felt blatantly denigrating, unaffectionate and patronizing. I never addressed her as "Gladys" or "Mom." Both would have been disingenuous, and she'd never invited me to do so.

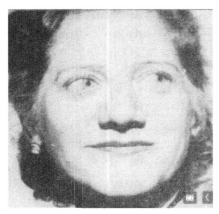 

Gladys Canty before I met her     Alan Canty, Senior before I met him
(my mother-in-law)           (my father-in-law)

Al's parents married in 1927. My father-in-law was articulate, decisive and confident, but never did I see him as humble, affectionate nor empathetic. He was complicated, introverted, brooding and habitually corrected people's grammar. In terms of appearance, he reminded me of an older George C. Scott in *The Changeling*. There was a heaviness about him. He smoked incessantly and preferred lecturing over listening. Mr. Canty often positioned his large frame in a hunched over posture, elbows on knees, while pointing his yellowed finger toward his caged listener—a habit I've never liked—and proceeded to lecture his disinterested audience. His perpetual cloud of grey smoke mingled with his receding grey hairline, sometimes eclipsing all his facial features.

"So, what do you think of the Cadillac Deville?" he probed through the fog. "I bet you've always wanted one."

Truthfully, I replied, "Not really. They're kinda an old man car, gas hogs. No. I prefer VWs." How was I to know he owned one?

I unknowingly erred again by sitting in a large, mint green, fan back chair in their cramped, quiet living room, positioned to oversee the dining room. It became clear this was the family patriarch's roost. Besides his love of amateur theater in a male-only venue, Al Senior's only other interests were watching television alone in the back room and collecting coins.

Prior to retirement, long before we met, he had a reputation for arriving late to work and bringing assignments home. He'd sometimes persist late into the night over a bourbon or two. In stark contrast with his wife, he used profane, sometimes shocking language, *liberally*. His family took no notice.

One evening, while visiting my in-laws, we watched home movies of Al growing up. My husband grew uncomfortable as we faced the miniature screen. There were typical scenes of backyard celebrations and "Buster" (his childhood nickname) as a toddler with various guests in and out of the movie lens. But what struck my attention most was Al was always alone. He threaded among the legs of adults holding a toy and spoke to no one in particular.

There were other omissions in the Canty household. For one, guests didn't visit, neighbors didn't stop. We never socialized on their enclosed back porch, or the concrete one in front, even on warm days, and their screened windows were seldom opened. Outside of Edna, I never met any friends or relatives. Their phone rarely beckoned, and when it did, it was usually Mrs. Canty's elderly sisters from Ohio. Music was never heard. It was always quiet.

His father behaved indifferently — even toward their cats. No one contradicted him. Eye contact was fleeting. Socializing took place in unofficially assigned seats. They never disclosed personal setbacks, acknowledged private worries nor mentioned regrets. Family photos were absent. Despite the multitude of questions tossed my way, I never knew much about their histories, let alone that of extended family. I felt like an intruder, a fifth wheel, a trespasser.

During meals, Gladys reigned supreme, encouraging everyone to "Eat!" while she nibbled and observed. No matter how much everyone consumed, she was disappointed. She put a lot of effort into dinners and prepared double what could be eaten. She preferred to serve, and a bare plate was her signal to fill it immediately. The table was set with fine bone china and silver flatware. Wine, when offered, was rationed in petite, lead crystal goblets, which were never refilled. Hot dogs, hamburgers and pizza never made the menu.

Life felt vaguely rehearsed in the Canty household. There was little spontaneity. No interruptions. No give and take. Disagreements were extinguished as soon as they began by a harsh look, a huff, or change of subject, feeling oddly like a game of Simon Says. Everything felt *restrained*, nearly…*staged*.

Al's father was a self-trained bachelor-level forensic "psychologist" for the Detroit Police Department. He never attended graduate school and his doctorate degree was honorary — awarded, not earned. He ignored the protocol of correcting others who referred to him as "doctor." My father-in-law made headlines in 1951 with a lecture on child sexual predators for the Detroit Council of PTAs. The large audience of administrators, teachers, and parents listened as he blamed "neurotic mothers" and frustrated schoolteachers for inflicting more damage upon children than sex offenders. He stated they created anxious children with their overprotectiveness and neuroses. After discussing sadism, window peeping, exhibitionism, impotence and pedophilia, he curiously ended as he always did. "There, but for the grace of God, go I."

Boisterous, informal dinners at my grandparents' downtown boarding house with extended family were much more to my liking. We congregated under a large chandelier passing mounds of steaming food and clattering dishes. Granted, the china was a little mismatched. Strict manners and punctuality took a back seat to simultaneous, animated discussions and outbursts of laughter. Slaps on the back were interwoven with food traveling north, south, east and west. It just felt festive. Dialogue grew loud and debates encouraged. I knew I belonged there, in the din of adult banter perched on a pile of phone books, peeking over yards of white, Damask tablecloth. I may not have understood the grownups' conversation, but I knew to my core everyone was included and valued.

My sister and I paid close attention to one boarder with eager anticipation. Whenever Wilber picked up an ear of corn, we elbowed one another and gazed in amazement as he gnawed in one long-winded effort, jaws like a chomping piranha, leaving no kernel behind without so much as one glance up, or pause, or gulp of air. It was an impressive accomplishment indeed!

(Left to right) My grandfather, Uncle Ralph, Uncle Bob, brother, father, grandmother and Aunt Marion inside my grandparents downtown boarding house on Pallister Ave. in 1960; one of many extended-family meals

It became apparent my in-laws were image-conscious, though they would vehemently deny it. I do not mean they were ostentatious or hosted parties to be noticed. No. It was demonstrated through dogged protectiveness at keeping the Canty name in rarefied esteem. It was never to be subjected to gossip, dishonor or rumor. Perhaps that's why they screened potential daughters-in-law so closely.

Over time, Gladys and Al Senior accepted us as a couple. There was little alternative. We shared meals at their house and ours and celebrated holidays. While Gladys initiated discussions about my education, her spouse appeared irritated and sidelined the topic, preferring to talk about city department heads in the news. He made it clear he and Gladys were on a first-name basis with local politicians, judges, and school board officials. This would later prove invaluable.

Al and me around 1979 in left photo. Right photo was taken about a year later. We were getting ready to go to a wedding. I was pulling him into the house to get ready.

Each year, Al and I traveled to Phoenix, often around New Year's, to see my parents. But, over time, Al preferred to be alone, declined invitations to watch movies together, visit the pool or sit on their veranda. He attributed this to having "worked so hard." Indeed, he seemed tired and we let him do as he wished.

At home we often strolled late at night under the towering elms of our neighborhood, sometimes walking two or more miles no matter the weather, and talked into the wee hours. Life was good, steady, comfortable. I was very happy.

One late afternoon Al arrived home with a new "selectric" typewriter, reading lamp and gift card for my favorite coffee stand for no reason.

He had my back.

By the summer of 1976, my Ph.B. (bachelor's in philosophy) was finished and I expressed interest in pursuing a master's degree. To underscore Al's full support, he arrived home a bit early the following day with another "just because" gift within a colorfully wrapped box as I sat on the back porch hoping to catch a breeze. Inside was a small, mushroom-colored coffee cup like none other. On the rim, a miniature figure pushed mightily, "denting" it outward resembling a creamer.

He eagerly explained, "This is a 'struggle cup' and that's you! You have it in you to finish grad school."

He sensed my nervousness at the idea and asked me to sit beside him as he drew a simple triangle.

"Look. See this wider bottom here? This group starts out in college. See how it shrinks in the middle? That's because half the students don't finish, for whatever reason. Then it's narrower at the tip. That's grad school. Same thing, see?" He turned and smiled. "Fewer students get there, so you have less competition the further you go! The only way a climber reaches the top is *because* the sides of the mountain are rough. So, it's more about persistence than anything." He gently lifted my chin with one finger as if for emphasis.

He refueled me. He inspired me. He believed in me! The treasure was prominently perched where homework was undertaken and served as a silent reminder that my goal was attainable.

> *By George, I really did it. I did it. I did it!*
> *I said I'd make a woman and indeed, I did.*
> *I knew I could do it. I knew it.*
> — Professor Higgins (Pygmalion)

Sunday mornings were refreshingly slow-paced, and we looked forward to them, sometimes going out for breakfast even when it meant waiting in a long line.

"Here you go," I said, as my hand extended an Ashleigh Brilliant cartoon ripped from the Sunday paper. It read: "*One of the best places in the world is anywhere with you.*"

He read it, smiled, studied my face and delivered a kiss on my forehead. He not only saved it, he laminated it and carried the cartoon inside his wallet from that day forward. He had a sentimental side.

These were the good years.

By 1978, I finished my master's degree and desired a Ph.D. Al's first reaction was subtly offbeat. "Well, think on it. Maybe a break is in order."

What was this? Al glanced away.

I invited him back saying, "But, my advisor says it's best to go while you're in the rhythm of school and reminded me tuition never gets cheaper."

Al hesitated, sighed, and halfheartedly agreed.

"You don't look enthused, Al. What's wrong? Is it the tuition?"

He glared at his water glass while he slowly rotated it in meaningless circles, considering his next words.

"Well, yes. But we'll manage." With weariness and displeasure, he added, "My book sales should help." He camouflaged his objection behind a forced smile and insincere words of encouragement.

The doctoral program grew time-consuming and challenging. It was a lonely time of "weeding out" students. The dissertation year was oppressive. Nonetheless, I finally walked across the stage certain of a rewarding future. There were two Doctor Canty's under our roof now!

My Ph.D. ceremony

In front of Rackham Graduate
School afterward

Al and me back home. I was so tired. The years of long days and weekends were finally over. I honestly believed it was all downhill from there.

Over summer I invited Al into a discussion of wanting to pursue a post-doctoral fellowship. He questioned the necessity of this altogether, reminding me, "*I* never needed it. You don't *either*."

We sat eating pretzels on our dark orange corduroy couch in the library. "Right, but it will give me double credentials, you know, in psychology *and* family therapy. Plus, I'm just over at the medical campus and I'd be earning a stipend. No more tuition."

He stared at his feet and twisted his lips into an unfamiliar weird sneer. He obviously wasn't enthused but wouldn't elaborate. I glanced at the clock and knew he'd dart away. He paused, picked up his mustard-colored thermos and shrugged, signifying *Fine, whatever.*

My post-doctoral fellowship program accepted three psychologists a year from applicants all over the United States. It was hard to express the honor felt in being selected. It was housed next to the new Detroit Receiving Hospital in the University Health Center Building on St. Antoine and E. Canfield in a futuristic-looking aluminum and orange building. The Detroit Medical Center was the largest single medical campus in the country.

Our fellowship schedule was splintered between the medical campus, nearby Mott Center for Human Growth and Development and suburban Grosse Pointe Psychological Center under Drs. Aaron Rutledge and Lois Martindale. The "fellows," as we were called, worked alongside medical residents, participated in Grand Rounds at hospitals, contributed to case staffings and served as core members of a treatment team for rare disorders, such as pseudocyesis (false pregnancy) and complicated cases (such as allergic reactions to anti-psychotic medications).

Finishing year two of my post-doctoral fellowship – almost done!

However, the decision to pursue my two-year post-doctoral fellowship had unknowingly violated the tiny, invisible clause in our marriage certificate. Much later I would understand we had become locked in an invisible, inevitable stalemate. The tectonic plates below us had shifted. His unspoken need to be needed, in control, had been nullified. I wanted reciprocity. Al wanted dependency. I wanted autonomy. Al wanted subjugation. The moorings of our marriage had loosened. We began to quietly drift apart.

# SEVEN

# THE NEWEST IN THE OLDEST PROFESSION

The sediment of Cass Corridor lured its newest nomad in late spring of 1982. Dawn Spens dropped out of high school to join her dropout boyfriend, Donnie. They'd fit right in because it was a place for the wanted *and* the unwanted.

Donnie Carlton had already established himself there, more or less, by working at an arcade near Woodward and Montcalm while "skimming a little off the top." Dawn was broke but Donnie clarified she must fend for herself. He confided to a friend she was skilled at fleecing men "with this 'poor innocent me' bit. She could rap. She really had a mouth on her."

While hosting a small party in their apartment on Montcalm and Park, one guest leered toward Donnie remarking, "I know a couple guys who'd pay her."

Dawn overheard and considered prostitution as an

option, despite having landed a little convenience store job. *How bad could it be?* she reassured herself.

So, Donnie explained to an older man in an Imperial, "My girl's looking for some action."

Donnie studied her quizzically after returning from her first sale with the thirty-five-year-old patron. She shrugged. No big deal. No outward signs of regret, fear or shame. In fact, Dawn was more upset Donnie asked her to shower before climbing in bed with him, than having a stranger climb on her. Spens then frequented Sabbs Market, offering "nooners" and "dome" to the executives in grey wool suits from the northern, "respectable" edge of the Corridor. She expanded her circuit to Second and Peterboro, a mere ten-minute walk from ground zero for drug trafficking in the region. She was in the game. She was Faux Real.

Spens had always been a quick study. She earned street cred with her youthful face and pitiful narratives. "I need money to eat." "All my stuff was stolen." Whatever the hustle required. She learned the lonely, gullible and plain lecherous would readily hand her cash—sometimes without sexual favors. She was glib. She was convincing. She was not someone to take home to mama.

John Fry scrutinized the confident, pretty newcomer from a calculating distance and saw opportunity, not a human being, an investment, not a teen gone astray. He'd been out of lock-up for two years when his bulky frame cast shadows in the red-light district. He was overweight, balding, opiate dependent with little volume control and excess of bravado.

The ex-con informed Carlton he intended to "sponsor" Dawn. By this time, Fry was an experienced flesh peddler, as he'd already forced Cheryl Krizanovic into prostitution with beatings and chokeholds. In a televised news interview years later, Cheryl explained, "I stayed with him out of fear. I had true fear. He threatened me. 'If you leave me I will kill you. I will find you. I will kill you.' I stayed."

Fry knew Carlton was smacking Dawn and planned to wedge them apart with that intel. John struck up a conversation with Dawn, aiming to win her confidence and interest. Gradually Spens offered John drugs—not much, but enough to predictably upset Donnie and lure the scruffy biker. This escalated the tension and distrust between Donnie and Dawn. She declared she wanted out, to which Donnie demanded they leave together. She refused, reminding him the money she made was by her and for her. Spens then left Carlton for Fry who in turn threatened to kill Carlton if he attempted to reclaim her. The young prostitute willingly teamed up with the older pimp and relocated to 644 Charlotte, near the Masonic Temple, in 1983. Spens had just inched closer to the edge of the cliff, but from her viewpoint, she'd chosen up.

The scheming duo launched.

Their new base camp wasn't much, and neither was their view, as their apartment windows overlooked cement and traffic. The four-story brick structure was built in 1927 when the nearby Purple Gang supplied Canadian whiskey to the Capone gang. The fifty-year-old décor consisted of old lead-based, lime green paint with blemishes of lath. The color of the worn carpet was anybody's guess, and city pollution etched windows on the south side to semi-translucent portholes. A century later, it still lacked conveniences such as off-street parking, reliable heat and a finished basement. They celebrated their new partnership with an avalanche of drugs and a long drive to Walled Lake. Dawn was a rock star now.

Within a year, Carlton was incarcerated for clubbing church bookkeeper Raymond Culver to death. Donnie had yet to turn twenty-three. Neither Spens nor Fry heard from him again. Dee sure called *that* one right.

Not only was prostitution and heroin plentiful in the crumbling Corridor, so was mixed jive, Fry's preferred toxin. The illicit powder was packaged in small, tan, paper coin envelopes. Dealers frequently applied their "brand name" to each envelope using a rubber stamp. These tiny pouches sold for approximately twelve dollars each. They contained a substance heavily diluted by lactose powder, laced with strychnine, the active ingredient in rat poison. This blend gave the user a jolt, simulating a novice's rush. Old-timers chased the same sensation of euphoria and disconnection. The tradeoff was extremely dangerous, of course. Most knew but shrugged. Overdoses were common. Less frequent, yet equally lethal, were allergic reactions to the witches' brew.

Mark Bando, retired Detroit Police Officer, vividly recalled the result.

I've seen mixed jive abscesses on junkies. They were a black circle, about one quarter to three-quarter inch diameter. The outer, concentric ring created a crater. The deep groove surrounding the black core was filled with clear liquid, which gave me the creeps to look at. Some junkies had dozens of these sores. Some dealers deliberately altered the contents of their product to induce overdoses on unsuspecting customers. The dealers played God; they determined who lived and died.

Bando knew the area personally, as he'd been assigned that corner of hell for ten years.

In 1982, Bando and his partner John Woodington were summoned to the office of their precinct commander, Daniel McKane. Commander McKane had evaluated the current out of control situation of street prostitution within his precinct boundaries and decided that a focused remedy was required.

McKane proposed that a special warm weather anti-prostitution car be started, to work on that problem from April to October. He hoped that accelerated enforcement would help put a lid on the situation. The two selected officers would have an unmarked, four-door, blue Plymouth patrol vehicle at their disposal, but could occasionally opt to patrol in a regular marked DPD scout car. The commander admonished his officers that they were expected to adhere to the highest standards of moral conduct. The 'whore car' would run for three consecutive summers, 1982-84.

The officers made their own hours and days off and worked varying shifts so that the prostitutes could not anticipate when the officers would be out. Nonetheless, the streetwalkers tried to dodge beefed up patrols by using fake birthdays and aliases, as most had pre-existing warrants and unpaid fines. To keep track of the twelve-hundred prostitutes in the three-mile area the two-officer team assembled so-called "whore books."

We had a North End whore book,

mostly for black females who worked north of West Grand Boulevard to the south edge of Highland Park. The South End whore book (Dawn's territory) was almost all white. Arrests were also made for pimps, tricks and related felonies, such as stolen vehicles, illegal drugs and carrying concealed firearms.

Officer Bando easily recognized a veteran hooker. He'd seen the transformation from vibrant, cocky teen to hollow-eyed apparition in a predictable sequence.

The process took place over months or years. These women started out healthy and beautiful. Some were prettier than Hollywood stars. The prettier ones were haughty, even indignant. They used their good looks to manipulate and intimidate customers. Being told what to do, being arrested, was alien to their perception of themselves and their place in the world.

The junkies blazed a clear trail *if* you knew what to look for. Custodians with the thankless job of cleaning up after them found it repeatedly. Heroin and mixed jive users ripped rotating cloth towels from public bathroom dispensers to use as tourniquets before inserting their version of heaven. Arcs of blood spatter confirmed their actions. Some dabbed toothpaste in the craters of abscesses to slow the pus from spotting their clothing. Some thought it had medicinal properties.

Not easily deterred, Fry dispatched Dawn to the grubby overnight truck stop near Michigan Avenue, east of Wyoming near the Congress Motel. She voiced no objection at becoming a lot lizard. Spens was a prodigy. But, for a parent, she could have only been a source of shame, worry and self-condemnation.

Officer Mark Bando ticketing a prostitute in the early hours on Cass Ave. around 1980. She had a day job in the suburbs. She, too, led a double life. (Credit: Ira Rosenberg, Detroit Free Press)

Many tricks were lonely, long-haul drivers hunting amorous company, but it was anyone's guess who among them was a freeway killer. Dawn must have known, in moments of clarity, that some serial murderers employed semi-trucks to control, conceal and transport victims across state lines. The FBI estimated that two hundred twenty-nine of one-hundred-thousand prostitutes became victims and that number did not include cold cases. But to this, and other dangers, she shrugged. Dawn considered John her protector, though he ordered her into danger. She regarded him as supportive, despite his expectation she'd turn tricks to support his habit. She told herself he respected her, yet he claimed she, "wasn't a fifteen-dollar whore. She was a fifty-dollar whore."

Typical for teens, she dramatically professed feelings for her new partner in prose.

*My love for you grows stronger with each day... I love you baby, so much it hurts me inside. It feels like someone is tearing my heart out. You are and always will be the love and light of my life... I yearn to lay in your strong arms. The arms that have protected and supported me... You're my whole life and will continue to be my whole life, for as long as you wish.*

Her fiend/pimp/punk rationalized his actions. As long as Dawn received cash—*beforehand*—Lucky didn't care what his for-rent woman did. In fact, Fry didn't want to hear about it. He figured everyone was a prostitute since everyone worked for something. Selling stocks was no different from selling sex. Fry smugly saw himself as a realist. He possessed *standards*, after all. He objected to Spens "having sex with any nigger." His hatred for blacks was legend in the Corridor, as it was rumored he "carved one up" outside a bar. Lucky Fry took offense to the term "pimp." He was Dawn's "sponsor." And Dawn wasn't a slut. She was his "working girl" who went on "dates."

Therein was another twist. How did an intelligent, suburban, high school would-be valedictorian turn tricks for a malodorous flesh-peddler in the dangerous Corridor before she could vote? *How does anyone choose to become rental property?* The risk factors were undoubtedly rooted in youth.

Spens was like many street sex workers, excluding those sold into trafficking, in that almost all come from abusive or neglectful homes with family disruption. Their childhoods were interrupted by parental incarceration, death, divorce, drug addiction or rejection and they became depressed. Future prostitutes usually found little joy in school, quitting early, severely limiting job options. Despite her academic success, Dawn left just short of graduation, increasing her social marginalization. These young women lived in unstable housing. Dawn was young, vulnerable, and nearly beyond the reach of safety nets. Prostitution was "survival sex" no matter how their customers fooled themselves into believing their momentary partner enjoyed it. Coercion and violence were simply job hazards. Dawn, like others, had a drug habit to feed, making her easy prey for pimps, bad cops, dealers and those with a penchant for viciousness.

Spens was a tad older than most beginners, but still a teen. Like her counterparts, she'd seen others struggle financially despite working hard. Typical for adolescents, Dawn could not envision the skin, hair, health and memories of her not-so-distant future. After drugs entered the picture, addiction followed and, with the enabling of Al, grew to crisis proportions. Support from the nearest and dearest faded. Dawn would age swiftly, grow more callous and risk her life *for* the life. She joined the group most easily and frequently killed of all women anywhere on earth.

A case in point was Linda Faye Wells who was shot in the face with a .32 caliber handgun. She was only 27. Her half-nude body was found on the back seat of an abandoned car at the rear of Auto City Motel in the Corridor in 1981. Ten years later Benjamin "Tony" Atkins (also known as the "Woodward Corridor Killer") would rape, torture and murder eleven women north of the Corridor and most were working as prostitutes. Atkins later admitted he hated prostitutes. His victims ranged in age between 21 – 45 and all were found in abandoned buildings. Not only did Dawn risk death, but prostitutes lacked the glamour of three-thousand-dollar-an-hour high-end call girls entertaining powerful politicians and celebrities, as well as the "victimhood" of hidden, trafficked women. There was no gauge to determine the wear and tear on Dawn's soul.

Prostitution was one of the few jobs where the pay was greatest for the least experienced. Many didn't survive past their thirties. Those that did were bitter, ill, broke and prone to post-traumatic stress disorder. They produced thick medical files, thin resumes and long arrest records. Many became mothers, a role they were no more ready to fulfill than an eight-year-old playing for the NBA. They consumed tax dollars with a revolving door of incarcerations and emergency hospitalizations for acute problems related to drugs, pregnancy and beatings. Some police thought it pointless to look for them if they went missing. It was less work if they *did* vanish. Besides, they rationalized, who'd miss them? Some officers were also tricks, blurring the line more. Death from accidental overdose, infections, homicide or suicide was shockingly commonplace. Some fatalities were impossible to confirm because of little cooperation and too few officers. Open season. During the years Dawn prostituted she risked one in a two-hundred chance of mortality. The leading cause of death on the streets she paced was homicide in a city that led the nation in homicide.

> *"A litany of headlights blinding her, she stands unsteady on the dotted traffic line,*
> *takes timid steps toward rolled up windows behind which any horror could crouch...."*
> ---Beatriz Fitzgerald Fernandez, *Shining from a Different Firmament*

Officer Bando, a man I'd meet much later, worked Whore Patrol throughout the 1980s and kept tabs on the fresh face from the suburbs.

My first encounter with Dawn Spens was preceded by word on the street. We heard about a new girl from the suburbs making a ton of money using a room above the market on Park near Sibley for turning tricks. One afternoon we spotted her a block north of there, loitering where there could be no other reason for a pretty girl from the suburbs to be there. We figured she would not yet have existing warrants. However, a check of her purse for possible weapons turned up a set of works (a hypodermic needle and syringe). This was an arrestable offense. Curiously, Dawn offered no resistance nor said a word when placed in handcuffs and driven to the 13th.

She evidently decided she'd deal with police through passivity. Her mind seemed detached—a good attribute for a prostitute who dealt with unappealing strangers. We tried to make conversation and learn more on the way to lock-up. She gave one-word answers. Oddly, she did not try the haughty trip. However, I believe she knew she could have maximum effect with minimal effort. To display any emotion was beneath her dignity. She displayed a shrugging indifference.

We parked [the patrol car] near the gas pumps at #13. We took a couple mug shots. What I will always remember about this encounter was how magnetically physically attractive Dawn was and that I felt nervous and somewhat shook up being in her presence. None of the other working girls affected me like that—before or after. I compared my perceptions with my partner, Woodington, and he said Dawn had the same unnerving effect on him.

Officers Bando and Woodington wanted to get Spens out of curb crawling. She was young, bright, healthy and had family ties. They contacted her father, Roy, and put her on the phone. Like Tallulah Bankhead, tears flowed. Mr. Spens invited her home and offered to come the following night to Chris & Carl's Café on Cass near Montcalm. She promised she'd show. Bando and Woodington did, too. They wanted a smooth hand off.

Roy Spens arrived punctually and joined the officers. The men on this rescue mission ordered coffee and awkwardly waited. Fifteen minutes passed. They stumbled for conversation. Twenty. Roy repeatedly glanced at the time, their cups, the window and his hands. What went through his mind as he made small talk with two Detroit cops on skid row, awaiting his honor student daughter who prostituted, injected hard drugs, and who lived with a felon many years her senior? Did he ask himself how she had become good at making bad decisions? For reasons known only to her, Dawn chose Lucky, mixed jive, beatings, arrests, sex with strangers and substandard housing over the lifesaver tossed her way. She claimed the street and the street claimed her.

Dawn Spens' arrest photo in front of Precinct 13 gas pumps
(Credit: Mark Bando)

Bando had at least two reasons to clean up the Corridor. For one, it was his assignment. Second, he could recall the urban oasis of years gone by. He took a girlfriend to the opera at the Masonic Temple. Now his headlights found whores and addicts cluttering the gutters, discouraging legitimate business. It soured his stomach to know girls as young as eleven were trained as prostitutes. Some were frightened runaways. Most were too off-course, uneducated and high to find their way back. The hustlers were locked in an undeclared war zone, turned out by families, controlled by pimps, used by customers and periodically sealed up by society. Many were considered "toss-aways" — but not all. Bando knew some were lured from affluent households with worried, educated parents. The father of one with a girl-next-door appearance was a police chief in Arkansas. However, pimps, tricks, and some members of law enforcement saw them as interchangeable, moldable and disposable. They were mere minions who served to please and were pleased to serve.

If Bando ever needed a reminder about the degradation, he preserved a note written by a newly deceased prostitute that read:

*It is so fucking sick in this neighborhood. It's sickening. Everybody is a stone dope fiend to the max. I'm going to get a good trick of mine to co-sign a car for me and get the fuck out of Detroit. My baby is not going to go through what I did. I'll get a better life for my baby if I have to kill a*

*motherfucker to get it.*

Officer Bando had no illusions about the damage inflicted to streetwalkers, their children, local businesses and the south-central chunk of Detroit. He'd seen his share of the walking wounded, the nearly dead, and even escorted some to Receiving Hospital. Bando and Woodington always wondered which overdoses were accidental and those that were intended. They never lost sight this was someone's daughter, sister, high school sweetheart or mother. Homicides were on the rise. It was as if law enforcement needed a smoking gun in the hand of the shooter standing over the deceased or a spontaneous confession of "yeah, I did it" to make an arrest. Cases simply kept piling up, which interfered with open cases being investigated. When it came to other felonies, witnesses failed to appear, and stories changed. The challenge to redeem the area was as fruitful and exhausting as sweeping leaves on a windy day.

As if solicitation and drugs weren't problematic enough, there was escalating homelessness, loitering and carjacking. Twenty-four-hour liquor stores with thick Plexiglas separated patrons from clerks under smoke-varnished fluorescent lights. Well-known locals bought and sold contraband at all hours. Empty, weedy, littered lots shared boundaries with burned out structures from a previously civil era along with packs of rats and an occasional cadaver. Nearly opaque bullet-resistant Plexiglas partitioned cab drivers and store clerks from customers.

One of many ironies of law enforcement in the

Corridor, is that many of the younger full-time prostitutes earned more than the officers that arrested them – including fines and court costs. Not surprisingly, under these conditions, the sex trade flourished in the Corridor. Fry ensured he'd get his cut. He knew sunlight wasn't flattering to the fast talking, embittered "senior" hookers. These "old" curb crawlers found better luck renting their high-mileage bodies under the veil of nightfall, usually charging fifteen-dollars a "date." However, this fresh face was netting him bigger profits with less effort.

# EIGHT

# STRANGE BEDFELLOWS

Gladys wanted to honor her son's fiftieth birthday and handed him five-hundred-dollars with a smile, commenting, "After all, you're a big boy now."

Al decided to celebrate this occasion by embarking on a fateful odyssey with shameful penalties. On the gray afternoon of November 30, 1983, he made a single, shameful choice. Powered with adrenaline and denial, he aimed his new car three miles south, toward the slums and red lights, with its promise of risk and failed dreams and guilty pleasures.

Al drove to the blighted area, propelled by the summation of his life experiences. He slid into another role, having yielded to his urge to "get away with something." He promised himself he'd behave better in the future, but not that night.

> *The house that Jack built is a house as real as any other.*
> *And Mother Goose is just as real as anybody's mother.*

*And Santa Claus is just as true as anything can be.*
*The greatest forces in this world are those we cannot*
*see...*
— Buster Brown.

The essential character of the Buster Brown comic series was centered on a young boy with a pageboy haircut and an American Pit Bull Terrier. The caricature, an only child, lived in the city with wealthy parents where he was mischievous and pulled pranks, usually alone. Most cartoons concluded with Buster delivering an extraneous, self-justifying "resolution." Buster's mother met his transgressions with spankings and shame, yet he showed no guilt, no learning. He was a sly boy. I was tempted to see parallels between the Buster Brown stories and the dynamics of my in-law's household.

So, it was my husband of nine years, the man I pledged to share all my married life with, "curb-crawled" in the deteriorating squalor of Cass Corridor, one mile southwest from where I was on medical leave. He must have known this short drive would jeopardize our lives as we knew it. This was "Buster's" mischievous, disgraceful tilting point, a detour leading to charades, dishonor and dead ends.

Al paused in the dirty slush at Second and Charlotte with a racing heart. An attractive, available teenager on "kiddie stroll" paced in below-freezing temperatures wearing a long, stylish leather coat that needlessly flattered her youthful shape. Gusty winds fluffed her long locks, which increased her allure. Her flirtatious glance beckoned him into her world of lawlessness and assured carnality. A span of thirty-two years both separated and connected them.

The rebel minus a cause smiled stiffly, awkwardly, as if wearing a mask and roguishly asked, "You workin'?" That's all it took to turn our world upside down, two self-destructive, self-righteous words from the mouth of a man who made a living encouraging others to be considerate and genuine.

The young hustler made a living with her mouth also. She leaned in, felt the gush of warm air, inhaled the new car smell and surveyed him with the eye of a pro. She decided he wasn't a cop, and purred, "Want to go out?" She wondered if he was a bookkeeper.

Al handed her ten dollars to obtain her number and name. "Dawn," she winked. "Dawn Spens." She didn't ask his name, nor did she care. Tricks were interchangeable. He was looking for a "GFE"—girlfriend experience. She was after cold, hard cash. They understood their implicit contract. He was just another faceless, errant husband looking for adventure. But adventure was a lot like water. In sensible doses, it was life-affirming. In massive doses, it could kill.

The disaster could still have been averted if Buster only paused to acknowledge the fallout from what he was about to do. If only he'd considered the impact to his integrity, marriage, his profession. But loyalty took a back seat to his need for pranks and lust on that wintry afternoon of his fiftieth year. He was not about to let this secret diversion pass by.

He was mind blind.

The five-foot-four-inch petite hooker from Harper Woods and her latest trick paired up hours later in the danger zone near the White Grove Diner, at 3131 Second

Avenue. He exchanged real life, with all its cumbersome accountability, commitments and regulations, for peril and frolic. His lust was palpable. So was her need for drug money.

The White Grove Restaurant at 3131 2nd Ave. - Detroit
(which hung on longer than most Corridor establishments)

The streetwalker charged fifty-dollars for the use of her agile body. They agreed their steamy rendezvous would occur at the nearby, narrow Temple Hotel at 72 Temple Street where rooms were rented by the half hour, like Spens herself. He excitedly, immediately agreed.

The yard outside the 1880s Romanesque Revival flophouse, situated between Cass and Woodward alongside a narrow alley, was paved over with asphalt. It's doubtful the original architects would have approved of the modified entrance with its six-foot-tall cinder block wall that surrounded cigarette butts, empty twenty-four-ounce Colt-45s, and secrets. It was more suitable as a barricade for an industrial building or to partition compost than frame a vintage hotel foyer. Over time, this unsightly obstruction received leisurely-applied graffiti, periodically concealed by grey paint only to be despoiled again. That night it exhibited puffy, large blue letters proclaiming "Rift," an expression unnoticed or unrecognized by patrons who scurried inside with more pressing matters.

The hotel originated from the Gilded Age where heavy ornamented glitz ruled the day and a ribbon of glossy paving bricks ran adjacent to the once-dignified entrance. The three-dollar charge per night per person included dinner back then. The Temple was erected around the time of Jack the Ripper, widely believed to be the first known serial murderer of prostitutes.

Temple Hotel(and bordello) at 72 Temple Street -Detroit around 1980

Pedestrians could glimpse careless, amorous patrons inside the second-story bay window some evenings. The third floor accommodated a seldom-used brick patio and narrow casement window with a green copper spire projecting skyward from the dormer. The tarnished adornment's only purpose now was to remind passers-by of the building's once refined origins. Mismatched brown asphalt shingles, from various attempts to heal the steep roof, added to the overall look of neglect and senescence. Mismatched wires and television antennas, some at odd angles, completed the disfigurement of the once impressive inn. Nearly every window on the first floor was ablaze that holiday season. Business was vigorous.

Before Dawn and Al established their rhythm, they met a temporary barrier, which consisted of no-nonsense ghetto grills (iron security gates) and two buzzers. They hurried past black metal coach lights toward the front porch capped under a deep, red, stone arch of the arthritic building to begin Act One Scene One of their respective role-plays as lovers. The Canty name was about to be smeared. Gladys would have been appalled.

A few "higher end" bedrooms had faded flocked crème and lilac wallpaper that somehow survived the ravages of time, use and "improvements." The hotel's two elaborate oak staircases, framed by prominent gothic newel posts, were pointed and large, along with carved chair railings above carpeted steps. Deep oak sills underscored tall windows, topped with delicately-carved molding. The firm staircase railings bore thousands of handprints from inhabitants and thrill seekers. Ironically, the building was erected when women were judged on their purity, manners, and modesty — but not tonight. The old structure was no longer opulent, no longer suitable for earnest business travelers, families, vacationers or prudent women. Its overall appearance had dulled to plain and functional.

It was understood that the first and second floors of thirty-four rooms was set aside for patrons who used a lot of bed linens. The third floor was reserved for "permanent" guests who paid weekly. Old grizzly, shapeless men lounged on dated, shapeless couches in the smoky lobby with unadorned light green walls. They swapped gossip, stories of conquests and spouted solutions to life's problems. Some knew a few "tricks" and police officers by name. Locally this bordello was known as "The White House," not for its paint, but for the color of skin screened at the entrance.

The two actors peered through a wire mesh cage to communicate with the uninterested front desk clerk, the keeper of the garden. His belief was all customers were alike, though he never looked up at them. The trick paid the admission fee of five-dollars plus a twenty-dollar room charge and adopted the name, "Dr. Al Miller." He'd always relished the theater. He forgot, if only momentarily, he had a wife, private practice, and ethical code for his profession. He was living up to his teenage reputation of being "book smart and life stupid."

Al was in overdrive.

Showtime. They walked shoulder to shoulder toward their Bower of Bliss, though on that chilly evening the halls were uncomfortably stuffy. Their passageway, illuminated by smudged vintage chandeliers of gaudy cut glass, dripped with pseudo-sophistication and visual clutter. The glow of the fixtures was reflected in the high gloss ceiling paint from which they hung. Whiffs of stale urine, perspiration, alcohol, cigarettes and old newspaper accompanied the squeaky corridor. Muffled tête-à-tête and impatient moans of metronome passion were audible behind some raised panel doors, demonstrating discretion took a back seat to fulfillment in the combination boarding house-strumpet nest. The Temple did not offer marble nor a pleasing view of Central Park.

He crossed the Rubicon.

Al's descent into dishonor was initiated. Their tryst hastily began with his purchase of what most tricks desired. Escorts knew it as a "half and half" — half oral, half genital sex. He wasn't particularly rough, nor loud, but no Don Juan. For him, the real world — and its routine — had vanished. He wished only to absorb that moment, that sensation, his wantonness. There was no more need for words. He sought immediate carnal healing for all that tarnished and twisted him emotionally. Al "Miller" immersed himself in an intimate thrill and yielded to the forged overtures of his young companion. Buster enjoyed the risk, the sheer "naughtiness" of it. It was no big deal to her. Dawn wasn't in love despite making love. Neither was he. Her hands, which slid over her customer's thighs, would one day use them in a way she could not then imagine. Dawn Marie's own right thigh, with a rose tattoo, intensified his rush. Their thin sheets became as tangled and stirred as the serpentine shadows cast upon the barren walls. She knew how to tease and please, ever-mindful time was money. His hyperventilating assured her he had what he desired but the young streetwalker was turned off by how much he was turned on.

Doc Al "Miller" found a way to turn the wrongs into a right on that birthday and he was satisfied. Al tipped Spens generously for her sexual expertise and expressed interest in a future ménage-a-deux before they slipped back into the weary hallway. She promptly agreed. It was just survival sex. He was on cloud ten.

*In the middle of the journey of life*
*I found myself within a dark wood*
*where the straightway was lost.*
— Dante Alighieri, *Inferno*

# NINE

# DESERT SLUMBER

Achy joints, raw throat, and fever stopped me cold. The "mono" virus zapped my energy for the third go 'round during our ninth year of marriage, stalling completion of my fellowship training. I reduced my hours but couldn't keep up. Winter was fast approaching and, after two months of worsening symptoms, my physician recommended a time-out. "You can go to a hospital or somewhere warm and rest."

We both knew he was suggesting a trip to my parents', away from damp, bone-chilling weather and deadlines. The thought of desert sunshine, sleep and quiet was appealing. Dr. Hillenberg added, "Your immune system is weak. The last place you should be working is an urban medical center. The last thing you should be doing is working ten-hour days. That's partly why you're not recovering."

This meant I wouldn't be home for Al's fiftieth

birthday which I had so wanted to celebrate together. However, between the urging of Dr. Hillenberg, my supervisor Dr. Rutledge, my parents' concern and the reassurance from Al, I caved. After all, was November in the sunny southwest a bitter pill to swallow? Dr. Rutledge offered to extend my fellowship deadline to meet the two-thousand-hour requirement. "You'll be further behind if you *don't* go. In your state of fatigue, you aren't much good for anything *but* sleep. You're learning habits of a lifetime. Take care of you. If your patients see you do that, they'll take better care of themselves too. Go."

Dr. Aaron L. Rutledge, my steadfast mentor

Likewise, Al commented, "I can't bear to see you so lethargic. This has gone on long enough. Your parents will take good care of you."

So, I boarded an outbound for Sky Harbor/Phoenix. Al had purchased an open-ended, nonstop first-class ticket to smooth my way, a straight four hours, with the explanation I'd receive "better care" if I weren't in coach.

*He's so considerate.* Sleep easily won out.

The jet floated over changing terrain thirty-thousand feet below, where grey sleet yielded to orange skies and smog was eclipsed by wind-swept palms. My parents embraced me, reliable as the sun setting over the dry desert.

Dad teased, "Do you need me to carry you?"

They'd prepared fresh sheets, homemade soup, a new pillow. Soon after unpacking, dusk descended. White Christmas lights glowed inside their stucco courtyard, and the three-tiered terracotta fountain splashed soothing water over the basins, pleasantly drowning out civilization. The restful sight was hypnotic and in full view from my bed. It was the best seat in the house.

"Your job is to get better," Mom reassured. "Mine is to get you there."

A warm breeze softly penetrated the decorative iron grates on the fully open window. My parents' two-bedroom house was perched on the western edge of the Painted Desert with the lavender Gila Mountain in the distance. It was exceedingly quiet, a world away from the cold hustle of Detroit. In no time I was dormant and hovered in bed eighteen hours a day, desiring no contact with the world. I was uninterested in conversation and food but craved icy fluids. Light bothered my eyes, and my throat was ablaze. Mom poked in occasionally, and their Golden Retriever sometimes slept nearby, without even demanding a pat on her old gray head.

I'd set my bedside alarm to coincide with 11:00 p.m. Detroit time and, what seemed like moments later, it obediently pierced the calm of the darkened guestroom. I reluctantly clawed my way back into consciousness, fighting confusion brought on by deep sleep, medicine and infection. For a moment, I couldn't recall why it rang as I slowly sat upright. My cold feet staggered toward the phone while my fevered shoulders felt gripped by invisible icy hands. Outdoor luminaries still glowed on that balmy night of November 30. They cast soft shadows on my parents' tile kitchen floor. They were asleep. I wanted to be hibernating, too. My pounding head tempted me back to the soft pillow and state of near lifelessness under soothing blankets. My throat felt rubbed raw with gasoline. Two rings. I perked up at the sound of Al's voice.

"Jan-Jan! What a surprise! You should be in bed."

I stifled a yawn. "I was. Just got up to call you. I feel bad I missed your birthday." I did my best to sing him "Happy Birthday" through my thick throat without coughing in the dim kitchen. *What was this? Tears? That was unlike him!*

"I'm just so worried, have been all day."

"But I'll be *fine*! It's mono, not yellow fever. I just need rest. I miss you. Did you do anything special after work, for your birthday?"

"Yeah. I treated myself to dinner at Chung's."

Al knew I disliked him eating there, at the frayed eatery on Cass and Peterboro, founded in 1940 in the once-thriving Chinatown. The worn-down, single-story restaurant with large red awning was open until 2:00 a.m. The late hours seemed to attract the local sinners and desperados. However, it was his fiftieth, I had no strength to protest and what was done was done. It saddened me to picture him eating his Chow Mein alone staring at the empty chair across him on this night that was supposed to be memorable. As was our custom, I asked, "So, what did your fortune cookie say?"

"Oh, the usual… Something about love as medicine or some such thing."

Our conversation was short, hardly what I desired for his half-century mark. The worry in his voice made my heart sink. His birthday had been ignored while he'd fussed over mine. Just this year he somehow tracked down a signed edition of Sharon Wegscheider-Cruse's book, a social worker I admired. And, if that wasn't enough, Al presented tickets to see Marvin Gaye at the Masonic Temple. I hated being apart. Hearing his voice made me miss him more. *We're separated by a third of the United States and a stubborn virus.* I did not then know we were also separated by a dangerous lie.

By week's end, I slept less. It was reassuring to be with my parents as I perched on the edge of the aqua pool soaking up vitamin D in the Valley of the Sun. My appetite gradually returned, my headache left, and I grew homesick. By day ten, I walked their dog on the nearby desert at sunup, and planned my trip home, just in time for the holidays.

*Ah, life is returning to normal,* I thought, as the 727 landed in light snow. Al's open arms greeted me on the evening of December 14 back at Detroit Metro.

My parents and me in Arizona, on our way to the airport - feeling much better

Arizona

Because of sick leave, I'd fallen behind in the required post-doctoral fellowship hours, so needed overtime to catch up. This negated some lunches with Al and more hours bent over paperwork in the evening. Fortunately, he showed no resentment for the interference and encouraged me to take whatever time was needed.

His patience smoothed out my rough road. I knew in my heart of hearts I was right where I was supposed to be. I was so proud to have him as my spouse, to know he had our best interests at heart. He respected me, loved me in sickness and in health. This would be one of those points in our marriage that would be memorable.

Detroit Metro; home again… (Credit: Detroit CBS local.com)

# TEN

# WHAT MIGHT HAVE BEEN

By mid-summer, I felt ill, out of sorts, just "not me." Fatigue weighed me down, turning slippers into lead boots. I became winded running upstairs. My hair had thinned. At first, these nuances were dismissed. Who wouldn't be tired putting in seventy-hour weeks year after year, commuting one-hundred miles round-trip for classes on a freeway under construction, completing schoolwork on weekends and caring for a house the size of an orphanage? Nevertheless, after three weeks of additional dizziness, low back pain and nausea, I made a doctor's appointment.

Dr. Hillenberg completed an assessment and unleashed a roller coaster with two words. "You're pregnant!"

I was stunned.

"Yup. Congratulations!" he said, over thick, rimmed glasses.

"But I'm infertile!"

He laughed and shook his head. "Apparently not."

I felt shock. Then panic. Then glee. Then uncertainty. Al was never crazy about kids. My concentration splintered. What would he say?

Before I caught my breath, he added, "And so I want you to see an obstetrician soon, tomorrow if possible. You're what we call an 'old first-time mom' so you need to be seen early and maybe often."

In the shower, I strove to collect my thoughts as my hand slid over my future child. No wonder I'd been tired. I needed time to wrap my head around the news and decided to ask a colleague with five children how she managed it all.

She explained, "My mother-in-law lives next door and our oldest are fourteen-year-old twins so they're a big help, too. Larry's mom moved near us when our fourth came along. I don't know what I'd do without her."

I couldn't see that applying to my life.

Dinner was much too rushed for such an important discussion, so it was delayed a few hours until Al finished work. But, by 7:30, as he wrapped up downstairs, I suddenly showed signs of a miscarriage. I contacted my doctor, who was equally concerned. Since I had no fever, didn't feel faint and my pain was on both sides, he gave me the choice to stay home and call later, or go to the hospital. I chose the former. He informed me this would take hours.

The physical pain paled next to the emotional pain.

"Why are you crying? Do I need to call 9-1-1? What's *wrong,* Jan-Jan?"

This wasn't how I wanted to tell him. This wasn't

supposed to end like this. This wasn't supposed to end *at all!* Between the crescendos of pain, I described what happened and what was happening and what would never happen. He paced, rubbed my back, glanced at his watch and brought cold washcloths.

Hours later the storm passed. I felt weak, confused and sadly empty. He sat on the bed, our faces barely illuminated by a dim buffet-style lamp and placed a hand on my perspiring knee. "You shouldn't have gone through this alone, Jan-Jan."

"I didn't. You were here. I just found out yesterday. I needed to let the dust settle before you knew, that's just my way." I tried unsuccessfully to get comfortable among damp sheets and continued, "I was planning on telling you tonight after your last patient. I hoped you'd be excited."

He waited for more.

"I wasn't sure about a nanny or what we'd do. I didn't know how you'd react. This wasn't planned, I know."

He sighed, looked away and finally said, "Wow, I'd be fifty-one. That's a little old for a new dad, but you would've been a great mom. I'm sure we could've dealt with it, you know?" He was deep in thought. "Sure, unexpected..." He sighed again then lay down. "You needn't worry, I wouldn't have left you or anything. Try to get some sleep." He kissed me on the forehead, turned out his light and peacefully slept.

I remained wide awake, reliving the gyrating events of the last forty-eight hours. His unsettling words echoed. *"Deal with it?" "Left me?"*

I was alone in my confusion, shock and grief for what could've been. Did I carry a son or daughter? Whom would the baby have resembled? What could their future have held? My due date was mid-March. I told no one else of the miscarriage because I wanted to hold on to it, to the pregnancy, at least in my mind, for as long as possible.

My "lost child" threw off my momentum. I'd lost my way. My friends had started families and took actual vacations. I looked at reports, not baby clothes. Instead of holding a newborn, I embraced books. For the first time in a long time, I questioned what I wanted out of life.

Al smiled at me the next morning, but I did not, could not, smile back. "I'm still spinning about the pregnancy and how it ended before it started. It was unexpected but I got excited. Your reaction was confusing. It's not just school and it's just not fair."

He paused, smiled and remarked, "Like I said, you would've been a great mom. What do you need? What can I do?"

I had no answer and shrugged. There was a chilly draft circulating between us. It was unfamiliar and unsettling and unspoken. I brushed it off as hormones.

I began a gradual transition to nurture my own practice in the Fisher Building while I reduced hours at the medical center. The conversion was easy since I'd been doing more supervision of first-year post-doctoral fellows than clinical work. The light at the end of the long tunnel was emerging. It had been an extended haul since Oakland Community College, but the years of all-work-and-little-pay were finally over. The day I held my acceptance letter to Wayne State a decade earlier released my dream. It seemed we were going to finally sit on top of the world when, in actuality, we'd begun to slide off.

Meanwhile, Al busied himself in his work and was

close to finishing the brick driveway. Even as chilly weather descended, his enthusiasm remained for hunting heavy street-paving bricks in old, almost-abandoned inner-city neighborhoods.

"Al, you could get clobbered. It's dangerous and probably illegal, don't you think?"

Al in front of the carriage house designing the brick driveway (drinking coffee)

He ignored the hazard and me. He might as well wear a sign saying "easy mark" across his back as he stooped digging up his treasures. This was only one of several ways he demonstrated indifference to risk. When he left his new car unlocked, peeled cash from a roll of bills, was jovial with strangers who did not welcome a conversation, left repairmen in the house alone, was careless about locking his office, he revealed his callous indifference to danger. He was equally confused by my alarm at this. His trivializing of risk, indeed, his *flirtation* with it, widened the wedge between us.

My life partner was a study in contrasts, but perhaps that can be said of any spouse. On the one hand, if he said he'd be home by six, I could set my watch by that. He predictably read the paper each weekend, regularly watched the local, annual Grand Prix races and seldom shopped for clothes. He drank coffee by the gallon, purchased from Kroger's, and seldom traveled anywhere without his beat-up thermos. He even took it into restaurants! I overheard someone tease him about it and he admitted it was "his blanket." He faithfully took his mother grocery shopping on Sundays. He was a creature of habit.

Conversely, his personal papers remain disordered, outdated and growing. He never organized the boxes of rusty car parts. He didn't care if dinner was at 3:00 p.m. or 9:00 p.m. and was forever losing his keys. He didn't mind spending eight-hundred-dollars to preserve our century-old elm tree yet balked at spending over twenty-dollars on shoes. He had five suits and wore three. No one ever accused him of dressing to impress and he was oblivious to the snowstorm of dandruff that spotted his shoulders and ashes that dropped on his little paunch.

A week into 1984 I described the car I'd been saving for, a slightly used red, five-speed, turbo-charged Thunderbird. "It has wonderful smelling grey leather, aluminum wheels, and a tach, Al!" I'd wanted a car like that all my life while I'd been driving very used Volkswagens. "It's an executive lease car from Ford Motor. My dad says it's just broken in! I know it's been maintained."

Al insisted on paying the balance for Christmas, despite the holiday being over.

"Well, only if we agree it's my graduation present, too!"

It provided reliable heat, quiet windshield wipers, a working gas gauge, *and* a defroster! I was *thrilled*. My shiny gift was nicknamed "Chili Pepper." Wherever we went I was confident it would not fail me. This signaled the years of lugging textbooks and generally postponing "real life" was worth it. Change was underfoot.

Over the following months, differences in Al's appearance and behavior surfaced, slow at first, but with more resolve. He was strangely cheerful, in a forced way. At other times he was engrossed and far away. He spontaneously arrived home early one day in a stylish coat.

"Al, such a change. I like it!"

"Yeah," he responded with a giddy quality, "I have some spontaneity left in me!"

He complemented it with shoes that cost more than twenty-dollars and a garish navy athletic jacket with "Cadieux Café Detroit" monogrammed on the back in orange. He kept the windbreaker tucked in his car.

Gladys noticed the changes and commented, "Isn't it nice he's sprucing up?" I thought it was welcome yet odd.

# ELEVEN

# SNOW JOB

The first shot across the bow was mistaken by Al as a cry for help. Spens "caught another case" — her seventh solicitation arrest — on December 7th, 1983. She needed two-hundred-fifty dollars in bail money.

Fry decided to test her new trick's interest. After all, "Doc Miller" had rented her body three times the first week alone, and John wasn't about to spend his money for her problems. The pimp wanted a face-to-face. He came. They met. John "Lucky" Fry dismissed Dr. Al Miller as a "goof" and accurately concluded he'd drifted far from safe harbor. And the joke was on Al since the DPD had already released his damsel in distress and she had watched the entire performance from upstairs. Moreover, her bail was inflated. It was a play within a play. She had a good laugh at Al's expense. It would not be her last. Al saw the bait, not the hook.

In December, John wanted to accompany his

younger brother Jim "Six Pack" to Gleason, Tennessee in Weakley County to see their father, Pete. More importantly, he wanted to pay respects to his mother's grave. Since Fry was concerned about Six's growing paranoid, drug-induced delusions from the rocket fuel he'd been ingesting, Fry demanded everyone "go around the turn" (get clean and sober).

He explained, "We can't help Six if we're fucked up. We're gonna get clean for Christmas."

How would they finance their holiday expedition? In unison, they sought to tap Doc Miller. Spens requested a modest three-hundred-dollars. By departure time the following day, Doc Miller did not bring it. He brought a thousand.

John, Dawn, Six Pack, and his family drove through Wingo, Martin and Dresden before they reached Gleason, Tennessee on an unusually frigid Christmas Eve. The tiny town of about four-hundred families off Hwy 22 was devoid of stoplights but boasted an annual Tater Town Parade and Coca-Cola fundraiser. They drove streets named Luellen, Janes Mill, and Pillowville which were a stone's throw from John's birthplace in Fulton.

Pete Fry wasn't particularly delighted to set eyes on his eldest son, John, but displayed curiosity over the young woman who accompanied him. As usual, he welcomed Six Pack warmly. He reminded himself repeatedly it *was* Christmas and his twin grandsons were there, so he tried to be superficially cordial to John.

Later, just as everyone was asleep, Six came to his father looking like the weight of the world was upon him.

"Pop, I want to ask you somethin'. Is it okay if me and the twins move here and stay with you? I think I'm gonna have to leave Janet."

The eldest Fry slowly lit another cigarette as he propped himself up on his makeshift mattress. "Why, you don't even have to *ask* something like that." With a slight smile he added, "Jim Dale, you know the answer."

His youngest, clearly pleased at his father's reaction, sat pensively in the near darkness. A look of urgency and seriousness swept across Six's tired face again and he cautiously digressed into a tangled monologue about "the devils" and how he needed to "get them" as he eyed his father's gun rack. Jim Dale "Six Pack" was without ground control.

Neither Pete nor Six knew Janet had shimmied quietly into the blackened room and remained tucked in the recesses of the corner. She'd heard every word.

Confused and tired himself, Pete Fry listened but dismissed Six Pack's ramblings as "crazy talk" and suggested everyone get some rest in the cramped quarters.

Sometime later, as December 25th commenced and everyone else had fallen asleep, Six Pack tiptoed into the glistening snow under a night sky in zero weather, clad only in pants. He sat inside his father's 1974 Gran Torino with his paranoid delusions and his father's twenty-gauge shotgun. He paused, aimed the barrel at his drug-distorted brain and pulled the trigger to end his life. The clatter was unheard from inside as the moon shone high above on new-fallen snow giving it the luster of mid-day.

Six's lifeless, frozen figure remained in its distorted pose until it was discovered at daybreak through frosty car windows to the horror of everyone. His shoulder was pressed against the glass and he'd turned blue.

John responded by stealing his father's Torino

before the culmination of the funeral and retreated north. Neither the blood-soaked seat, his father's wrath nor the ugliness of Six Pack's suicide deterred him.

And the drama did not stop at the Mason-Dixon Line. Upon their return, Spens was rushed from the Homewood Manor for medical care none too soon. She was amped-out from injecting the inner-city poison again and admitted to nearby Detroit Receiving Hospital. Her rank abscesses predictably burrowed into her leg, spawning a life-threatening infection and spread dangerously close to her femoral vein. She long ago "earned her wings" — injected drugs the first time — and paid the price. Even a veteran could err in shooting too little or too much, missing that sweet spot of euphoria just this side of overdose. So many variables — condition of the vein, the purity of the product, stomach contents, time since last dose, and so on.

Surgeons immediately intervened and found the large, life-supporting vein ravaged, but not permeated. Spens refused amputation. Physicians warned she could've easily bled to death, had she stalled one day more.

> *You will stop using drugs one day.*
> *Either before or after*
> *your heart stops beating...*
> — anonymous

Doc Miller played the odd role of imposter-physician and concerned trick. His rented woman was rightfully skeptical as he reviewed her chart. His bedside manner seemed clumsily staged.

The stolen vehicle from Gleason remained parked outside Homewood Manor ever since their holiday exodus back to Detroit. What others saw as a car John and Dawn saw as another scam.

"Hey, Al, I found a car!" Dawn said with artificial excitement. "But the guy wants the money now." She looked as if she would cry. "I need eight-hundred dollars real bad. I need this car and this guy is going to sell it to somebody else if I don't get it!"

Dawn proudly displayed the money to John moments later with childish glee, which confirmed they had a genuine goldmine in Doc Miller.

# TWELVE

# LIES GOOD-BYES & ALIBIS

"Open up!" Detroit Police pounded on apartment #202 at 644 Charlotte.

It was January 1, 1984, two months after Al's red-light birthday at the Temple. Detroit's finest had been summoned to investigate a report of shots fired. The officers found nothing but had prior knowledge the tenant was wanted on a fugitive assault warrant #109506 from nearby Dearborn. The wanted man was John Carl Fry. They "invited" him to resist arrest, thereby getting a chance to "tune him up," but he obediently surrendered. He knew the drill. Bando later told Woodington his eyes looked "like those of a killer" and "he was destined for bigger things."

644 Charlotte - Detroit (near 2nd Ave)
where Fry and Spens first lived
(Credit: The Detroit News)

Lucky attracted unwanted attention from law enforcement for a while, no doubt a byproduct of his grandstanding. Bando and Woodington had monitored him for two years, ever since they received a distress call from the "Travlers" Motel on Cass and Temple, alleging abuse between Fry and Cheryl Kraznovic (aka "Twiggy"). The officers made it a habit to not only carry weapons, but lug a camera, "bum gloves"—for handling disheveled drifters—and thickening, handwritten Whore Books. Officer Bando's notations under John Fry read "fiend/pimp/punk."

After Dawn's hospital discharge in mid-January, Al taxied his paid-for-companion on another spending spree—with a peculiar twist. Her latest whim was to purchase Al a gift, though she was habitually broke. No matter. Al slipped her five-hundred dollars for his gift. She ended up selecting two men's coats; one for her pimp/boyfriend and one for her trick/shopping partner paid for by her trick/shopping partner. She shoplifted other items to pawn for drugs with Al's awareness. He found it amusing.

The harlot's subsequent arrest for solicitation was March 24. John again requested bail money from Al but this time he declined, demanding to know why she was locked up for soliciting at all since they "had an understanding about that." John deflected the question. Doc Miller scurried to 1300 Beaubien to pay her a visit. Oddly, he accurately signed the visitor log "Al Canty."

Dawn's 10cc love affair with the street poison dominated her life and body. Again, Bando recalled:

"Her looks had drastically deteriorated. She was pale. No longer vibrant. Her eyes were tired and sunken from stress, a poor diet, erratic sleep and heroin use.

Anyone who went to bed with her around then would have discovered dope-related flaws, like abscesses from shooting mixed jive in places not visible to me. Rumors on the street said she was shooting in the artery on the side of her vagina, which was reportedly a desirable spot for mainlining and getting an immediate rush. It was hard for hookers to reach there alone, so they hired a guy—for about twenty-dollars. On the street, he was known as a "hitman." It took an extra-long needle with a black fastener on top called a "groin spike." If we found them, we knew she was mainlining there.

The Mobil gas station on Clifford near Henry had a filthy restroom. Some hookers would go there and sit back on the toilet while her hitman stuck the long hypodermic needle into the correct vein and sent her into brief ecstasy.

The street life was showing. Dawn was no longer compelling. She was an average street whore. Considering her competition, she was still equipped to make money, but no longer extraordinary."

Officer Bando recalled the two slackers were:

...world class manipulators. Dawn could coldly exploit anyone who displayed a need for her, with ruthless efficiency. Her partnership with Fry more or less guaranteed mayhem. It was only a question of whom their victim would be, and when. I believe they brought out the worst in each other. It was Dr. Canty's mistake, and their good fortune, to allow his obsession with this monster to control his life. It would become a fatal attraction. Sadly, they fit together like a jigsaw puzzle.

Al Miller wanted a faux dinner date before traveling home for a second meal as Al Canty. It was the spring of 1984, five months since Doc Miller had been giving and receiving inner city lip service.

The invitation, on the surface, sounded innocent but the young prostitute ran it by her pimp anyway. Fry's sage advice was, "It's better to get paid a hundred dollars to eat than a hundred dollars to fuck."

So, the two role-playing lovers dined at Chung's, the skid row restaurant Al favored, under the glow of a thin, paper lantern with the blessings of the bloated flesh peddler. Buster shared his fictional account of his life as a bereft, lonely widower over his wonton soup, not that Spens asked. He embellished. Why not? Doc Miller delivered a soliloquy concerning his rented house in Grosse Pointe that he had vacated after the crash which tragically claimed the life of his prostitute, drug-addicted wife. As for himself, he subsisted in an insignificant apartment near Detroit Receiving Hospital and worked day and night. The din of traffic and sirens easily penetrated the walls of the two-star diner, which interrupted his plaintive narrative, periodically giving Dawn a break.

Al Miller dropped by to kick it with John again who'd long ago regarded Al as a poser, not a player, a "wigger without the swagger." Al longed to appear streetwise in his customized, synthetic jacket, though he was just a college-educated, cheating, suburban husband with an attractive bankroll and magnetism for the seedy side.

Al invited John to the *Gaiety Bar* on Cass and Charlotte later renamed *Charlotte Lounge* — shown in the opening credits of *Beverly Hills Cop 1*. The darkened, red décor consisted of a large collection of international belt buckles, spent bottle caps, smelly sardines on crackers and a trunk load of stories designed to be overheard. The listener made the call where fact blossomed into fiction. The regular clientele consisted of dreamers and schemers, outlaws and in-laws, the nearly grown and the almost dead. Many steadfastly worked on their cirrhosis a pint at a time. Fry ordered a beer with whiskey, so Buster had the same.

Charlotte Lounge (formerly The Gaiety)
3107 Cass Detroit
(Credit: Rachel Caudill)

Dawn, downtown age 19
(Credit: Mark Bando)

Al inquired, "So, ah, how did you get into the protection business, John?"

John sensed a river of contempt flowing beneath the show of admiration and neon lights. He'd always detested the pretense of congeniality, though relied on it himself from time to time.

Settled in for another recital, "widower" Doc Miller drifted into a legend of triumphant medical cases, though no one expressed interest. He hadn't noticed that the eyes of his captive audience had thoroughly glossed over. His rented woman tuned him out. John groaned up his sleeve. Street acquaintances rolled their eyes behind his back.

He'd become a subordinate clause, the butt of a joke visible to anyone but him. Like Dean's signature character in *Rebel Without a Cause*, all Al ever wanted was to fit in since his first day in kindergarten.

Perhaps the imposter sensed he'd lost ground because he began to deliver breakfast on a more-or-less daily basis. No one asked Doc Miller the obvious question of how he found time to escort his escort to the malls, provide transportation for drug runs, play pool, procure groceries and leisurely read the paper in the middle of the day with "such a busy life at the medical center." Some mornings the thespian simply dropped food off or sat alone to read, much like his Sunday visits with his mother. It's as if he was sliding into the role of his father, always pontificating about "his cases" at his confined gathering. His chatter was as genuine as a three-dollar bill. He never noticed his audience had long ago developed a radar for detecting shams.

Buster was a habitual performer and learned to screen out the chatter of truth-telling. Life was a cat-and-mouse game of tempting fate and living to retell the glorious victory. "I used to play pool," Al lied again. "I supported myself through college one year with a pool stick." He cocked his head back, feigning a Tombstone serious expression and amplified, for effect. "I lived out of my car and traveled from pool hall to pool hall to earn tuition."

Not a word of Al's bohemian tale was true, of course. Al Senior, in fact, footed his son's tuition bill, all eleven years of it, including the car he drove. Al Senior was hell-bent on having one legitimate Ph.D. in the family to compensate for his lack of one.

Fry watched as Doc Miller placed the cue ball behind the head string directing it to travel slightly left of its intended line. Fry felt his opponent reasonably skilled.

So it was that performing was in Al's blood. Doc Miller offered to usher a skeptical John Fry for a dope run. Dawn remained behind, still nursing surgical wounds from the draining of yet another odorous abscess. She'd poked and smoked the inner-city venom for a while now, and her body was riddled with imprints of earlier indiscretions. Fry was leery of Al's request. He didn't warm up to the idea of tricks getting cozy, never had. He'd always gone *past* careful.

Spens persisted over the phone. "But, we're out of H," she pleaded.

Lucky bent his rule and climbed into the Buick to make small talk. Al launched into a plausible monologue of drug smuggling in and around Harper-Grace Hospital.

"I know guys who boost morphine from stock supply and wholesale it to cabbies who turn another profit."

However, Al had never worked at Harper-Grace, nor did he ever know such "guys." As the unlikely duo searched Second Avenue for the toxin, Al Miller grandly pointed out unmarked cars and cabbies supposedly awaiting drugs. "Those are cops, and they're watching deliveries from Harper."

Fry warned, "Don't you get involved in that shit, Al. I've been around this kind of thing all my life, and you definitely don't want to do time." Fry hated to pretend to like people who pretended to like him.

Al Miller dropped John off and watched as he returned with ten bags of mixed jive paid for in cash by his benefactor and driver.

In the Corridor, the driver was not known as "Al Canty, psychologist." He was sugar daddy-medical doctor Al Miller. In the Corridor he was not a law-abiding, hardworking husband. He was Doc Miller, who acted tougher than everyone knew he was; a chump, a risk-taking loner with money to burn. In the Corridor he was not a devoted son needing the approval of his elderly parents. He was a gullible, timid widower with no family at all.

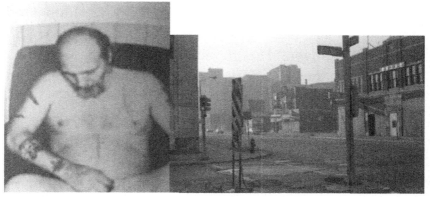

John Fry "on the nod" again     Cass Corridor; Peterboro & Cass Ave
around 1975 (Credit: Metrotimes)

In early April 1984, Al unexpectedly arrived on Sunday and pounded urgently on the freeloaders' door, feeling large and in charge. Spens and Fry scrambled to pull themselves together as the bidder hastily got to the point.

"So, what would it take for you to bow out, John? How much?" Doc Miller did not see he was rowing with one oar again.

The pimp was caught off guard and on the spot.

Minutes passed. No resolution. Fry took Spens aside and asked if she wanted to go with "the pinhead." She did not. But their veins demanded the rush, and they weren't about to seek legal employment or chance withdrawal. So, they conspired to squeeze him. Negotiations followed. Would two-thousand-dollars and a plane ticket to any destination John desired be enough?

"No." John raised him to ten-thousand and a ticket.

"No, John."

Momentary standoff. Al countered five-thousand, no ticket and a promise to never see Dawn again? *Sold!* The men agreed on a payment date of April 13. John later bragged to Gary Neil that Plan B was to cash Al out and "leave to start over." He offered Gary half the bounty if he helped with the hit. Gary wisely refused, but that did nothing to deter Fry's lethal intent.

With an ensured supply of cash, the duo's drug use swelled from casual to corrosive. Dawn consistently mainlined, which caused blood vessels to swell. Her "groin hit" injections were unfavorable for the solicitation business, except she rarely solicited anymore, and Al's erotic demands were comfortably low. Injecting between her legs signaled veteran status as it was always a last resort. Most addicts knew the risks: deep vein thrombosis, leg ulcers and reduced blood flow to limbs. Unchecked, the legs and feet slowly dissolved into fetid, rotting tissue. Amputation could not be ruled out. Even if the vascular system was spared, nerves could be damaged, leaving chronic pain or numbness behind. However, life was a roll of the dice, and maybe, just maybe, Dawn promised herself again, she would really kick the habit.

*Live as if you'll die today.*
---James Dean


Leaves had started to yellow again when Fry's friend, Frank McMaster drove south from Petosky to see an old flame. While he awaited Al's reliable arrival and their first introduction, Frank overheard Dawn bellow from the back.

"Hey, fuckin Al's comin' over." She followed with a smirk saying, "I got a sugar daddy that beats all them whores on the street."

Fry confessed to Frank he was thinking of leaving Dawn "'cause of her snotty attitude" and "her mouth." Fry added, "I think I gotta dump her." With John, you never knew what that meant.

Frank Dale McMaster coming out of DPD in 1986
(Credit: WXYZ, Detroit ABC affiliate)

Al was becoming well-known in the Corridor. His brash displays drew attention from predatory locals with a nose for that kind of thing. Afterall, whatever was done for show was bound to be seen. Over time, Doc Miller spent more hours — and money — driving the hooker around to obtain drugs, pontificate about his alleged work and read the newspaper, than enjoy any half and halves. This illustrated that his paramount need was for an audience, trickery, and flirtation with scandal. She never had it this good. He felt likewise. She could fake interest, loyalty, attention, even arousal. It was only for an hour or so a day. Oddly, her benefactor never kissed her nor held her hand. What might have escaped Dawn's notice was the thinning of her hair, intermittent nose drainage, drowsy eyelids, track marks and general corrosion. She'd lost the dewy freshness of youth. She was a veteran. Did Al recognize the gates of heaven had rusted?

# THIRTEEN

# INCANTATIONS, SECRETS &
# SHOES

Friday, Apr 13, 1984, the lives of fabricated Doctor Miller, M.D. and genuine Doctor Canty, Ph.D. imploded.

My mother-in-law telephoned urgently. "Something's wrong with Buster! He won't say anything when he answers the phone! I've called several times!"

Chili Pepper was pushed through the gears in congested westbound I-94. The official start of this nightmare was 1:20 p.m. Eastern Time.

Once at his side, my eyes set upon on a confused, silent...robot. Al purposelessly ran his tongue over his bottom lip. He was pale, perspiring, staring, hyperventilating, drooling. He looked through me, wide-eyed and fearful. He seemed...shorted out. My brain flits through pages of memorized symptoms. *Diabetic shock? Caffeinism? Pulmonary embolism?* I dismissed explanations as soon as they entered my head. *Renal failure? Allergic reaction? I don't know! I'm not a medical doctor! Meningitis? Stroke?*

I took a deep breath, paced and stared nervously out the window... *Psychotic break? Nutty schedule...? Catatonia? Conversion Disorder?* Psychosis rarely manifests for the first time in middle age. I rifled through his papers in search of opened mail that could've explained a shock. Nothing. Next, I hunted for open medication bottles. My mind froze. I couldn't *think!* Throwing my hands in the air, I privately admitted *I am too new at this! I'm lost!* I called his answering service to ask if he'd received any urgent calls.

"No. It's been quiet. In fact," she added, with curiosity, "it's been quiet for weeks."

Suddenly I heard the waiting room door open and found two pleasant women who were startled to see me, even more so after being told an emergency was underway. As calmly as possible I explained that their appointments would be rescheduled. A hastily written note was taped on the entrance after their departure, the door locked, and lights turned off. *Now what? I'm supposed to know what to do!*

Waves of electricity surged through me as I called Dr. Rutledge, my steadfast mentor. He immediately sensed my alarm. "Sure! Come. I'm waiting."

It was reassuring that Al would soon be seen in a Level-One trauma center under the eyes of a senior psychologist.

We descended the nine curling floors of the Fisher Building garage as I summarized his symptoms in my head, knowing I'd be asked to provide them. I tried to funnel my entire education into what I'd seen, what my gut instincts told me, while I pushed through the gears in city terrain alongside a very confused passenger. This man beside me was my husband, yet I did not know him. He was my life partner, but we were no longer confidants.

Within minutes, we descended again into the medical center's underground garage then trekked up to ground level. Another bank of elevators brought us to floor three. We walked the maze of long, carpeted corridors with floor-to-ceiling windows around the central courtyard as I held Al's hand. He was clammy. He was perspiring. He was absent.

Dr. Rutledge immediately greeted us along with a senior physician. "I'm glad you called. Catch your breath and review what's going on."

His colleague took vital signs while they listened to my hasty summation. "Ah, okay... Acute onset. Docile. Altered mental status. Some echolalia and echopraxia, but mostly mute." *I'm losing my grip, my train of thought!* All eyes were on me as I consciously slowed my breathing. "No changes of medication, diet or weight. No new stressors."

The physician asked about current health conditions, routine medications and recommended a tox screen, CBC and neurological evaluation.

Al occasionally mumbled, stared at the ceiling and held fast to an expression of sheer terror. He nodded mechanically, slowly, illogically. He was perspiring and pale.

*I'm his wife, not his treating source! This isn't fair! Please help us!*

With forced calm I asked, "I don't want Al hospitalized at Lafayette, Northville or Receiving. Any chance we can get him into U of M?"

Dr. Rutledge hung up the phone and answered, "It'll be expedited tomorrow. Contain this as best you can 'til morning, as there is no bed in Ann Arbor now. Take him to the nearest ER if he worsens. If not, U of M will be waiting for you."

We headed home in near silence with my mind divided between the road and his ramblings. *Please, Al, come back! Why is this happening? I don't think I can do this!*

Once in familiar surroundings, away from traffic and questions, Al became docile and quiet with a meaningless grin. He needed me as his wife. In the morning, he would need me as his advocate.

Al ate little and made no eye contact during dinner, muttering aimlessly, interspersed with periods of silence and jack-o-lantern grins. "You are snow." "Cass." "Have I been bad?" He stared off wide-eyed and pale. Minutes passed. "Did I stand tall?"

I interrupted the pointless incantation. "Al, where are you?"

"Cleansing. Cadieux." "Buster. Bus. Buster."

He appeared defenseless. He sounded like a scratched record. He behaved like a stranger. *Where was he? Did he know me? How could this have happened?* I fought tears.

Al insisted on wearing his clothes and shoes to bed with his arms rigidly at his sides staring intently at nothing. He would only lie atop the bedspread without a blanket. "Can't get in, get in. *Can't.*"

"But you're cold, Al."

"Am I tall? Cold. Cold."

*Morning can't come soon enough! Please be okay, Al, please!*

That was a Friday the 13th in living color. The night was long, filled with uncertainty and wondering how we arrived at this point.

Early on Saturday I drove us to my friends on the west side. Her husband, John, generously took over the additional thirty-five-mile trip to Ann Arbor. Al was confused, oddly stiff and broken.

"What are you seeing?" I gently probed.

He just stared vacantly and moved slowly as if in a waxy trance.

"Am I bad? Five-thousand dollars."

*Did he forget our taxes? Is that what brought this on?*

"John…" he muttered.

"Yes. John's driving."

We hit a bump. Al blurted, "Cadieux Cass! John! I'm bad." He pulled his shoulders together like a sleeping bird and whispered, "Do you love me, Jan-Jan? Do you? Am I tall?" This repetitious, scrambled mantra persisted for miles.

Once inside I was handed an avalanche of forms and shuffled between offices and hallways. Then we waited hours. A physician interviewed me since Al was mute again. I was of little help, though wanted to solve the riddle as much as him, undoubtedly more. How could a healthy man without a history of bizarre behavior, criminality, drug abuse, sudden stress, nor head injury abruptly decompensate in his early fifties? He'd withstood the rigors of graduate school, kept a complicated schedule and worked steadily. There had been no major changes in our life. No psychiatric history. Tox screens were negative. Other medical tests led nowhere.

"Follow the blue lines on the basement floor." The

139

maze of cement corridors led to more physicians, questions, exam rooms, forms, and waiting. It seemed everyone in a lab coat had no time to digest the "necessary" paperwork.

Noon came and went. We tried to ignore our hunger pangs that marked the hours this bewildering journey had taken.

As I sat with yet another psychiatrist I again explained, "He's grown preoccupied, distant. And his schedule! He's been working longer hours." *Like ships passing in the night.* "He's started to miss deadlines. Maybe the IRS? And, uh…the refrigerator door was left open a dozen times. Yesterday he displayed echolalia and was docile." I combed my brain for more. "He's asked to use my car, but he just bought one, for himself. That's strange, isn't it?"

"Maybe…" the noncommittal psychiatrist answered.

"He drinks a lot of coffee."

The admitting doctor was uninterested in these speculations. "Any major upsets, bad news? Sudden stress? Big changes?"

"No. Nothing. His father died about three years ago. He took it hard, but I doubt that has anything to do with this." The young doctor waited for more. "He's kinda…let down, or upset I recently finished school, my post-doctorate I mean."

"Oh, tell me more about that, about his reaction. Does he seem depressed?"

"Depressed? No!"

"Does he mention suicide?"

"No! Heavens no! He hasn't been giving things

away or talking about leaving. No one close to him has ever committed suicide that I know of."

"Does he ignore his hygiene?"

"No. In fact, Al is taking more of an interest."

"Does psychosis run in his family?"

"No. But he looks terrified. I think he's hallucinating."

Glancing over, the psychiatrist agreed.

"Oh, and yesterday I think he called me 'Mommy,' but he was mumbling so I'm uncertain."

We telephoned Al's mother to ask if he'd had an earlier episode such as this.

"No. Never." She was adamant.

The young professional in a lab coat was baffled.

"Any run-ins with the law?"

"No. Never."

"Any major issues at work, like being demoted or fired?"

"No. He's self-employed."

"Any domestic violence of any kind?"

"No."

"Talk of divorce?"

"No." *Does thoughts of divorce count?*

"Major issues with your children?"

"We don't have kids."

"Did anyone threaten him lately?"

"I don't see how. He's either at work or at home. He's never mentioned such a thing." *He doesn't mention much of anything…*

"Disagreements with in-laws?"

"No. My parents live out of state."

"Any major financial problems?"

"Not that I know of, but he handles the bills."

The psychiatrist struggled to make sense out of Al's ramblings, odd facial expressions, long silences and refusal to make eye contact.

We saw busy staff through exam room doorways. *Do they get how tough it was to get Al here? This started well over twenty-four hours ago.* We'd grown weary and hungry. It was near dinnertime.

Low cloud cover and drizzle obscured the darkening horizon, and the three of us wanted and needed to get on the road. I couldn't wait to crawl into bed and stifled a yawn. The intake process had mercifully come to an end. There was fewer staff bustling about at this hour and the intercom had grown quiet. John silently handed me my coat as we stretched and stood to leave. There was nothing more to say or do. Celia looked as tired as I felt. Dusk shown through the windows. We softly stepped toward the exit.

Suddenly, a thunderous, deep vibration erupted overhead. It was windy, it pounded, and rattled the walls and our nerves. Brilliant pulsating red and white lights flashed through the wet windows while the gush of air rhythmically smacked rain against the panes. There was shouting on the roof! The deafening pounding grew insistent and intensified. We scanned the ceiling in unison for clues. Al shrank into a fetal position. The floor quivered. The desk shimmied. The framed certificates clattered. We were beneath the heliport! Two helicopters had landed overhead! Al was petrified and unexpectedly animated. He sobbed and removed his ever-present glasses.

"They're coming! They're coming for us all! The

wicked! The evil! They're *coming*!"

Al stroked my thighs on his hands and knees. I moved. He followed. "They're bad! You're pure." He was frantic. I suppressed my own panic and hoped the psychiatrist would just *do* something.

"I've been bad! Birthday! Pure as snow, as snow, as *snoooooow*."

Twenty feet above us, the air continued to be spliced.

"Snow, snow, snow!" Al blurted.

The psychiatrist seemed lost as he glanced at his watch while grasping the phone only to replace it, as he recognized the futility of trying to speak above the racket.

The heavy thud of boots and shouting continued overhead.

"Buster, Bus. Buster, Bus!"

Seconds passed like minutes.

We stared at one another not knowing what to say or do. Al was escalating.

None too soon the frantic clatter gradually yielded to an eerie howl, then a deep, mechanical hum. Feet stopped running and flashers halted. The vibrations gradually faded. Finally, there was only the gentle sound of sleet. Al's incantations dwindled along with it, to a childish, wretched, whimper.

The clean sheets in the quiet, dimly-lit hospital rooms looked appealing. If nothing else, this experience illustrated just how stressful psychiatric admissions were for a family. I vowed never to forget it.

The nurses quietly asked us to leave, as they guided my shattered, vulnerable husband toward his spotless room down the shiny hallway. He still refused to remove his shoes, accept a blanket or eat.

"Can I come with you? Have I been good, Jan-Jan?"

As we walked away, Al pitifully called out over his shoulder, "Mommy! Mommy! Don't leave me! Take care of me. Don't leave meeeeee!"

That April 14 brought light evening sleet which reduced visibility and promised a miserable drive home. In all, the "expedited" admissions process took a grueling ten hours plus a two-hour drive each way.

The late hour, exhaustion, lack of food and long drive in the early wintry mix took precedence over trying to understand. We were drained. Al was now a castaway to some other faraway place and time.

The hospital, then Ann Arbor and Ypsilanti, progressively dissolved behind us. I'd been on the other side of Pluto in a house of mirrors for more than a day. It was hard leaving him behind but harder to imagine him at home.

Once in my own vehicle on the last leg of the trip back, I reflected on how far we'd strayed from the serenity of our early years a decade ago when we walked and talked for hours. Now we'd become mere roommates. It was painful, not to mention mystifying. In the past months, he'd been gone a great deal. Now he was far away emotionally. Was this fixable?

Chili Pepper finally pulled onto our wet driveway as I cut the ignition and the window wipers halted. Big flakes from late evening snow silently blotted out the glass, but not my worry. It was 8:30. Dark. Quiet. The world looked deceptively at peace. Had it not been so chilly I would've slumped right there, rather than exert the energy to get to bed. I felt ninety. The house never looked so dark, so unwelcoming.

We visited in the blue and grey Day Room for six weeks after the hospital staff inspected my purse, bag or envelope. They scribbled notes discreetly behind the nurses' station window. The stringent drill grew familiar.

Back at the Fisher Building, I reluctantly looked around at his jumbled mess of ashtrays, mail, newspapers, coffee cups and dry cleaning in his office. *Ugh.* I started with the unopened mail to prioritize and organize. My anxiety rose with each slice of a bill since most were overdue. Some invoices were minor — magazine subscriptions. Some were uncomfortable — phone bill. However, one stood out among all others. His health insurance was close to lapsing. *If his hospital bill isn't covered we're screwed!*

The deeper I dug, the worse it became. *How could we be in the red with all the hours he's working? We don't go on vacations, haven't bought much for the house or spent it on clothes or entertaining. It doesn't add up!*

One small paper, in Al's handwriting, floated to the carpet. "Mother is the ultimate passive-aggressor."

*Is that how he sees Gladys? Someone who vented her anger indirectly? What happened between them?*

Hours were spent sorting and disposing of paper. In the process, unused Detroit Receiving Hospital envelopes surfaced, which was odd. And then two from Harper Grace and one from Henry Ford Hospital. I shrugged my shoulders and tossed them.

His checkbook was overdrawn! Did he set up a savings account as promised? Did he gamble? Medical expenses I'm not aware of? Bad investments? What had happened to his income?

I paid what I could, but it didn't make a dent. I couldn't ask my parents. They weren't even local. The damage exceeded six-thousand dollars — more than thirteen-thousand today — not including income taxes! And this was just what I knew of. *It might as well be a million.* I kicked myself for getting Chili Pepper.

There was only one place to turn — his mother. I was angry with myself and him for this mess. Since we'd never asked her for a penny, I hoped she'd be receptive. It would be clear this was a loan, not a handout.

Gladys was thoughtful and gracious. "It's no way to live. Everything should be jointly owned. That's what we did."

I couldn't have agreed more.

Small talk and description of life inside the protective hospital walls dominated our visits. Over time, news from home was interwoven with his discharge plan. I wanted to shield Al from the money problems I knew of, for *now,* but planned on spreading out our financial papers in view of both of us in the near future, for a heart-to-heart. Enough cloak and dagger!

In early May, as Al's release approached, I halted and scrutinized the view from the hospital's five-story parking garage. Fragrant pink blossoms clung onto the trees surrounded by emerald grass. *When did spring arrive?* Mother Nature pulled a fast one. With the focus on damage control, nurturing my own practice, finishing my post-doc, commuting to the hospital and taking care of the house, spring snuck up on me.

The day before his discharge, May 8, Al's hospital summary was handed over. The report advised against a return to work for ten days and then part-time for a week.

Cutting down on coffee wasn't a top priority but couldn't hurt. No medications or follow-up were recommended.

The report shed no light on the cause of Al's acute decompensation but did reveal some new facts. Mrs. Canty had privately disclosed to the attending psychiatrist that Al *was* jailed for multiple unpaid tickets in his late teens — twice. In addition, she covertly informed staff Al *had* been hospitalized earlier for "bad nerves" following his divorce. The report quoted Gladys as saying, "Maggie left him since she paid all the bills. He sobbed and blamed himself, grew listless and quiet. His father took over his practice for a few weeks."

*But he was a bachelor-level non-psychologist! How'd that happen?*

Additionally, the discharge report stated Al "fell apart" after receiving a draft notice in 1951. He wrote a brief note to his mother which she preserved. It read:

*Dear Mommy:*

*Before I went to bed, I thought I had better get off this letter to my best girl. I don't mind this Army life so much, but it's not like being home...*

The summary also revealed that Al Senior admitted his son to The Haven, a private sanitarium in Rochester, Michigan rumored to have treated the rich and famous and ever careful of confidentiality. That meant this was actually his third psychiatric hospitalization. Buster was reclassified 4F and entered outpatient treatment with Dr. Awes, who saw him intermittently since. And Maggie and

Al divorced in 1972, not 1967 as he had told me.

I was brimming with questions. Why falsify his divorce date? Why did Gladys lie and deny during the admissions process at U of M? What was his diagnosis at The Haven? Why did his first wife pay the bills if he was working? Apparently, appearances in the Canty family trumped honesty even during emergencies. Most pressing was to figure out what prompted the previous two psychiatric hospitalizations. There had to have been a common denominator that pushed him over the edge.

The draft notice would have demanded him to function in a new role away from familiar surroundings, to be surrounded by others who removed control from him, and his previous divorce was certainly tough on him. He didn't do well being on his own. Yet, what did that have to do with his *current* life? I shook my head and set it aside. I was exhausted. This was not the time to ask Al about it, and Mrs. Canty would not have discussed it. But the report did validate I was an outsider, sidelined by both Al and his mother. This confirmed the veins of my husband's mystery ran deeper than I ever realized.

# FOURTEEN

# DISCHARGED, RECHARGED

On the drive home, awkward gaps in our conversation surfaced like jarring potholes. Small talk substituted for genuine communication. "The cats miss you. They'll be glad to see you."

He nodded.

"There's a new neighbor in that house on the corner, the one with ivy-covered arches. You always liked it."

"Oh," is all he offered.

The blossoming countryside blurred like pink and white curtains. He wasn't being rude—just flatly uninterested. More silence.

Miles and minutes dragged. I was mindful not to upset him but wanted to reinforce the discharge instructions. "You work long hours."

He returned an obligatory nod.

"So, maybe we could exchange the honeymoon we never took for a ten-year anniversary trip. Hmmm?"

Again, he was preoccupied.

I hesitantly added, "It'd be fun." I wasn't convincing because I wasn't convinced.

More lane changes. "Please take it easy."

He nodded.

*Did he hear a word I had said? Was he discharged too soon?*

It became painfully obvious he had no more intention of heeding the discharge instructions than the traffic citations decades earlier. With sudden urgency, he announced, "I need to stop by the office and check my mail!"

His words wedged me into an impossible predicament. Was it better to violate the reasonable discharge recommendations, or upset him hours after release? A compromise?

"We'll stop if you agree it's only for fifteen minutes and that you'll take the rest of the week off, okay?"

As we crossed the threshold to our offices, he halted and looked disgruntled.

"While you were gone, I straightened up piles of jumbled paper."

He stiffened. "Why? They're *my* papers!"

"Well, it was a mess. Expired coupons, junk mail, useless receipts, old magazines… They covered the table, chairs, and even littered the floor. I just thinned it out but kept what you needed. I was careful. See? I didn't throw out anything impor…"

"What *else* did you do?"

I began to feel interrogated, in Alan Senior style. "Well, your suits went to the dry cleaners, and the carpets were washed. They smelled like cigarettes and dust. I canceled two of the magazines you never read. Why pay for them?"

He grew indignant.

I grew annoyed.

"Look...I'm trying to help," I said with forced patience. "I wanted things easier for you and to reduce expenses, if only a little. Your crazy schedule... You didn't need to come back to a mess. In fact, you were advised not to come back here at *all*, yet. *Remember*? This is why!"

He grew glaringly angry.

I wasn't far behind. "It's just that..." I counted to ten. "Look, we *both* need to get away from work, from here, for a bit. You've been working six days a week and I'm still catching up from the medical absence from having mono. Remember? I missed your birthday. I wanted to ease your stress, that's all."

Then my husband, who'd been supportive, complimentary and gentle, snapped, "I never *asked* for help! I never *needed* it! You should *trust* me. I will go back to work. I *will* drink my coffee, and I will be fine! You're overreacting."

*"Overreacting?!* Al, if you didn't need help, why the unpaid bills? And, by the way, one was our health insurance!"

He clenched his jaw.

"If you didn't need help, why were you admitted to the hospital?"

He blurted, "You think because you're almost done you can *take control?*"

His words were a punch in the gut. *"Take control? What's *that* mean?"

He turned and glowered. "Just what I said! Do you

think I need *mothering*?"

He exhibited a snarl, never seen before.

His remark struck me as odd because he *did* call me "Mommy" during his hospital admission, but I let it go.

We left our offices with a heaviness. I had miles to consider my reply. Upon arriving home, I turned off the car, faced the stranger of a husband and cherry-picked my words. "Things are different from my point of view, Al. You *did* need help. You could not speak. You slept and showered with your shoes on! The bills are current, thanks to your mother. The house is clean. I got groceries. The cats are fine. And you're *angry*?"

I inhaled and waited for eye contact that would not come. "Your patients were told you had a medical emergency. I struggled to figure out their contact information. I only did it to take pressure off."

He scowled in stony silence. His breathing was audible.

"You didn't *ask* me to do it, Al, but it never occurred to me it would *anger* you. I'm not taking control. We're supposed to be a *team*, that's what you always said!"

He strangely smirked and nodded in disbelief.

"For goodness sake, Al, I would hope you'd do the same if it was the other way around!"

Right or wrong, I was on a roll and couldn't stop. These issues had been smoking and were ripe to ignite. "I don't even know what caused the hospitalization and the treating staff didn't either. You know that makes it harder to prevent a recurrence. Anything you want to share on that?"

More silence.

"Was that your first hospitalization?" I waited.

"You aren't meeting me halfway here. I'm tired of being shut out by you and your mother! You must do your part and listen to the discharge instructions."

My patience had run out.

"Al, if you don't lay low and you slide backward, I *refuse* to hold this together a second time. Do you hear me, Al? You violate the discharge instructions, and you're on your own. I refuse to rescue this all again, especially considering how my efforts cause resentment. We're not a team! We're ships passing in the night."

That was, undeniably, a low point. We sat side by side in the well-appointed car I regretted purchasing but might as well have been conversing from two continents. We never had these confrontations, and maybe they were overdue but, nonetheless, were ill-timed. He left the car, shutting the door forcefully. A face-off so soon after his discharge? I fended off tears again. I was frightened, exhausted and very confused.

Naps substituted for sleep. I stared at the darkened ceiling and listened to my husband's breathing which I had missed, until then. I felt defeated, alone, outraged. The last six weeks unsettled me more than I cared to admit. He'd heard my words but not my intent. How did we slide here? There was such a disparity between where we *should* be and where we *were*. It was spring. We had our health. Our long-anticipated goals were within reach. His practice was steady. But what did it matter if we'd become strangers who scheduled fifteen-minute dinners? I faced the probability he'd leave for work tomorrow. My ears hadn't heard his departure yet, but my heart could feel it. It would signify he had left common sense, and us, behind.

A couple weeks later our phone rang during

breakfast. "We're so upset. I can't believe it! Your father just paces!"

"Mom? You sound so different."

"We put Ginger to sleep Wednesday. I thought nothing could be worse. I can't part with her bed and dog food." Words dissolved into tears as I waited. "Then last night, while we were out, someone broke in. It's a mess! They got your grandma's ruby ring—the one Dad wanted you to have—and a pocket watch and... We didn't sleep. We're not even sure what's missing yet."

I ached for their double loss. They must've startled the burglars since the hanging lamp near their back-slider door swung as they returned. And they smelled cigars and stale perfume. But the most valuable thing stolen was their peace of mind. I was thankful they were unharmed. They were thankful their dog was not around to *be* harmed.

Local police eventually arrived but found no witnesses, fingerprints, tools or prospects. They did find a baggy of white powder curbside and reasoned the intruders were addicts feeding their habit.

Hours later, the same day, Al called with unsettling news.

"What?! You locked it, right?"

"Ah, I *think* so..."

Not only was I confused by the news of his car theft, but also because of *where* and *when* it was taken. "You were parked outside Receiving Hospital?"

"Had to drop something off."

I regretfully no longer trusted him with my wellbeing and resented feeling like a sidecar, a "hack" on a motorcycle. I was weary of living in the dark regarding finances, talking to the back of his head and feeling vulnerable. There was a nagging sense the other shoe was going to drop and that he was holding back secrets. He'd become unreliable and unavailable.

"Al, let's put a security system in *this* week. Something is wrong. You can't sense it?"

"No, but you're on edge."

"I am—you're right! Remember when my parents had *their* car broken into last year, right in our driveway out there while we all slept? Now yours is gone."

I documented the interior of our house with photographs and captions making educated guesses about their corresponding value then rented a safe deposit box and assembled an emergency folder hoping it would never be needed. Photocopies of credit cards, driver's licenses, insurance cards, birth certificates, the house deed and such were added. For good measure, I stuck an envelope with cash inside and the never-worn diamond ring from my mother and started a savings account "just in case." *It's better to be careful than clueless.*

But, for the first weekend in memory, Al was in the carriage house organizing car parts! Maybe he sensed my resignation?

"I'm dejunking," he announced. "I'm gonna sell some of this stuff."

*About time.* While he was busy, I claimed a parking stall for my Thunderbird.

That day was a doubleheader because he opened up in ways he previously had not. The topic of the *Indianwood* manuscript, which brought us together over a decade ago, surfaced. He admitted it was somewhat autobiographical. "I went through some of the same stuff with my parents. I couldn't get angry. We were the perfect family, ya know? I

155

had mixed feelings about them. I mean, how could I get upset when they provided everything, and bailed me out?"

His facial expression was refreshingly transparent and, for the first time in ages, he looked directly at me and struggled to formulate his thoughts without evasiveness.

Al's furrowed brow framed his clear blue eyes, his hands gestured conflicting emotions. "Ma pampered me with fancy meals and never allowed me to help. But there was this unspoken rule, a condition. They wouldn't tolerate letting me be me! They were always in charge, like restricting me. I couldn't become autonomous or different from them."

I listened intently and glimpsed the man I fell in love with a decade ago, but without my heart softening. Where had he been?

Me around 1984—I was sitting at my parents' kitchen table after a big meal.

The conversation ended when he abruptly stated he wanted to borrow Chili Pepper. "I'm going to get it detailed and gassed up."

"No. It's half full and supposed to rain. It can wait, but thanks."

"I want to do this for you." He was insistent. Was this his apology for our recent confrontation?

"I know, and I appreciate it, but weren't you going to stick around? Besides, I'm just leaving for the garden store to get...."

But before I could say "geraniums," he was off again. Now I was looking at the taillights of my *own* car. *Damn him!*

By September, I'd given considerable thought to Al's comings and frequent goings, his evasiveness, psychiatric hospitalization, overdue bills, and canceled lunches. He'd started to consume liqueurs and stopped taking walks. His mission was avoidance. Leisurely baths, television, going to bed early, errands with his mother and long hours at the office allowed almost no time for us. Was that his goal? Gone, too, was his interest in our future. Did we even cross his mind?

He'd become midnight sneaky in the middle of the day.

And there were smaller things. The day he took my car for detailing I found a crumpled McDonald's bag on the backseat. Al never ate fast food. The detailers sure didn't leave it. *So, where did it come from?* And what about his psychotic ramblings during his hospitalization? He'd mentioned "Cass," "cleansing" and he'd "been bad." It was all collated in my head, and I found the opportunity and determination to ask. "Al, there's something I need to ask."

He turned and walked into the guest room, glaringly at odds with his normal behavior. A giveaway I was on the right track.

"Remember on our way to Ann Arbor, you were talking?"

He nodded cautiously.

"You said you were 'bad' and mentioned Cass and your birthday." He held his breath. "I need to know what that meant."

His quizzical face turned boyish. "Aw, Jan-Jan..." He looked around awkwardly.

"Confused," he replied. "I thought it was me because of fatigue. See, I've been supervising a therapist... She had someone who... Well, she scheduled someone who is a prostitute...and this female therapist got in over her head. She saw her outside a clinical setting. That's unethical, you know. I must've confused myself with her. I wouldn't do that."

He'd never mentioned such supervision and his brief look of shock did not escape me. He hadn't made eye contact and he swallowed hard before speaking. He spoke in too much detail and was off point. Why take more interest in his appearance? On the other hand, he wasn't much of a Casanova. Far from it. How would he find the time, anyway? As far as I knew, he wasn't hanging out with men that cheated.

"And you expect me to believe that?" I asked, more to test his resolve than anything. My intuition jabbed at me. If he hadn't been cheating, what was it?

He indignantly replied, "How could I do that when I'm either working or here?"

Stepping closer I said, "That's my point. You *aren't* here! I see more of your taillights than you! And even when you're home, you're far away."

He denied his guilt, terminated the conversation and brushed past me to ponder the television. He'd given me the go 'round again.

I followed him downstairs intent on learning more but halted to study him from a distance. What was he up to? What preoccupied him? How could infidelity be verified one way or the other? Did this have anything to do with the hospitalization? But the painful truth was, did it matter? We'd had a good run, but I sensed a dead end ahead. I found myself seeing an imperfect person perfectly.

He was a thousand-miles gone.

*Men don't pay hookers for sex.*
*They pay them to leave.*
---anonymous

As he waddled away with his odd Charlie Chaplin walk, I saw us dividing assets and parting ways. Moreover, I'd be clueless why. He'd been considerate to my family and, generally, easygoing. He wasn't into drugs and worked hard. He'd never laid a hand on me and rarely been gruff. But we were as unable to connect as railroad tracks. It was clear that deny and lie were his standard defenses. It hardened my heart.

The following week Al mentioned, over a hasty breakfast, he'd added jail consultations to his full schedule and needed an early start.

"*Wait! Timeout!* The *jail?* You don't *need* more work! C'mon, Al! Why did you agree to that?"

159

Skirting the question again, he replied, "Oh, Jan-Jan... It's just temporary."

I knew his mind was set, so I suggested an alternative. "Okay. Well, I'll go *with* you. It might be interesting. Besides, I have the credentials now."

Al hastily screwed the lid on his ever-present thermos, shaking his head, and bolted away exclaiming, "No. It isn't a great place! It's no place for you. It literally *stinks*!"

This decision robbed us of even more time together and I was determined to stop it. I insisted he quit the jail work altogether three weeks into it. He shook his head in opposition.

"But you said it was *temporary*! Are we having financial problems?"

"No. It's just... Well, it's complicated. It's taking more time than I thought."

"What's complicated?"

"Not now."

"You mean not ever! Look, if we aren't having financial problems just *quit*! We never *see* one another!"

"Look, we'll talk it over at dinner tonight, okay? Gotta go."

As usual, I faced the back of his head. My husband, and our marriage, had become a bewildering, wearisome blur.

I was offended and confused as the screen door separated us again. In a hurry. Always in a hurry.

Our shrinking schedule shriveled more, which forced dinners into mere fifteen-minute slots between his work downtown and home. His appetite dwindled to where he just shoved food around. Was there any point in preparing a meal? Was he not well? I needed the precision of a control tower to schedule time with him. Then Al canceled our lunch dates, which we'd arranged to compensate for our break-neck dinners. Would he become hospitalized again?

I revisited the matter of our finances as I thought about those neglected invoices in his office. No collection calls had arrived, but what of our age difference? What if he collapsed under the weight of his insane schedule? I needed to know.

Over dinner, I brought up a subject he'd resist. "Al, let's sit down this weekend and organize our schedules and finances. We need to be co-signers on all accounts in case of an emergency. I don't have a clue where we are financially. If we understand where we are, we can decide how much we *should* be working. If we don't need the money, scale back! If we do, I'll put in more hours and..."

"Sure, okay. Soon as I'm free. It's an idea."

"No, *not* as soon as you're free and it's *more* than an idea! Stop putting me off."

"Well, not Sunday, I'm going to be with Ma." He added a reassuring smile that failed, this time, to appease me.

I wondered if he'd changed or if I ever knew him at all.

# FIFTEEN

# REACHING FOR THE BOTTOM

The threads that bound the three schemers together had begun to chafe. Fry smirked behind Doc Miller's back because "the chump" never challenged him about the pretense of staying out of Dawn's life as promised. And Buster didn't remind Fry he'd bought exclusive use of the prostitute before his hospitalization. And Dawn never wanted to leave her bestie to be with the Doc. It appeared a rupture was inevitable.

Al had gifted his friends a thousand dollars a week. This was week twenty-two.

The Doc had a reputation for being in the black in a community with bottomless needs and marauders who roamed in search of plunder. He was an easy mark, an outsider. Even better, he was predictable and known to be unarmed.

Al Miller again toddled up to the ghetto apartment soon after his discharge with his head in the clouds and his mind on grandstanding. Like a magnet attracted to steel, a thug jabbed a knife tip against Al's clothing, piercing it slightly, and demanded cash. He knew Doc Miller by name. Al was no Jesse James. He froze with fright. John, ever vigilant about protecting his free cash, challenged the challenger. John didn't say a word. He didn't have to.

The knife that penetrated Doc Miller's clothing failed to penetrate his denial and minimization of risk. He refused to see he was drowning in the shallow end of a cesspool, and no lifesavers would be forthcoming- not from me, not from Gladys, not from anyone. He had to do it alone.

Twelve deceitful months had elapsed since Al ran with scissors; a full three-hundred-sixty-five days of payouts, lies and tempting fate.

It was fitting that the traditional first-anniversary gift was paper. That suited Spens and Lucky perfectly — so long as it was green with dead presidents. Al gave. They took. Yet, the game had grown tedious.

Fry unloaded onto a neighbor, BJ, while he drove, in late fall. "The doctor's fucking up. He's not paying me the money he should, and I'm gonna take him *out* if he don't get straight!"

"Yeah. Heard that, Lucky."

B.J. assumed John Lucky Fry was just blowing off steam again. He threatened violence regularly and carried it out periodically. A week later Fry was still on the same tirade. B.J. recalled the trick in the black Buick. He'd seen him buy groceries, jump dead batteries and loan his car to someone in a jam. Fry's anger caught B.J. off guard, as did Dawn's.

"He's a fuckin pinhead. I wouldn't fuck him. He's lucky I suck his dick." Apparently, she used her mouth to earn money *and* alienate others.

Spens grew demanding. Like most young women, she wanted new clothes, a change of pace and freedom to do as she pleased.

Perhaps Al sensed his strumpet's restlessness and fell back on a familiar snare. "You're college material, you know? You should go to college and become my receptionist. I'll even pay your tuition." Did he see a diamond in the rough?

She smiled with false flattery; she always had the gift.

Meanwhile, John no longer believed Al Miller was a "doc from Receiving Hospital." Or that he was a widower. Or that Miller was his last name. "He's duping us," he angrily complained to Dawn. "And the trick works in the Fisher Building."

John, an expert on deceit, was irritated with Al's lies and pretense that he had to be out of Dawn's life. *He* was the alpha, Afterall. A shakedown was in order. So, he and another addict devised a scheme to jolt Al into believing Dawn needed John's protection, to lay the groundwork for John to slide back into her apartment. Fry took a page from the playbook of the genuine close call in May. As Doc Miller predictably arrived, a decoy cokehead thrust a switchblade toward his ribs stopping short of skin. John sprinted out, on cue, chased the faux assailant away and plausibly told Doc Miller the "snowbird" had caused problems before and that he was worried about Dawn's safety. Al suggested Fry move back, to which John offered a crocodile smile. The Doc never even requested his five-thousand-dollar refund.

Dawn was growing weary of the entire game to the

point where she told a friend she could "get enough money from Al to leave John and start over." With delayed insight she added, "Al says John's a bad influence."

As trouble in paradise resurfaced, Ray Danford received an unexpected call from his old friend, Al Canty, shortly after Thanksgiving. They agreed to meet at Marcus Hamburgers in Hamtramck—a historically Polish community surrounded by Detroit—on McNichol's Road. They frequented the eatery as teens. Like Al, the business was immune from change. It offered the same down-home, grease-coated menu from 1949. Even the prices were retro.

Ray became a family man years ago. He worked steadily and kept in touch with Skip, Donna and the others from Southeastern High but hadn't seen Al in a while. Ray sensed there was something on Al's mind, but he didn't get to the point. Nonetheless, they agreed to meet, now and then, as their schedules allowed.

Back on Casper, Al saw himself as a pal to John, *to his face*. He pontificated on the history of Detroit, though John never asked. He postured as an authority on James Dean, without anyone expressing interest. He tried to discuss motorcycles; a subject of which John clearly had the upper hand. Al was running out of script and his audience was clearly bored.

Doc Miller finally unloaded his transgressions onto Ray one afternoon over onion rings and grumbled Fry was a "pain in the ass." And, as for Spens, "She's yellow, Ray. She's *killing* herself with drugs." He stopped short of adding, "that I furnish her." Seemed the thrill was going.

Ray was Dee's counterpart for Dawn. Both were old high school buddies whose wise counsel was dismissed. If Ray couldn't reach Al, who could?

It turned a new year; 1985. Fry needed clarity on this weird triangle that restrained him the previous fourteen months. He wondered, "What's Al *really* up to?" And, more importantly, "How much more can we squeeze outta him?"

"That's it! That's where the punk lives!" He called and spoke with the house sitter over the holidays.

"No, he isn't here. He and his wife will be back next week. Can I take a mes..."

John slammed the phone with self-righteous indignation and roared, "God-damn mother fucker! The pinhead's *married!*" Fry never tolerated being on the *receiving* end of lies.

Upon Doc Miller's return from the Grand Canyon, he used a new ploy to increase his allure. "See? This is my rental." Al dangled a photo album in front of them that detailed the household items and their approximate value. They studied it with dishonorable intentions. Fry and Spens quickly surmised this was where Al and his very alive wife resided. Al left the album behind for them, and others, to scrutinize and memorize and itemize at their leisure.

So, Spens and Fry discovered Doc Miller was married by early 1985, that he worked in the Fisher Building and lived in Grosse Pointe. They also had the layout of his house, the contents of each room, the make, model and color of the Doc's car and his real last name. Fry finally felt he was back in the driver's seat.

*You can tell who the strong women are.*
*They use their lips to speak truth,*
*their ears for concentration,*

*their hands for earnest work,*
*their heart for compassion and*
*their eyes to see injustice.*
*They're the ones who build up other women*
*instead of secretly fracturing their foundation.*
---anonymous

The young woman from Elkhart Street, the prostitute who would claim in court she was a helpless victim, suggested, "We could blackmail him. We could blackmail him good." Knowing the Doc was married did not deter her. It made her more determined to bankrupt him.

Change was underfoot. Fry and Spens were bored with their cramped Corridor apartment and rented a bungalow at 2518 Casper off a back alley near Pitt Street in south-central Detroit in the Springwells neighborhood. Ironically, Governor Lewis Cass also established the area in 1818. Their new dwelling lacked a ring of litter and boasted a lawn with a covered porch. This rental was in the Sixth Precinct, near W. Vernor Highway and Central. They tried to clean up in other ways by enrolling in a methadone clinic — again.

Their new neighbor had a little girl who took a liking to John. He made funny faces for her, and she saw him as a great, harmless polar bear. He occasionally brought her candy from a beer run. He had a way with kids and came to their defense. A few months earlier he found Six Pack's twins being mistreated by Ike, his sister-in-law's new man, following the suicide of his brother. Lucky discovered Ike had locked the twins in their room for two days while their mama was forced to do tricks in the next room. Ike was on a bender. The kids had soiled themselves, and Ike had rubbed their faces in it for punishment. John wasn't gonna have any of it.

Upon announcing himself with a, "Get up, punk!" Fry discovered an absence of food, dirty, frightened kids and their mom with a black eye. Janet admitted when she tried to help the twins Ike punched her.

Fry ignited! He broke a table leg off and held it as an exclamation point. "Got somethin' for ya here! I said get up, *bitch!* You like to fuck with women and kids? Come on, fuck with *me!*"

Ike dashed out the door.

Fry later griped to Frank, "I should've killed that dirty, slimy sonovabitch!" Frank knew if Fry had his favorite weapon, his baseball bat, he likely would've.

Al sensed he held a losing hand but turned to his friend for a rebuttal. Al's bragging-by-installment brought back memories for Ray, which seemed comical *thirty years ago.* His thoughts recoiled to when Al boasted of dating a student from Henry Ford Community College in 1969. Carla was a twenty-three-year-old single mother. Al gave her money, a used car, unsolicited advice, and too little space. She broke it off when she felt like a paid-for woman. Ray recognized the pattern. Al preferred the chase, pranks, control, and props over transparency, loyalty, and flexibility. He'd substituted charisma and confidence with adrenaline and lies. Al faked cancer, used a so-called "aphrodisiac" from a druggist and once kept detailed logs on a classmate. His shams were immature, ill-fated and contrived. His old pal never knew Al to be faithful nor insightful. Ray realized Al had again aimed for the sand trap instead of the fairway, but he was no longer amused.

Al portrayed himself as the victim, which Ray didn't buy. "A whore from the Corridor? Large sums of money?! Been goin' on for over a *year?!* C'mon, Al!" Ray tried to talk sense into his old pal, to no avail. Al kept his friend close, but his enemies closer, putting Ray in an impossible dilemma.

"I told 'em I'm Al *Miller,* Ray. Dr. Al *Miller!"* Al brimmed with adolescent confidence.

Ray recalled Al Miller as a racecar driver his friend had cheered on at the dirt track at Schoenherr and Eight Mile as a teen. And their trip to Chicago in their twenties when Al brought a hooker to their room. Al later bragged he paid her with stolen money from a girlfriend. The next morning, he suggested Ray distract the clerk so they could avoid paying and, on the way back to Michigan, stopped to mail a postcard from the Chicago YMCA to his mother, to say they were staying there. It was all about appearances, the next scam, being in the driver's seat.

Later Al discovered a scrap of paper while visiting Casper. There it was in black and white—his correct name, business address, business phone, home address and home phone. The jig was up. He hadn't been off the grid. This was month fifteen of the charade. *Buzzkill.* The performer dashed to his old therapist, Dr. Awes, who found him appropriately panicked. Like Ray, she encouraged him to examine the hole he'd dug for himself and advised to stop digging.

But there was another scrap of paper Al didn't find. One side listed groceries while the other said, "Al: Arrange to spend time 'alone.' Go out to lunch at least once per week. Maybe out to dinner or you fix him a special dinner. 'After work' is the best time. This is to prepare to get a nice chunk of money before goodbye."

The news wasn't any better at work. Doc Miller discovered that Dr. W. Alan Canty had overdraft alerts from Comerica Bank. *Had the notices come to the house, too?* They'd even frozen one account for frequent overdrafts.

This was a game changer, of sorts.

Not long afterward, Doc Miller failed to show at Casper and deliver cash. Fry felt it was time to show him who was boss. The following afternoon Al's new car was stolen in front of Receiving Hospital. Message sent. Message decoded.

The Buick was eventually recovered but needed repairs and was in the shop causing Doc Miller to find alternative transportation. Much to everyone's surprise, Al arrived in the Corridor in a newer red Thunderbird.

"I borrowed it from a coworker's daughter," he fibbed.

He could've come in a horse and buggy for all they cared, as long as he brought cash. Fry shrugged, climbed in and sat in front of Dawn as they ate carryout from McDonald's. Fry informed Al that Dawn needed transportation as he savored the grey leather interior. John detected a whiff of perfume.

*Hmm. Wonder if this is the Doc's old lady's ride?*

Dawn selected a 1975 white Thunderbird on July 3rd and Doc Miller obediently handed over the sixteen-hundred-dollars in cash to purchase it. Buster simply could not turn off the way deceit turned him on.

Lucky had been busy inventing new scams to "squeeze" Doc Miller, to kick-start his planned California escape. He connected with an old pal on the coast and calculated the cost and route of the two thousand-mile trek. Dawn was up for it. Detroit bored them to death anyway.

"Ain't nothing here for the takin' no more."

Lucky guarded his traveling money like a snarling mama grizzly. One foot was out the door.

# SIXTEEN

# I'LL HUFF & I'LL PUFF & I'LL BREAK INTO YOUR HOUSE

"Can you visit next month, Mom?"

I intended on bringing my parents into a discussion of my marital doubts and gain their input. The months since Al's hospitalization had not been rosy. I felt depleted and locked out.

"Sure. We'll come at the end of July."

I sent for an Arizona psychology license "just in case." There was no denying it. My 34th birthday passed uncelebrated, unnoticed and underlain with more evasiveness.

Nights were the hardest. Sleep was evasive. It was then I felt the loneliest, the most defeated. One night, very late, I sat inside our darkened back porch staring out at Essex, our side street, I admitted I had no reason to stay.

This was a backyard cookout for Al's high school pals. They are the last photographs of Al. In left photo Al is standing in the garage doorway with coffee. I'm standing up serving. In the right photo he is the fourth from the right in blue shirt with a white coffee cup. His new Buick is on the completed brick driveway. This was taken shortly before he was killed.

In preparation for my parents' arrival, the yard needed attention. After a particularly heavy rain, I ventured out front to yank dandelions which slithered out like a crop of carrots. Three heavy lawn bags later, a man pulled to the curb in an old Dodge Aspen and smiled. I didn't recognize him. He was friendly, appeared to be in his thirties, cleanly shaven with sunglasses and a full head of straight, dark hair. He looked to be of American Indian descent.

"Is this Al Canty's place?"

"Yes. He isn't home yet. I'd take a message but can't." I exhibited my muddy palms to show my predicament. He laughed.

"Okay. I'll call later."

Our house on Berkshire in Grosse Pointe Park, Mich.

*That was odd. If he had our phone number, why not just call? Was he a patient?* His car drew my attention also because it was old, dented, loud and smoked. Those vehicles were rare in our area and typically owned by teens getting their first taste of freedom, not grown men. However, nothing seemed menacing about him. Unfortunately, by the time Al arrived hours later, the driver's name was long forgotten. Al characteristically shrugged it off.

My application to practice in Arizona arrived. It was an open door, proof of my wish to depart. I read it carefully but set it aside for now. I had never been a quitter. I never imagined marriage to a man who would become so indifferent, so evasive.

My savings habit became a higher priority, and anything possible was paid off. We'd been together for almost a decade, and while most of it was positive, my husband's increasing absence had taught me to live alone.

Soon after the stranger drove by, odd calls started, usually in the witching hour. A heavy, slurred, male voice with a southern accent asked for some woman. "Wrong number," I said each time. He hung up when I finally asked his name. I dismissed the calls as drunk dials. I mentioned them to Al, but he appeared uninterested. Half a dozen hang-ups invaded dinner. How could one person dial the wrong number so many times? Was he that wasted?

My parent's plane would land in two days. With the guest room ready and refrigerator stocked, I tackled the backyard with annoying mosquitoes and humidity which Michigan summers guaranteed. An attack was launched on the hedge, then the weeds. The sun made a welcome appearance which afforded an opportunity to "bake" porch cushions in the glorious summer heat. Red and purple annuals placed welcoming pops of color near the back steps and buoyed my spirits.

After a late lunch, I refreshed my bug repellent and charged the north perimeter of the backyard. The lilacs were fertilized, and dead branches trimmed as far up as I could reach. However, something peculiar riveted my attention. Under the kitchen window to my left, I discovered three fresh-looking cigarette butts. They were as conspicuous as a candle in the dark.

These little warnings could not have been old, given the past rainy weather. Al had quit smoking. I'd never started. Because of their location, no pedestrian could have tossed them. No workers or guests had been around. *So, whose were they?* Once again, this uncomfortable, prickly sensation erupted at the nape of my neck. It was the same creepy premonition as when I pushed for a security system. This internal guardian announced an unnamed danger.

I studied the dampness for footprints but only saw mine. I'd been tugging a stepladder and tossing tools around for half an hour, which had disrupted the soil. I recalled then it takes about seven minutes to smoke one cigarette, so if they belonged to a single person it was likely the trespasser stood there for at least a half hour. But *who* and *why?* Were they from the unfamiliar driver in the old car? The man who called with the slurred voice? A complete stranger?

I quickly took a rapid inventory around the perimeter of the house. My instincts were leading me more than logic, and I wasn't even sure what to look for. *Al's never around when I need him.* Nothing was remiss. I returned to examine the kitchen windows. They were high enough that someone would have needed a boost to get inside and, besides, the screens were intact. The lilacs were too thin to support an adult. However, it was possible to slip through a *basement* window. One sill looked cleaner than others. The first-floor windows were fastened at night, but I hadn't checked the security of the basement in ages. I was relieved the alarm system had been installed and our belongings documented. *Come to think of it, where was that album of property photographs?*

Once inside, I fired up the security system but was unsuccessful in trying to locate the photo album of our belongings. I called Al. His answering service picked up. Sensing concern in my voice they asked, "Everything all right?"

"Well, it can wait. Please make sure he gets the message to call home, okay?"

Despite the heat and incomplete yard work, I locked the first floor. *Who'd been outside watching? Would they return? Maybe one of Al's jail cases? What did they want?*

What was my next move? With the doors locked I carefully slid my sandals off and silently descended the narrow, back basement staircase without turning on a light. *Should I call 911? And say what? 'I found cigarettes?' That'd go over well…* Two more steps. *Maybe I should leave?* Fifth step. *Should I wait for Al? No, by then I could grow a foot.*

My hand slid down the cool basement wall while I strained to pick up any sound. Four more watchful steps led to the dark recesses of the old house. My breathing quickened. The chill of the cement floor ran up my legs producing goosebumps. I questioned my decision, held my breath and stood wide-eyed as my eyes adjusted to the dimness. I quietly searched each room, while I glanced over my shoulder. The basement windows appeared locked and undisturbed, but I wasn't actually tall enough to touch them. I inhaled the air to detect any hint of cigarette butts or anything unusual. Then, on my hands and knees, I crawled into the low, dusty, black cavity under the front basement staircase past a few spider webs. I found one old red marble, a dirty popsicle stick and a wrinkled, legal-size envelope with a ring of keys inside. One key looked like it fit a car, another to a door and two small ones to a file cabinet or padlock. Their age was anyone's guess. Five rooms later, nothing else turned up.

I rummaged the upstairs hall closet again for the emergency photo album and found its empty box. Had it contained social security numbers and other information? I could not recall, not in my present state of mind.

By the time Al arrived, it was past dusk. He barely put his thermos down as I launched.

"Where've you been?! You didn't return my call!"

"Working… Why are you upset?"

I almost shouted, "Seems you're *always* working. Did you bother to check with the answering service? Someone was standing at those windows studying the house!"

"Well, did you call the pol…?"

"*No!* I didn't call the police, I called *you!* It didn't happen tonight, but *recently*."

"Did you see them?"

A little warning went off in my head. I became eerily calm. "Why did you say *'them'*? Why do you suspect more than one?"

"Oh, come *ON!* It's a figure of speech. I don't even know *IF* someone was outside. Start over. I'm listening."

I exhaled slowly and carefully worded my statement. Al looked amused.

"That's it? Cigarettes? You found three cigarettes… They could've been there for ages…"

"No! *Would you take me seriously for once?* I'm telling you they're *new!* It's been raining before today!"

"Jan-Jan, calm down! I got you the alarm system. Do we need a dog?" His smile usually defused me. Not tonight.

"Don't *belittle* me!" I backed away, crossing my arms. "Besides, the alarm system wasn't for *me*. It was for *us*. Something is wrong, and you refuse to see it! You don't listen. Just like those creepy late-night calls! And something else. Where's the album of our property pictures? It's gone."

Al looked my way and said, "Geeze! Okay. I left it in the car. I'll get it."

He hastily retrieved it with a look of irritation.

I clutched it to my chest like a family Bible. "Why did you take it? Why does it stink of cigarettes?"

He shook his head and tried to brush past me. Blocking his retreat, I emphasized, "Al, I asked you a question."

"No. You asked me *two*. I took it to show Ray, at lunch, that's all. I thought it was a good idea. Thought him and Jeanne would like to make one. I was bragging about you. I'm going to take a bath."

This was code for "stonewalling" or "eluding." He hid in plain sight.

*You've been so unavailable. Sadly, I don't know why.*
*your heart is unobtainable, though, Lord knows, you kept mine.*
— Adapted from *I'm Not the Only One* by Sam Smith

Left alone in the half-lit kitchen with my singular anxiety, I stared out the now-closed, darkened windows facing the lilacs and tried to shake off a feeling of pending danger. I couldn't help but imagine a stranger out there staring inside. *Did I have an overactive imagination? Why had we been singled out?* Small beads of perspiration dotted my forehead.

Dismissed. Unheeded. Sidelined. Al's attitude was *infuriating*.

July 12 rolled in under a damp blanket of stifling humidity and heat. Al woke early and suggested we travel into the office to finish the move to join our practices.

"C'mon. We'll get breakfast."

*What? Had he read my thoughts the other day, or are we back to the same ol' dance? Does he want to talk things over or acknowledge it is over?*

179

Al went out of his way to take us to the very table where I'd proposed marriage a decade earlier, though it seemed a century ago. Back then I was a deliriously happy, dumbfounded almost-adult. I had such optimism. But now… I'd never seen anyone so pervasively preoccupied. There was no rewind. In my saddest moments, the times with greatest clarity, I admitted the truth was blurry while his lies were clear.

At our new offices, Al emptied the last boxes and straightened furniture. I rearranged my bookcase for the third time, without satisfaction, and half-heartedly organized my desk, wondering if I'd be boxing things up again soon. I felt glad my parents were en route. Al offered to hang three certificates for me and curiously mounted two side-by-side with one in the lower right quadrant, leaving space in the bottom left corner.

"Why didn't you put them in like a 'T' shape with the bottom one centered?" I asked. As inevitable as the tide turning, his enthusiasm evaporated again.

With sadness and irritation, he complained, "'Cause you'll get something *else* to put there." He pressed a finger inside the blank space to emphasize his point.

Huh? Was this fatigue speaking or something worse?

That day should have been joyous, celebratory, gratifying. It had been a decade in the making! We had sacrificed so much to achieve this very moment in time. All the weekends devoted to reading and writing, the tuition and textbook expense, the postponing of recreation, the occasional overnight in Ann Arbor during snowstorms, relentless commuting, years of counting down to the day we would join our practices, selecting and decorating our new office suite... I'd put my heart and soul into it! We'd arrived at our destination, but it felt like the wrong stop. Did this mean from here on out I'd be traveling solo?

Al's new office on the left          My new office (at end of the hall)

# SEVENTEEN

# FAREWELL

The following morning began as routine and seamless as the summer Saturdays preceding it but would end like no other. The heat and oppressive clamminess quickly built. I'd purchased Al a short-sleeved grey shirt recently and, to my amazement, he came downstairs wearing it, along with my favorite suit. He predictably topped off his old thermos as he had countless mornings before. Still in my nightgown, I accompanied him into the stagnant morning haze to the edge of the bricks in bare feet. He pecked me on the cheek, waved goodbye and aimed his car toward a hazy future. I returned to sit in the kitchen nook with steaming coffee. *He spends more time with that thermos than me.*

Al returned moments later.

"Forget something?"

"Yes. Just wanted to say I love you. I apologize."

"For yesterday? Forget it. You were tired."

I could not muster up the interest to even ask for clarification nor the expected response of, "I love you, too." I would later regret that. He toddled away with his familiar Charlie Chaplin walk, glimpsed back, squinted in the daybreak sun, and waved farewell. Gone, this mystifying, evasive husband of mine.

The weather deteriorated by mid-morning. In anticipation of my parents' visit, I went for last minute groceries before the skies loosened their full fury.

As I again stared down Essex to the horizon, the idea of detaching from Al, my practice and Michigan unnerved me, but I needed a contingency plan. My concerns were inconsequential to him. And as for the immodest Tudor... Why was he so connected to it? He was seldom home, never worked in the yard and rarely ventured to the carriage house to even touch his boxes of car parts, let alone restore his old vehicles. *He wouldn't have noticed if I painted the living room hot pink!*

By afternoon, I'd become drained. The annoying midnight calls had disrupted my sleep, along with muggy weather and discouragement. The ground floor was secured, the attic fan set in motion and lights extinguished. I quickly fell asleep as rain steadily pounded the steep roof and journeyed through copper gutters and spilled into city sewers.

Storm clouds had gathered across Wayne County.

*KaBOOM!* I jolted upright from a dead sleep. The rumbling smack of nearby thunder jarred me as my nostrils confronted the distinct smell of ozone in the downdraft of an intensifying summer storm. The rain rained down—hard! The downpour hammered gables, wetted windowsills and rattled the blown open shutters.

The wind heaved the tips of the tallest trees in gyrating directions as if in a tangled dance. The boiling skies darkened and triggered streetlights to flicker a mid-afternoon S.O.S. I sprinted around the Tudor securing windows, drying woodwork and unplugging items that power surges would damage. Chili Pepper was pulled inside, then the news turned on. A helluva storm was predicted.

Al called around 3:00 p.m. "I'll be home around seven. Hamburger's tonight?"

"Okay. How's the rainstorm there? It's ramping up here."

"Oh. Hadn't noticed."

That could be his middle name, so blind to danger.

"The news predicts we could lose power. There are small branches all over the yard already. The drive home could be tricky; can you leave early? Your patients don't need to be out in this."

"It'll be fine. See you in a few hours."

"Well, okay. Be safe."

With power outages predicted, ice was placed in the saltwater tank for added protection of the anemones, flashlights gathered, then candles. The attic fan strained to circulate heavy air. A trickle of perspiration dripped down my spine, and I grew uncomfortably sticky. A couple of reports demanded attention, so I turned on calming music to help focus. But, the century-old elm in our backyard was a distraction, nonetheless. Even larger limbs stirred in the gusts which caused green leaves to descend like confetti. They formed a delicate bracelet around the base of the century-old trunk.

Around 6:00 p.m., dinner was started, then I

retreated to the library to listen to the news again. Hail appeared. Sustained winds of twenty miles per hour, with occasional gusts three times that, huffed through Wayne County. The rafters groaned. The blue spruce outside the dining room slapped the casement window repeatedly as if it demanded entry. Hail hugged the curb in the middle of July.

When I turned off a faucet my scalp registered a small tingle. Lightning momentarily bleached the kitchen walls to a sickly white and the lights blinked. Our trio of cats quivered under the dining room table, their blue eyes wide and glistening with fear. As the barometer quickly fell below 30.00, my apprehension rose. The gauge mirrored my own feelings about our future.

# EIGHTEEN

# BLOODBATH

Spens and Lucky drifted back into consciousness again, following another jag of drugs. The methadone clinic was, again, a dim memory. They never were quitters. John still seethed over his conviction the "money was funny," having suspected Al wanted to "push out."

Al's strumpet called him at work to plea for money. Apparently, she thought of nothing else. He was upset by her intrusion and admonished her never to call him at work, but the line had been drawn in the sand and, after eighteen months of deceit, drugs, and demands, boundaries grew murky and were open to testing.

He'd lost control of his private amusement.

That one call, that one communication verified the play was over. His cronies from Casper Street knew his real name, where his office was, his business phone number and that he'd been misleading them for months. What else did they know?

At 6:30 Al locked the door to his office, walked away from the tower, toward his final performance as Doc Miller. Did he sense the punchline coming? Al Miller approached the now-familiar corner of Peterboro and Second under an angry sky, a sky as angry as the pimp who climbed into the passenger seat. The trio arrived at the Casper house where Fry found a soggy eviction notice hammered into the siding.

"Well, looky here," he laughed. With thick sarcasm, he sneered, "Got extra cash to put on the rent? Wouldn't want to leave this fuckin' dump or miss another goddamn winter!"

Ignoring his temper tantrum, Al dropped him off and drove Dawn to purchase more street poison.

It was a final boarding call.

As they returned from the drug run Fry hungrily anticipated more cash. Al had already given an excess of one-hundred-fifty-thousand-dollars—three-hundred-fifty-eight-thousand-dollars currently—over the preceding eighty-four secretive weeks. Then Al delivered a bombshell. He could not, or would not, deliver another dime. John predicted this doomsday was coming. The haze of drugs reinforced his entitlement and urgency, anger, and skepticism. The straining hinges loosened John's madness. Dawn was alert from the sidelines, powerless to intervene against the inevitable.

Without warning Al uncharacteristically barked, "It's *my* money! I can give it, or I can take it. I can do whatever I want! If you don't like it, *fuck you! Fuck you, John!* I don't have to justify *anything* I do to you!"

The undersized, bespectacled psychologist from Grosse Pointe Park took one last defiant step forward. John did not back up. Al Miller-Canty did not back down. Dawn backed away. The storm which hovered throughout Wayne County seemed to intensify outside the bungalow on Casper Street. Even then, it did not match the emerging hurricane inside. Al foolishly defied John Carl "Lucky" Fry—a former biker devoid of a conscience, nearly twice his size. A convicted felon unable to delay gratification. An addict who surrounded himself with thieves, prostitutes, pushers and con artists. An opportunist who bragged of his transgressions. A parasite who never accepted "no" for an answer. A tyrant who put others in the hospital—and probably the grave—because they defied him. How *dare* Al arrive empty-handed!

*"How do you know I'm mad?" said Alice.*
*"You must be," said the Cat, "or you wouldn't have come here."*
---Lewis Carroll

Doc Miller shoved the alpha male's shoulder. No one ever, *ever* pushed Lucky. Not even in jest. The beatings John suffered at the hands of his ax-handle-wielding father made him incapable of turning the other cheek. Someone had to pay! Fry instantly registered rage-filled disbelief.

The madman tripped over an unnoticed stool, which intensified his wrath. His face moistened and immediately grew flushed. His blood pressure spiked. His closely-spaced beady eyes drilled into Al with homicidal fury. Fry's breathing had grown audible and labored, as did Al's. Perspiration dotted their foreheads. The buttons on Fry's plaid shirt nearly detonated. Adrenaline and mixed jive reinforced his escalating madness and weakened his restraint. Doc Miller's fate became inescapable.

With tunnel vision, Fry locked his predatory glare onto Al as a lion preying upon a lone gazelle. The callous man beaten with fists and clubs and words found a target worthy of his seething fury. His greatest advantages were surprise and brute strength. His victim was contained. Everything else was irrelevant. For all Al's playacting, for all his bravado, Al failed to recognize the Corridor gave no second chances, no rescues. Nor did he know a Louisville Slugger waited behind the grimy door jamb. The tornado inevitably, furiously, touched down.

Despite John's bulk and narcotic-saturated body, he released a frightening burst of speed. The slayer grabbed the familiar club with perspiration-coated hands. With righteous indignation and velocity of a pro athlete, he forcefully swung the bat in a flawless arch, having aimed it directly at the right temple of his defenseless target. *Contact!* He pummeled him not once. Not twice. But three times. Al's ever-present eyeglasses hurled across the killing room, shattering upon impact. He staggered, was dazed and crumpled onto the thin, grimy carpet. The hooker raced past the prey and pursuer into the blinding downpour. Her trick was convulsing. Her pimp was boiling. Flashes of lightning enhanced the slaughter with a gruesome freeze-frame effect. Lucky delivered another commanding blow across the fractured forehead for assurance of death. Al's lifeblood gushed from his mouth, eye, ears and the gaping crevice on his temple. *"Get up, motherfucker! Get up!"* bellowed the murderer toward ears that no longer heard.

Stillness. Silence. Deadness. Human tissue coated the Louisville Slugger, carpet and ceiling. Blood splattered

Fry's murderous arms in telling red arches. The heartbeat he heard could only be his own. He scrutinized the underdog as the seizures of his victim gradually, inevitably subsided. John's hands slowly loosened their sticky grip on his tool of annihilation as he unlocked his gaze and took one slow step backward. The frenzy diminished. In the eye of the tempest, the only sound heard inside the squalid house was rain that coated death-smudged windows. The Corridor lived up to the hype again. *"Detroit. Aka Amityville."*

The strumpet cautiously returned, dripping from rain and fear. Before her, on the floor, she witnessed the silenced remains of her sugar daddy, the pinhead no one in the Corridor took seriously. She repeatedly called him a "chump" to his face and "fucking pinhead" behind his back. It had been a game, a free ride, a prostitute's dream come true. He'd been so laughable, so gullible, so manageable and oh-so-generous. She considered him fortunate to receive her lips on his body. She wanted to blackmail him. He wanted to sideline him. They both merely tolerated him. Then they eliminated him.

*Murder is not about lust*
*and it's not about violence. It's about possession.*
---Ted Bundy

Scarlet rivers erupted from Al's splintered head which saturated the worn carpet and new grey shirt even though everything—for him—had faded to black. He had a lifetime of words he would never say. Decades of places he would never travel. And lies he would never utter. An unnoticed clump of scalp gripped the rug. Gone was Dawn's meal ticket, the person who'd lavished her with gifts, cash, transportation and veil of respectability. Gone was John's drug supplier and ticket out of the slums. Gone was the dishonorable psychologist from the golden tower of the Fisher Building.

Al passed from one world to another.

John clicked back from the homicidal frenzy and barked, "Go make money!"

Spens hastily tiptoed around the lifeless, cooling body back into the raging night. What crossed her mind? Spens somehow turned two tricks in the damp back seat of strangers' cars under the ill-tempered skies.

The counterfeit physician, the trick with the implausible story was changing before him. His pupils had dilated and his jaw relaxed. His fingertips were blanched.

John dragged Doc's still-limp body to the grimy bathtub and raised his feet. Fry again studied his prey, his handiwork, his object of ridicule. Fry pressed a hardened blade against Doc Miller-Canty's defenseless, pale neck and effortlessly slit him from ear to ear. Vessels gushed thick, odorous, beet-red fluid. Panic and reality finally broke through the fog of rage, narcissism, and heroin. John lit another cigarette, grabbed the Doc's keys and angrily went in search of his only eyewitness.

Al's lifeblood dripped down the tub drain as John drove through pelting rain and widening puddles trying to find the former valedictorian from Harper Woods. What did she witness? Where did she go? Had she confided in anyone? He needed to know. Now! Finally, Fry spotted Spens in an all-hours, harshly-lit Coney Island near Springwells and Vernor Avenue sitting near an older man. Lucky ordered her into the car. He wanted more dope, more time and answers—right then! Should he trust her? Dawn climbed in wet and nervous and handed over her meager earnings from her grimy "dates."

The savage with the temper and the woman with the abscesses returned to stare at the silent man with no future. Since November of 1985, he'd brought gifts, drugs, and lies. He was the gullible golden goose who reliably delivered money in exchange for dependency, a dirty secret, and a guaranteed audience. He left a comfortable life, thriving business and wife who respected him to volunteer for the real-life version of *Requiem for a Dream*.

The murderer admitted aloud, "He can't stay here. Too many eyes in the hood." He fixed another syringe and waited for its numbing effects to coat his brain. He lit a cigarette. Then another. And a third. He debated his limited options.

The killer lumbered into the kitchen and clutched a large, serrated Ginsu knife. He discarded the grey shirt and trousers of his lifeless victim and stripped down to his own underwear to avoid the inevitable bloodstains to come. John climbed over his prey, which had drained and waited and stared back for over two hours.

John started with his head. He ignored his victim's open eyes and hovered the shiny, sharp blade next to the left of Doc's lukewarm Adam's apple and pressed down firmly. A few more pushes and Fry decapitated his inconvenience. Next, he detached his hands near the cuff line but paused to steal his watch. Last, he amputated his room-temperature feet. Lucky made several messy trips to the basement.

It was easier than imagined.

He wrapped Al's head, hands, and feet individually in newspaper and shoved these identifiable body parts into separate green plastic lawn bags. The executioner ordered Spens to fetch the brown suitcase. John stuffed the packaged carnage in the refrigerator, which proved monsters *did* exist. Fry felt contempt, not regret, exasperation or remorse. Al Canty was nothing but a damned irritant—dead *or* alive.

2518 Casper St. in south Detroit where Al was murdered. (It is now torn down.) (Credit: Michael Green, The Detroit News)

Living room of the Casper house at the time of the murder. The small stool to the left (above) is the one Fry tripped over during the homicide. (Credit: WJBK News Detroit Fox affiliate)

Where Al like to sit and read the paper when on Casper
(Credit: WJBK News Detroit Fox Affiliate)

# STANDING BY

*Live Aid,* a three-hour special, was a welcome distraction from the aggressive storm of July 13, 1985 and my weariness. The special broadcast, from Philadelphia and London, was designed to raise funds for famine relief in Ethiopia.

The heat index rose to ninety degrees in The Points yet still my attention was riveted by Mick Jagger, David Bowie, Tina Turner, Black Sabbath, and a paralyzed Teddy Pendergrass, who'd made his first appearance since his near-fatal accident. Tragic, full-color footage showed Ethiopian drought, disease, and famine. Segments of dusty roads with weary refugees carrying dying children were heartbreaking. Dead farm animals... Tear-stained faces... Governments planned an ill-fated global relief operation. In the second hour, Santana and Madonna performed.

Dinner was overdue. I grabbed popcorn to tide me over. *He's delayed by the weather. He'll be home soon.*

Millions tuned in to hear *Live Aid's* anthem "We Are the World" which reminded viewers, "people are dying, it's time to lend a hand to life, the greatest gift of all."

In stark contrast we had rain... *Oh*, did we have rain! A second wave of the Saturday storm pummeled the area. Night had fallen. The clock shockingly insisted it was 10:10. *Three hours overdue?* I telephoned his office but only spoke with his answering service.

The sweltering storm hadn't cooled the agitated sky. It was still a muggy eighty-one degrees. Gutters released torrents of water. *Where is he?* Lightning decolorized the interior of the house again. It was as if the night was angry. Forgotten dinner ripened on the stove while pangs of fear replaced pangs of hunger. The coach lights were illuminated to greet Al upon arrival. But something felt wrong—*terribly* wrong. Again, that prickly sensation of danger returned. The aura of dread was not to be silenced. *Wait! His spare appointment calendar!* It suddenly seemed to hold the key to his delay. *Who did he last see and when?* I seized it in sweating hands but found nothing. *Blank! What?!* My eyes scanned barren pages in disbelief. *No appointments?*

By eleven, nausea had set in. Adrenaline pulsed my temples. Pain robbed me of clarity. My feet vehemently pulled me into his darkened home office again where my dim reflection revealed my anxiety. I froze, not reacting to distant thunder. I stared at my blanched image. My breath paused. I felt oddly detached from everything and everyone.

"He's dead. He's not coming home. I...know...this..." I said aloud.

This belief was *unshakable*. It was unfathomable. It

was surreal. And it seemed a little crazy. How could this be...*known?* In a sliver of time I was isolated, perilously cut off from my surroundings and absolutely aware something evil, something unfathomable, had occurred. My breath felt stolen. My thoughts locked. Time stopped.

A boom of thunder and lightning snatched me back. My pulse quickened. A throbbing headache returned. *No! He's just...late. Surely, other, plausible explanations existed. Another psychotic break?*

Pacing and panic exhausted me. Rain and lightning chilled me. The humidity finally broke. Broad puddles dotted lawns, alleys, ditches, and parking lots throughout the tri-county area. The temperature yielded. My stomach was knotted.

I reluctantly phoned my next-door neighbor, Jim Saros, and asked if he'd accompany me to the Fisher Building explaining that, after 6:00 p.m., everyone had to sign in and out of the tower. Jim immediately agreed despite the weather and late hour.

"She never calls for help," he commented to his wife, as he grabbed his keys and headed out.

That section of downtown wasn't great on weekend nights. I was glad to be accompanied by a large, confident businessman. "Can I see the sign-out log, please?" I asked the guards.

There it was, his signature. Plain as day. Time: 6:35 p.m. We headed up to Al's office. Jim asked me to wait in the empty hall, concerned Al might have had a heart attack. He groped for the light switch, looked around, stepped back, and shrugged his broad shoulders, stating simply, "He isn't here."

The night skies cooled and soft drizzle dampened

streets. Once home I called the State Patrol, local emergency rooms and Grosse Pointe Park Police. He'd vanished, swallowed up by the night. The house never felt so cavernous. The frayed, upholstered chair in his home office drew me as I sat wrapped within his heavy, striped bathrobe to quiet the goosebumps. With the phone on my lap, and the room dimly illuminated by outdoor lights, I dozed.

Daybreak, Sunday, July 14. Three hours of broken sleep, no food, and surges of adrenalin left me feeling ill. I struggled to formulate a plan while I gazed out windows at dull, early morning mist. My head felt stuffed with cotton. It was much too early to call anyone and what was there to say except, "He's gone"?

Sunday afternoon was consumed with a search for clues with my friend, Celia. We returned to the Fisher Building and discovered, to our surprise, Al had polished both desks and finished organizing.

We paused in the windowless, marble hallway. I suggested we search nearby bathrooms, though Celia was not enthusiastic.

"He could have had another breakdo... Like, maybe he commit... I'm saying we don't know what we'll find."

Electricity in that part of the skyscraper was out due to large-scale, so-called "improvements" demanded by Burroughs Corporation. We regretted not bringing flashlights as we gingerly opened restroom doors.

"Al! You here? It's me, Jan-Jan!"

The only sound was our echoed voices. We paused.

"Ces is here, too. *Al?*"

We inspected the shadowy interiors of the men's and women's restrooms as far back as we could see, but illumination was minimal. After the first two stalls, we could not even see each other. We slowly slid our hands along the cool marble walls and heavy stall doors and probed with our shoes.

"Al? You here?"

Nothing. No sign of life or death.

We walked to the nearby Detroit Police Substation to report him missing, where two officers were on duty, at least *officially*. One interrupted to casually call out her Burger King order. She held her puffy hand in front of our faces as if she directed traffic. The other officer forbade another word while glued to a prizefight on his black and white, pint-size television. A pause in the action released him to look up momentarily. He understood but made no further eye contact.

"Check his friends? You get in a fight? Sure 'nuf happens. How 'bout the hospitals?" He was glued again to his entertainment. "Lady. Like I said..."

"My name isn't 'Lady,'" I interrupted. "It's Dr. Canty." My anger was simmering again.

"Well, *Doctor*, call the morgue."

His words kicked me in the gut with the intensity of the athletes he studied. We backed away from the worn counter, Celia put her arm around me and asked him, "Can *you* do it?"

"Uh, nah. Can't even take no report 'til he's been missing twenty-four hours. That's the law." It's clear this concluded his interest and involvement.

We reported him missing at a different police station, since, technically, we hadn't *seen* him for twenty-four hours. What else was there to do?

Celia had her own family to attend to and drove me

home. I paced inside the house I never wanted, closed my eyes and called my parents. "Can you fly in earlier?" I hadn't needed them this much since I was hospitalized for a tonsillectomy as a kid. They immediately sensed my alarm.

"Why? What's happened? Is it Al?"

"Yes."

"What?! Is he back in the hospital?"

"No. Not *that*... Mom, he..."

"What? You sound *awful*."

"Well, he didn't come home. I haven't seen him, not since Saturday. I expected him yesterday for dinner. He hasn't called. I haven't been to bed. The weather... It's awful. I've checked everywhere! Even went to his office around midnight with Jim. I don't know what else to do!"

Her voice yanked down my defenses, and I sobbed. If only she could crawl through the phone. Phoenix felt past the Milky Way.

"Celia helped. We went downtown. We filed a missing person's report. I don't know what else to do..." I said for a second time.

She repeated the fragmented story to my father, who was aware of some sort of emergency.

By late Sunday still no word. *Nothing*. It was as if he'd been absorbed into the Bermuda Triangle. Time for a different approach. I phoned WJR-AM—located in the same office building as ours. They interrupted their broadcast to ask for information about "the missing psychologist from Grosse Pointe Park."

I also telephoned his longtime friend Ray Danford. Had he seen him? Ray sounded alarmed but didn't know his whereabouts. "I don't know what to say, but if I hear anything at all, I'll call. Try not to worry." He could be counted on.

Meanwhile, I apprehensively phoned Gladys and again relayed the series of events that had, so far, led nowhere. "Can you reach people you know and get them searching?"

She asked me to come for her.

As darkness fell, I offered to put up a bed for Mrs. Canty, but she preferred to face the front window in a straight back chair where she waited and watched. Neither of us ate. This frail, elderly mother of the missing man remained on guard all night in her ever-present cardigan hoping her Buster would return. She declined even tea. I tossed and turned upstairs trying, unsuccessfully, to sleep. We could not unite even in the face of a shared nightmare.

Daybreak Monday found us closer to nowhere. A heavy stillness and sense of futility hung in every room. It'd been over forty-eight hours since I had more than cat naps. I offered to drive Mrs. Canty home, but she wavered.

"Of course, I'll call the minute I hear anything, and you do the same, Okay? It's on the radio, you've made calls, and Ray is helping."

She looked weary and understandably upset. She was in her late seventies and looked every day of it this dispirited morning. Gladys had not eaten nor changed her uncharacteristically wrinkled clothes since yesterday.

"Your cats need food, and we can watch over both phones and houses if you're home. What if Al shows up there? All we can do is wait."

She slowly agreed and walked in a gingerly manner with her back bent. She said not a word on the short trip to her home. Gladys quietly unlocked her darkened, silent house of antiques and memories and stepped inside. The mother of the missing psychologist hung her head as she delicately closed the door to life as she knew it. I had never seen her cry in the ten years I'd known her, and she did not do so then.

Gladys Canty was well connected in the city. One appeal paid off. Detective Greg Osowski received a missing person's report from the police commander and contacted me immediately. "Your husband… What are his habits? Close friends? Girlfriend? Does he gamble? Has he gone missing before?"

We covered those bases and more. At 8:30 that evening, Osowski returned to the Fisher Building to chat up some guards and garage technicians.

An insignificant story appeared in the Detroit Free Press, which introduced our private nightmare to the public. Around lunch, a local television crew knocked on our front door. I hesitated to speak with them but needed assistance. Time was not on our side.

"No. You may *not* take my photo," I emphasized, but they stole one anyway for the evening news while I answered a phone call. It annoyed me no end.

They were supplied a description of his car, recent photo from our trip to the Grand Canyon and his license plate number.

My parents' eagerly anticipated flight arrived at 2:55 p.m., Monday, July 15 at Detroit Metro. Their reassuring hug triggered a flood of tears. Back home, my mother instantly detected rancid food on the stove, still waiting in the summer heat since Saturday. It had escaped my attention along with showering, changing clothes and breathing deeply. From my perspective, the last seventy-two hours had been one long day, not distinct twenty-four-hour periods. Mom threw away the rotten hamburger and advised, "You need to shower and get into clean clothes. C'mon back and I'll fix you and Dad lunch. You need a nap, too. You're ragged."

The hot water comforted. Food was moderately appealing. Sleep remained impossible.

Ray arrived unexpectedly at my office three days into Al's disappearance and explained it was urgent. He'd always struck me as a modest, sincere, bashful man. I wanted to know what Ray knew, but the timing was problematic. He was ashen with dark circles under his gentle eyes. He struggled for eye contact and tried to get to the point but spoke in fragments. He fought tears and removed his ever-present bucket hat (that he referred to as his "fishing hat") which revealed thinning hair the same color as Al's. His fingers trembled as he sat hunched in Al's chair while my patient waited in my office. He never achieved eye contact.

"Uh… How much do you know about the…the, ah…*dopers* Al saw?"

"You mean patients? I don't know much about them. I'm not supposed to — ethically, I mean. Why?"

"Well, he started hanging out with 'em on, Cass. Not doing drugs…just… He *saw* them."

Ray seemed confused or torn, and he confused me. I couldn't track his thoughts, but then again, I was running on cat naps and caffeine. Ray paused as if he had more to say but left without making eye contact. I felt he never got to the point.

Later I told my father about the cigarette butts, odd late-night calls, wad of keys under the steps and described the stranger who stopped by while weeding.

"Who do you think he was?" Dad asked.

"Someone from Recorder's Court maybe? Probation cases? Al said they owed him back pay. If that's it, I don't want felons around our house."

"Hmmm…let me call and see what I can find out."

My father reappeared and added to the ever-growing puzzle. He shook his head and reported, "The prosecutor's staff said Al doesn't work there. Never has."

I was stunned. "Huh? Al said…."

Yes. That was the emerging pattern. Things became muddier and clearer simultaneously. I also described the crumpled McDonald's bag in my backseat after it had supposedly been detailed and Al's evasiveness about money. My father grew angrier at Al by the minute but didn't say so. He didn't have to. I could easily read him. His mind vigorously tried to make sense of it.

Later that week the *Detroit News* published its first wave of detailed information about Al's disappearance on page 9A without an author. It read:

> Grosse Pointe Park psychologist vanished after seeing a patient in his Fisher Building office at 6 pm. His wife said he was stopping at Kroger's on Kercheval, but store personnel could not recall seeing him. She last saw him 8:30 a.m. Saturday. Dr. Canty is 5'10", 170 pounds with reddish-blond hair and tortoise frame glasses. He was wearing an olive-green suit and a gray, short-sleeved shirt carrying a gold thermos. His car, a black 1981 Buick Regal License 712KZK, is also missing.

One television reporter confidently speculated it was a "Successful abduction. More details at 11:00." They confused my spouse with his deceased father. Sketchy-looking strangers were interviewed on the news defined as "friends of the missing man and his wife." If they got *that* wrong, how could I believe anything they said?

Three detectives darkened my office doorway shortly afterward. Each appeared the size of a football lineman dressed in no-nonsense dark suits with official shields. One ducked slightly to clear the transom as he stepped inside. They were all business. I felt intimidated and reassured by their presence and nearly snapped to attention. They stood shoulder to shoulder through their clipped, purposeful questions. "Does anyone worry you? People he owes money to?" "Does he frequent prostitutes?" "Do you have a recent photo?" "Can we see his office?" "Have you had any unusual phone calls or people driving by your house?" "Has his behavior changed?"

As they departed, it was my turn. "What are the odds this will be solved? That he'll be found?"

They exchanged a hasty, sober, knowing glance. One countered with, "We're certain it'll be figured out, and soon."

I exhaled. That was a glimmer of hope.

We continued to search also. My mentor, Dr. Rutledge, contacted C. Patrick Babcock, Director of the Michigan Department of Mental Health, on Thursday, July 18 theorizing Al could have succumbed to another mental crisis and become re-hospitalized somewhere in a mute condition. Dr. Watkins was chosen to spearhead the urgent hunt. He discreetly contacted every psychiatric facility in

Michigan, then all non-psychiatric hospital admissions. Dozens of hours led nowhere.

We held out hope that wherever Al was, he was there by choice and he'd soon return. The coach lights remained illuminated day and night. I glanced at the struggle cup and recalled the afternoon he presented it, explaining it would give me the strength to endure the challenges ahead. I hoped he was right. I was certainly struggling.

# TWENTY

# DISASTER CONTROL

Around midnight Fry bellowed at Dawn to retrieve the dead weight from the refrigerator. The weapons, broken eyeglasses and blood-stained clothes had been shoved into a fourth bag. Doc Miller-Canty's thermos was the last to go. The deed was exceedingly past reversible. They placed the chilled remains in the getaway car, the same vehicle driven by the divided man earlier. They were headed four hours north to Emmet County, to enlist the help of Frank McMaster.

After another round of drugs, the butcher and the butchered slid northbound on I-75. It was gonna be a break night. En route, Fry tossed Al's torso into a dumpster off Buchanan near 35th and his arms behind a gas station near Springwells and the I-75 ramp. Dawn was on the nod as she occupied the passenger seat in Al's car-turned-hearse. Fry stopped to toss more body parts onto a littered, wet embankment of a freeway ramp in Auburn Hills near Joslyn. Spens asked what happened.

I-75 runs N-S between Detroit and Petoskey.
Grosse Pointe is on the immediate east side of Detroit.

Lucky smirked, "Just throwin' away some garbage."

The former biker and valedictorian pushed further north under the dark, misty sky with the hands, head, and feet of their silenced passenger. Headlights reflected damp, green exit signs on their northerly progression. Flint. Saginaw. Grayling. They quietly drove northwest under pre-dawn darkness toward Alanson, past Indian River up to the tip of Michigan's Lower Peninsula.

The runaways were within an hour of their destination when they switched drivers somewhere between Grayling and Gaylord and continued under drying skies. Fatigue had finally settled in. By daybreak John, Dawn and the heavy suitcase had arrived unannounced at McMaster's Emmet County cabin, and he wasn't enthused to see them.

*This can't be good news,* Frank groaned to himself. He'd never been fond of Dawn. "Prima donna," he muttered. Frank never liked how she talked trash about other hookers and snubbed John's friends—him included.

Frank looked quizzically at the Buick.

"On loan," John quipped, as he insisted on getting rid of the incriminating items in the trunk. He needed a place to bury his sins.

McMaster suggested a privately-owned spot in the woods. Lucky intimidated him too much to ask questions, let alone deny him.

Sunday was devoted to spouting half-truths and deciding upon a burial spot for the satchel containing the nuisance. John bragged to Frank about the cargo, but Frank dismissed it as another bloated story. The two men, in the black Buick, with carnage in the trunk, drove past Pellston Airport and turned east off U.S. 31 onto Douglas Lake Road near South Fishtail Bay. Blue signs indicated the property belonged to the University of Michigan Biological Station. Frank directed John to a seldom-driven logging road.

"Turn here, it's a dead end."

Fry snickered. "Sure is!"

They reached a section reserved for roadkill. "Good enough," Fry announced.

The sun was in tandem with humidity and mosquitoes. Frank dug a shallow hole and realized he was burrowing himself into a jam with every shovel full. The swarms of miniature vampires insistently buzzed around the gravediggers' moist, exposed flesh. John released the heavy suitcase and smirked, "Bye, Al."

Dusting off their hands, they planned the rest of their day. A half hour later they burned the contents of Al's wallet in McMaster's wood stove and disposed of belongings owned by the man stuffed in the bog.

Meanwhile, Fry and McMaster went on a triumphant beer run. They drove past the shadowy, makeshift gravesite in the late afternoon mugginess, confident they'd buried their culpability. Fry chuckled as he referred to the area as "Doc's private cemetery." Frank and McMaster shared a good laugh. Fry waved and muttered, "Bye-bye, mother fucker!"

The secrets surrounding the fate of the fifty-one-year-old missing psychologist were destined to be buried along with him for all eternity. The gravediggers reassured one another they knew how to get away with murder. Three hundred miles separated the body parts from the murder scene. There were no witnesses. Evidence inside Casper had been removed and the car would be gone. There was no money trail because Doc paid cash. Their alibis had been fabricated and coordinated. The co-conspirators would soon go their separate ways and Fry envisioned himself sitting under a palm tree on the west coast with or without Spens. Maybe he'd hook up with his old biker buddies.

In time the public's attention would wane. The house on Casper was rumored to be scheduled for demolition. The investigation, they agreed, would be relegated to the back burner of the overworked Homicide Unit. Theories of what happened would grow stale. Justice would neither be denied nor available, merely suspended. W. Alan Canty's file would join the other 164,000 unsolved cases nationwide and the missing Grosse Pointe Park man would become a mere footnote in the history of Detroit.

By late Sunday, July 14, the executioner and his accomplice rewarded themselves with a job well done. It was over. They cleaned up then proceeded to nearby Mackinaw Island where they strolled the boardwalks and mingled with the tourists. Their actions lent credibility to the odds that, on average, someone unknowingly walks by a murderer thirty-six times in their lifetime.

The fugitives bought the latest *Detroit News* the following morning and saw the search warrant story on page one. John arrogantly dismissed the investigation as a futile game of tag yet privately, told himself he'd never be taken alive. Dawn wasn't so convinced they had a home run on their hands. She read the article and rewound the entire freeze frame murder in her head.

Someone else picked up the article. Doris DeDecker, formerly of Recorder's Court Clinic, turned to her spouse. "Look at this. I haven't seen him in years. It brings it back to me... When you diminish somebody, when they feel no self-worth, they're open to seeking the level of self-worth they have." She then paused with more seriousness and added, "They're gonna find him in some dumpster."

Later in the week, the duo returned south toward Wayne County with another half-baked plan, as Frank dutifully followed in his own vehicle. California would have to wait until they took care of Doc's car.

A friend tipped off Fry that police cruisers had circled the area and may have entered their rental, causing John to frantically abandon the idea of selling the Buick. Plan B was to round up a car thief instead. Gary Neil came to mind.

"But I can't boost the ride without a fucking *title*, man. You know that! Isn't that Doc's car? Where is he?"

"In five different states, mon," he replied, with a fake Caribbean accent.

"What happened to your move west? Thought you were parting ways."

"It backfired. He *pushed* me. He pushed me over the goddamn edge! He had to go."

"Well, I don't want the car and I sure can't sell it."

"Fine! Then let's *smoke* it."

Fry and Neil grew reckless. They darted through traffic like wild arrows, snubbed stop signs and cut corners across private property. Panic had finally registered. Frank reluctantly followed, trying to avoid attention and keep his own alarm under wraps.

In an unguarded moment, Frank challenged John's account that Dawn wasn't even in the bungalow at the time of Al's murder. "John, that's bullshit."

The killer replied, "Well, what the fuck you want me to say? That she was packaging when I was cutting? Okay, so it happened that way. But don't tell Dawn I told you. She don't want nobody to know she was there."

The con artist searched urgently, haphazardly for a way to dump the new car, which had no value now, not even to a thief. John charged Frank's car window at about 11:00 p.m. "*Fuck* it! We're gonna strip it and smoke it. Get some gas!"

Frank dutifully purchased the incendiary at an all-night Mobil, becoming more deeply involved in the cover-up. Fry struggled to remove salable, unidentifiable auto parts as his hands trembled from drug withdrawal, pain, fatigue, and apprehension. Frank grew impatient. "Let's roll out! Forget the rims! Let's get *rid* of it!"

Frank grudgingly tailed John and Gary into the ominous, humid night to a neglected industrial area devoid of pedestrians, traffic and streetlights on Federal east of Livernois near an abandoned, cinder block, two-story warehouse. It had been painted a sickly sea-green a decade earlier, made more revolting by one dim fluorescent light and garish graffiti tags. The first-floor windows were bricked over, and a ghetto grill spanned the narrow door. Fry knew this forgotten area was seldom patrolled, as it was sandwiched between two police jurisdictions and sparsely populated. Freight trains did sprint through nightly on Class Three tracks with speeds of 40-45 miles per hour but never stopped. The raised track blocked visibility from the opposite side. The trio planned to be in and out.

Al's Buick in police impound lot. I was charged for every day it sat there.

Elsewhere in southeast Detroit at that hour, a detective spotted a familiar snitch, who he observed surreptitiously from the deep shadows and haze for a few minutes. It was 1:30 when he was curbside.

"You know where Dawn is?" he casually asked.

"Yeah. She be hangin' with John somebody. Word up he's a *crazy* one. He don't *need* to pack [a gun]. That Dawn woman got a trick named Doc. He's a good John."

Osowski's intuition told him this was a valuable lead. The informant briefly blocked the detective from his cruiser to repeat her warning. "I'm tellin' you…John be off his rocker!"

The precinct files immediately churned up a rap sheet and last known address for Fry, and within minutes, the rental on Casper was under surveillance.

The snitched called with more. "They be trying to unload Doc's car near Livernois."

Not long afterward, a young man by the name of Jim Campbell, a surveyor assigned to the central south side, called Police Headquarters and reported finding a scorched car near some railroad tracks which matched the description of the Buick announced over the radio.

Another top cop became involved, Inspector Gil Hill—who made an acting debut as Eddie Murphy's boss, Detective Todd, in *Beverly Hills Cop* the previous year. The information was dispatched to Osowski who quickly located the cremated car and immediately knew Fry had tried to conceal evidence and did a lousy job of it. But, then again, he smirked; Fry *was* a dope head, not a professional thief.

On Wednesday, the 17th, Detroit's finest had a plan. They rounded up six so-called "hostages" for questioning. This number might lead to information and deflect attention away from the helpful snitch picked up in the sweep. Al's disappearance graduated to page 2A.

Day five. A signed search warrant authorized Sergeant Gerald Tibaldi and six others to enter the modest alley home. It sanctioned them to acquire, "Any identification, personal effects, blood or other effects relating to the disappearance of the person last seen wearing a greenish jacket, slacks, and gray shirt in the company of John Carl Fry and Dawn Marie Spens with a last known address of 2518 Casper."

The case was assigned to Bernard Brantley and Marlyss Landeros of the Special Assignment Squad whose responsibility it was to ensure an airtight paper trail and that witnesses showed. Detective Brantley was formal, perceptive, hurried, to the point and rumored to be Hill's replacement upon the inspector's anticipated promotion to commander. Landeros was a tall, slender woman of color who knew her way around the block. She was attentive, insightful and efficient — without being curt. She'd been in law enforcement longer than would be assumed. Little escaped her notice.

Search warrant in hand, they first inventoried the outside of the rental then executed the warrant. A mere glance revealed evidence typical for shooting galleries and that something serious had occurred. The bungalow was sparsely furnished. Its "décor" was an amalgamation of litter, overflowing ashtrays, missing air vents, dirty laundry, old newspapers, scattered plastic bags, unopened mail and half-filled Styrofoam cups with sticky residue. Curiously, three cinder blocks were plunked in the living room for no discernible reason. There were syringes, bent spoons and an assortment of plastic milk jugs with yellow liquid on a shabby table — undoubtedly their altar of excess. The summer air had a sickly stench and flies buzzed against smudgy windows trying in vain to escape the squalor. The seasoned detectives immediately noticed missing carpet, brain matter on the ceiling, two bloodstained towels on the floor of the small living room, eviction notice and clump of my husband's reddish hair with scalp still attached, recklessly overlooked on the thin, contaminated carpet.

A technician followed a blood trail downstairs to a cardboard box for plastic leaf bags under the steps. It was entirely circled with more blood. A concrete laundry tub concealed bright red liquid in a recessed groove of the drain.

Officers in the kitchen bagged an empty Comerica bank envelope, stethoscope, and book entitled *Psychology of Industrial Conflict*. They found the hallway smeared with waist-high uneven red streaks. A further probe turned up a folded scrap of paper containing the name and contact information of the missing man, evidence of a connection between Dr. Canty and the persons of interest. They took numerous measurements and photographs to document their discovery. Neighbors confirmed the "Doc" was a well-known visitor, within the last few days in fact, and that he drove a new black Buick last seen on Saturday.

Fry bragged of his deadly intentions to several threadbare acquaintances, unaware of the damage it could do. He and Spens left a trail of evidence a police cadet could unscramble. Officers wondered if it was Johnny Fry's narcissism that caused his carelessness. Perhaps his incessant drug use? Blind rage? Sense of urgency? Probably all the above.

# PART TWO

# THE DOMINO EFFECT

# TWENTY-ONE

# CIRCLING THE WAGONS

It was a quiet ride home Sunday morning, July 21. The grit and decay from our early meeting with Inspector Hill was jammed into my pores. My father took over the forty- minute drive as I lay curled in the back seat of my own car with my head on Mom's lap. Dad had a chokehold on the steering wheel. Mom stroked my hair as she had decades earlier and cradled me in her arms. Each of us tried to digest the ghastly news.

Conversation was minimal. Words could not express what we'd been told. My brain toiled slowly and felt bruised or shorted out. *My husband, a probable murder victim inside some back-alley house with a pimp and prostitute that knew him? Our money problems were real and caused by him throwing it away?* It occurred to me the Corridor had something for everyone. For his assailants it offered victims to fleece. For Al it was a walk on the wild side, and I was able to fulfill my academic dreams and then some.

And all three objectives had collided.

Observing through the rear window, past Mom's profile, nine-story buildings yielded to expressway overpasses and familiar green signs along eastbound I-94. The rhythm of road expansions felt soothing. Our speed quickened, along with lane changes, truck noise, and deep preoccupation. Sunlight flooded the back seat, and I caved into an island of safety after nights of sleeplessness. In the shelter of Mom's arms and warmth of the sun, I nodded off. I wanted to remain there, blissfully out of touch with the ugliness of this world.

I later awoke to the majestic trees, sidewalks and stop signs of my tidy neighborhood where orderliness belied the anguish inside the car, inside our heads and between our glances.

News of Al's burned-out car was out before we arrived home and now included Al's dated photograph from the back cover of *Therapeutic Peers*. Staff writer Peter Lochbiler contributed to the article, which said:

### Missing therapist believed slain

Detroit Police suspect that missing Grosse Pointe Park psychologist, W. Alan Canty, was slain and are seeking two people for questioning after raiding a house in southwest Detroit that Canty reportedly frequented.

Police said they searched the bloodstained single-family house at 2518 Casper Wednesday night after receiving a tip that a man who lived there boasted he killed the 51-year-old therapist, who has been missing six days and that "police will never find the body."

No one was home, but bloodstains were in the kitchen and basement, said Homicide Inspector Gilbert Hill. Detectives are also seeking a woman Canty visited regularly in reported attempts to steer her off drugs and prostitution. She was not a patient of his, but Canty often gave her money, police said.

The article contained a detailed map of south Detroit with arrows designating our home, his charred car, office, and house on Casper.

The media's actions increased my father's worries and protectiveness. He knew I'd been avoiding the news, which worried him. "For your own safety and ours, you should know what you're dealing with. I know it's hard, but we need to stay together, even going to the store."

Dad proceeded to read an article from the news the day following our meeting with Gil Hill entitled "*Canty case figures still on the loose.*" It contained the suspects' mugshots.

"Do you recognize the faces or names of these two?" Dad asked.

"No. Never seen them. Geeze, they look hard."

"Well, memorize their faces and don't go near them if you do see them. Call 911, then me. In that order. Okay? Promise?"

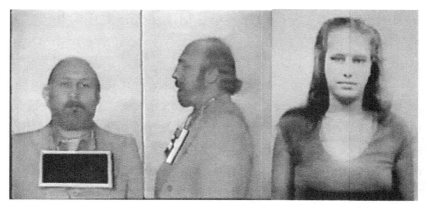

Mug shot, John Fry
(credit: Mark Bando)

Mug shot Dawn Spens

The article indicated Fry was spotted with the Buick Tuesday shortly before it was discovered incinerated near a vacated area of 5700 Federal Street.

Hill was quoted as saying:

> If we had a body, we'd have a murder warrant. By Thursday we had statements they allegedly made; they were seen in the doctor's car, a witness saw the burned-out car shortly after he saw them in the vehicle. We executed the search warrant and found blood. The rug had been removed between the living room and bathroom. There was a huge amount of blood in the basement. There was a lot of indication something very serious had happened…

The three of us sat there with ugly bulletins that tore a gaping hole in normalcy. They were incomprehensible, unfamiliar, frightening and, worst of all, authentic.

Mom grew visibly upset as we discussed locks,

security codes, drawn drapes and keeping lights low. She blurted, "Let's just all go back to Arizona. We're not safe here!"

Her heart was in the right place but leaving was out of the question. I anticipated more contact with Inspector Hill, had the cats to consider, wondered about leaving the house unoccupied and had bills to pay. Dad read my thoughts, paused, and declared, "From now on no one answers the door but me, understand? Same for the phone and it goes off the hook at dinnertime. The outside lights stay lit all night, and I'm going to sleep downstairs for now."

"Dad, you're scaring me."

He calmly stood and answered, "The situation scares *me*. I want you and Mom safe. No one drives anywhere alone. Got it? Not even to your office. Not until they're caught."

"But what if I need to..."

"This isn't negotiable!"

I felt twelve again. But, in this situation, I agreed.

The following afternoon Dad installed security grills over basement window wells and a padlock and bell on the garden gate. He insisted we park inside the garage. "And no more leaving first floor windows open at night."

Day six. Strangers began to ask intrusive questions without a need to know. An elderly neighbor, who was usually tactful, spotted me in the garden and offered her unsolicited opinion over the top of the iron gate. "He's committed suicide, don't you think?"

I was shocked by her insensitivity, which reinforced the removal of the phone from its hook and even being outdoors in my own yard. My father ran interference with the bigger world from then on. Mom adopted the role of keeping us fed, on schedule and in clean clothes. Sleep was elusive, even with steadfast parents under a shared roof.

Tension grew as days passed. I felt guilty having my problems spill over onto my parents. This was not their battle, though they'd disagreed.

One evening after dinner, Dad sat next to me on the back, screened porch on the striped glider in near darkness. He quietly explained he'd just watched the news. Anticipating another installment of repulsiveness, I interrupted, "Not more. Not now, Dad. Please? I can't sleep as it is."

Dad patiently, quietly explained, "Don't forget how much you have already endured, everything you've faced –starting with the incubator you were in. One day you'll look back and see how strong you are." He paused and looked weary.

Studying his tired face made me more agreeable. I had to meet him halfway. "I know, Dad, it's just so scary and confusing."

"Remember the poster in your room over your desk in high school?" he said after a few minutes. "It said, 'We don't grow when things are easy. We grow with challenges.' That's you. It started when you were born prematurely and underweight and look at you now, a doctor. You're stronger than most despite your size, and you aren't alone."

I smiled, and he put his arm around me as I rested my head on his shoulder. We glided back and forth which allowed a sense of peace to briefly return. My breathing slowed. For a moment, things even seemed normal and uncomplicated. I began to yawn and thought about how peaceful it *would* be to escape to Arizona with its violet mountains and solitude.

Then Dad cleared his through and interrupted the calm. "Well, I wish I had better things to report, Jan. A young neighbor of the man they're looking for, Fry's neighbor, was on T.V. His name is Michael Oliver, and he overheard Fry threaten to kill Al. That doesn't mean he did, but he sounds dangerous. This Oliver fella also said he…"

"Stop, Dad. I don't want to hear it!"

"Jan. I'm not telling this to upset you. Information is power, right? You cannot stick your head in the sand. We have to be prepared mentally for what may be coming."

I teared up but the look of exhaustion and concern on his face softened my protest again.

"Anyway, the neighbor remembered Fry and the woman from the mug shot, the prostitute, Donna was it? No, ah, *Dawn*? Well, he said they took off with garbage bags Saturday night. What was in them, no one is saying. Saturday was the night of the storm that you told us about, remember? The police are trying to find those bags."

"They're that important?"

"Yeah, guess so. And they're on the loose, but I doubt they'd come here. They have no reason to. You don't have anything of theirs and they probably know the house is under drive-by surveillance. They're probably on the run."

"We're being watched!?"

"Yes. Inspector Hill coordinated it."

"I can't decide if that makes me more scared or more relieved. The fact that he thinks it's necessary…"

Mom joined us, dishtowel in hand, having

224

overheard everything.

"Mom, I've said it before, but I am so thankful to have you as parents and that you're here."

Mom teared up, trying to look calm, and replied, "We know, honey, we know, and there is no place we'd rather be than by your side."

We sat listening to crickets and staring at the tile floor that Dad and I installed the previous year. I loved doing projects with him. He was patient and skilled and funny. The weekend we laid the tiles he pressed my finger into the grout and said, "The world will see you were here." I laughed. That was life *then*. Lighthearted. Safe. Unaware.

Dad finally stood and replied, "Let's get some shut-eye, okay? Maybe tomorrow will bring better news. All we can do is hope for the best but prepare for the worst."

The burden was showing. Mom and Dad looked like refugees and moved with apprehension and fatigue. What would tomorrow bring?

# TWENTY-TWO

# THE ME BEFORE

The five of us seemed in perpetual motion inside the little brick bungalow in a religiously and ethnically diverse neighborhood of blue-collar and entry-level management workers. Each nearly identical home had postage-stamp lawns, a single-car garage, and minuscule cement porch, all framed by a lush cascade of towering elms.

How could so much animation unfold within eight-hundred-sixty-three square feet of living space? The neighborhood was so dense we knew when neighbors served dinner. Car restoration was a frequent pastime on summer Saturdays with Dad, my older brother and various onlookers. Mom was often in a flurry in the compact kitchen preparing complicated meals. My twin and I alternated between music, Monopoly, Girl Scouts, plotting against our brother, and an assortment of outdoor activities dictated by the season and latest whim. I took piano lessons and accepted my father's reading challenges during school breaks. We had what my mother called, a "menagerie"—which I assumed meant pets. One winter we added to it by rescuing a huge box turtle from certain death on a busy, frozen street and provided her temporary refuge in our bathtub until spring. We named her "Helen" after Mom's friend. When warm weather finally returned, we placed her on a heated black boulder in Edward Hein's Park, near fertile green ooze. Helen stretched her neck toward the sun and, in a flash, submerged herself in the murky water to reclaim her long-awaited, life-affirming freedom.

My childhood home on Annchester in Detroit. Many happy memories there.

Summer road trips carried us across to ghost towns, museums, seashores and mountains. Sometimes the menagerie came. On these excursions, Mom served meals at sixty miles per hour. It was amazing how she could convert a station wagon into a diner.

Unlike my future in-laws, my parents were uncomplicated. Their expectations were as clear as the consequences for violating them. They issued no empty warnings, accepted no excuses, didn't believe in bailing us out of a jam and didn't tolerate delays. These were "teaching moments" they said. Most rules were reasonable. Some weren't. When I suggested which was which they countered, "When you have your own house, you have your own rules." They were a formidable duo, and we dare not attempt an end-run. Yet, through it all, it was clear they loved us, and they were in love.

We somehow managed with one bathroom, one car, a "party line" (shared phone line), and no electronics. Dad expected us to entertain ourselves "without batteries or a plug." We had chores in exchange for a small allowance and generous "vacancy policy" for friends to spend the night. Some weekends we were in an overflow situation.

One of my oddest memories from childhood was of a downtown Christmas trip that Mom established as a tradition. She would take my sister and me to J.L. Hudson department store on Woodward Avenue, to the three-story Winter Wonderland display culminating with a Santa chat amid glistening trees, the sound of carols and the intoxicating smell of cinnamon and pine. We'd often meet our cousin Mike and Aunt Betty there. One year we disembarked from the bus, the three of us, and were confronted by an honest-to-goodness flasher, complete with trench coat. We pointed and laughed, causing the show-off to appear "taken down" by our lack of shock and awe. We ended up comforting Mom who was undone by the graphic display. When we returned from the holidays, my teacher asked us to tell the class about something interesting that happened over the break. I did.

My mom with us at home around 1953. I'm on the left.

Me with my twin around 1955. Again, I'm on the left.

Other childhood memories were bleak. The race riot in the summer of 1967—the second for Detroit—dealt a TKO. I wanted to see the turmoil firsthand but was a year from driving, so my friend's older sister drove us before the evening curfew was enforced. The riot was near my grandparents' house, so no map was needed. We exited at West Grand Boulevard, turning right onto 12th. The odor from incinerated buildings, along with funnels of black smoke, pointed the way. Police stood alongside soldiers. Both had rifles. Some wore gas masks. Glass littered the streets. Witnesses gathered in tense groups. We had second thoughts about witnessing history in the making once we heard a Molotov cocktail (petrol bomb) explode in a storefront ahead. We withdrew. The memories did not. The heart-wrenching stories ranged from a police officer killed two days preceding his retirement, to an innocent four-year-old who took a stray bullet. Businesses were ruined. Racial tensions grew.

Sometimes bias was underfoot under the roof of my childhood home. My older brother's football scores and car predicaments dominated dinner conversations repetitiously, seeming to cover the same ground. And I resented he was occasionally allowed to drive my father's salmon-colored '57 convertible Thunderbird while my sister and I were denied because of gender. It made no sense. I'd observed him trying to break the sound barrier in his yellow 1932 Ford hot rod and 1959 Harley Davidson rigid front end. We knew he'd amassed two speeding tickets and considered blackmailing him with that intel. There was also a sliding scale for curfews based on gender, not conduct. Biology was destiny...

We moved to the suburbs in ninth grade in part due to Dad's job. The development of freeways made it easier for my dad and others to live and work in the suburbs. This concrete expansion drained the city of revenue, jobs and skilled employees. It also drained the schools of students and one hundred ninety-six buildings were eventually closed, including my old elementary. Packard, Hudson, Studebaker, and American Motors perished, along with their subsidiaries. Steel plants took a hit, too, from increased use of plastics.

Besides Dad's job we also moved due to changes spawned by the controversial forced bussing in the Detroit Public Schools brought about by the landmark Brown vs. Board of Education decision of 1954. My soft-spoken sister came home with a black eye, graffiti appeared in the halls and class sizes were unmanageable. The kids in busses clearly didn't want to be uprooted and we were all keenly aware of racial tensions.

My world suddenly changed.

We didn't know what to make of it, but it seemed to us that the adults didn't know *what* they were doing. None of us found it easy. My parents tried to explain it, to no avail.

Another element in my parents' decision to leave Detroit was the numerous teacher strikes — demanding basic school repairs such as adequate heat and rodent control, along with higher pay — which eventually led to walkouts. Over fifteen-thousand students left Detroit schools between 1966-1971.

By the time we moved my brother had already left Michigan. My twin and I never adjusted to the new school with the old linoleum. We missed our friends. In the move we gained our own bedrooms, yet it didn't seem a worthy trade-off. Having to leave my piano was another downside, along with the loss of authentic Italian cooking next door and my softball team. One positive outcome was I grew closer to my sister.

Another blow came in eleventh grade when the dreaded summons arrived. All juniors were ordered to meet with the offensive school counselor down the hallway that smelled like Elmer's glue and felt like a tunnel, to plot the post-mortem. College? Work? Military service? He was a nasty little man. A school bully of sorts. He smelled stale. His stinky breath, dirty fingernails and condescending attitude earned him a reputation envied by no one. I'd been successful in dodging him. It was a sport among the juniors.

"Well, you transferred from college prep to co-op, right?"

"Yup. I wanted out earlier in the day, so I switched."

"I see. So, you also dropped band?" He viewed this as proof of laziness, of the complacency of female students. Drawing a haughty, disapproving, long breath, he exhaled

231

in my direction, nearly sending me to the floor. "Well, not *everyone* is destined for college. How did your parents react?"

I shrugged. "They're not pushy about that."

"Hmm... Says here you passed shorthand, so you have thoughts about becoming a secretary?"

"Secretary? No, no. Would *you* want that?" It was close to crossing the line, but I didn't want to play ball with this spiteful, smug, wanna-be. I *hated* school, this one in particular! He was relentless.

"Why aren't your grades consistently high? Your aptitude tests are promising, although math stumps you." He peered through his smudgy glasses, groped my transcripts and built to a snobbish sneer.

"Aptitude is nothing without opportunity. School feels like a sentence."

He made it personal. "I notice you wear makeup. My grandmother disapproved of young women doing that. Why do you need eyeliner?"

Even at seventeen, I knew *he* crossed the line. I was *incensed*. "Because I don't see anything wrong with good hygiene and attention to detail." I silently added, "*You should try it*." Around and around we went.

I needed to escape his cramped office with stagnant air, fluorescent lights and ugly, dated calendars hung at a slant, but he wanted to spar. "What interests you?"

"Freedom."

"I mean what kind of *hobbies* do you have or want to have?"

Thinking hard to deter him, I replied, "Watching baseball with my dad and making chains out of gum wrappers. They look good on Christmas trees." I kept my enjoyment of science, art, traveling, music, cartography, geometry and other things to myself. We were matching wits as far as I was concerned, and my older brother taught me long ago how to win.

He cleared his throat, tapped his chewed No. 2 and shifted in his squeaky, Cold War era chair. My eyes glanced up at his loud, ticking wall clock for the third time. *Ten less minutes to graduation.* I missed my old school friends.

"Did he attend college, your father I mean?"

"No, neither did."

Resigned to my dismal fate, he stood, glared down, and dismissed me with his final comment. "Aptitude tests can be wrong."

"Then why use them?" I countered. My future was unclear, but *anything* was better than those senseless restraints. He represented everything I disdained about public education, men and social norms.

A common refrain was to work hard and pursue what made us happy. But that was my dilemma as high school graduation approached. I could not connect my interests with any vocational path, and my parents were noncommittal. "Do what makes you happy," they advised. Predictability ceased. Confidence was eclipsed by doubt. I had determination without direction. I'd always planned ahead but found it difficult to look further than I could see. I sought more guidance on my future.

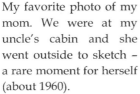

My favorite photo of my mom. We were at my uncle's cabin and she went outside to sketch – a rare moment for herself (about 1960).

Me with my parents, sister and neighbor's dog. This was around 1969.

So, as graduation loomed, my smoldering desire for additional schooling faded. I began my after-school job at the National Bank of Detroit in Inkster, another lesson in what I did not want out of life. I yearned for adulthood, but how and where and with what goal was unclear. Mom warned, "Don't be in such a hurry to grow up; it's not all it's cracked up to be." No truer words were spoken.

The high school counselor's disparaging remarks stung two years later while questioning my ability to succeed in community college. I worked tedious minimum wage jobs as a file clerk and moved in with friends who occupied a nearby turn-of-the century dilapidated farmhouse, in Farmington, hoping to locate my future. But, like the house, I was at a dead end.

Sheer boredom pushed me to register for one English Literature course at nearby Oakland Community

College (OCC). To my delight, it was *nothing* like high school. Who knew? The class was organized and thought-provoking, the homework relevant and doable. One course led to three, then full-time and an AA degree. It occurred to me I might be capable of transferring to a university but worried about tuition. My parents made it clear not to ask for a penny. In fact, once we left home, we dare not ask for anything.

My admission to Wayne State launched the happiest days I'd ever known. Little did I realize it would also propel me into the darkest days of my life.

My undergraduate days at WSU. I'm standing Cass and Warren around 1972

I always dreaded walking under Baltimore RR bridge on my way to/from WSU, especially after dark (Baltimore and 2nd Ave)

# TWENTY-THREE

# STREET CLEANING

Destroying the Buick got Fry thinking about other loose ends, among them his Aunt Dorothy ("Dot") Wilson. He'd recklessly told her about his plans to kill Doc Miller in an unguarded moment. In fact, she knew entirely too much. Dot had to go, too.

For reasons known only to Fry, he called his aunt on the 21st to warn her he was coming. Her nephew "Six" once cautioned, "If anything happens to me, have it looked into. John will be the death of me one day." And she'd seen, firsthand, the beating, and bite marks Fry inflicted on a former wife in the '70s. She was terrified. Seems he had sent many bridges up in smoke. Dorothy Wilson had every reason to be fearful.

Dot frantically phoned anyone she could think of for help—*except* 911. Fortunately, one call was to her neighbor, Ray Brewer, a thirty-year veteran detective in the Fourth Precinct who'd just walked in, anticipating a quiet evening at home. He, in turn, called for backup.

John frightened Dot to her very core, which caused her to fly out her back door in slippers into the darkness toward her sister's nearby. She never forgot "Six Pack's" warning: "Never cross John. He *will* kill you." She was a believer.

Under the safeguard of darkness, Detective Brewer slipped outside too and, through the gloom, spotted a large, balding man with tattoos and baseball bat inching toward his neighbor's porch. A young woman accompanied him who appeared unarmed. Brewer quietly and quickly approached the suspicious man and requested identification along with an explanation of why he was walking with a bat in the middle of the night in a residential area. Fry calmly ignored him. Lucky did not know backup had arrived nor that officers William Johnson and William Deck had already closed in wearing athletic shoes to conceal the sound of their footsteps.

Fry remained coolly detached. Deck silently coordinated with Brewer, then swiftly pressed his chilly .38 Smith & Wesson against the back, sweaty flesh of Fry's recently shaved head. John halted and spoke calmly, too calmly for Brewer's taste. Moments passed without movement. Dawn watched intently, realizing they were outnumbered. It was 12:45 in the morning, Monday, the ninth day since the murder, the 609th day since the duo met Doc Miller.

Moments later the California-bound culprits were apprehended near Schoolcraft and Heyden, near Brightmoor. Fry had four outstanding warrants for shoplifting in Petoskey, contempt of court for failure to appear in Allen Park, assault and battery in Detroit, and a traffic citation in Saginaw. That was more than enough to hold him.

Off-duty police officer Sgt. Brewer who captured Fry.
(Credit: WJBK Detroit, Fox 2 Detroit)

Dawn's own outstanding warrants for solicitation allowed her to be arrested as well.

From the back of the patrol car, John quietly assured his sidekick they could not be found guilty of anything. "No body, no heat, remember?"

He woefully underestimated the evidence inside Casper and the eagerness of Oliver and other neighbors to divulge his comings and goings. Fry believed to the bottom of his chilled heart that there, "Ain't nothin for them to bag or flag. The car is torched. Relax. It's all good."

Spens leaned closer to his murderous arms and whispered, "Don't worry, Babe. I'll never say a word."

With or without her, Fry was California dreamin'. This was a momentary delay, a test of his superiority.

The cuffed accomplices arrived at Police Headquarters in the witching hour and were curtly separated. Spens was led to women's detention on floor eight, and Lucky to the all-male ninth.

Officer Brantley gave Spens her options. None were pretty. He was as tired as he was cranky. He spelled them out and told her to think on them. This was Dawn's turn to endure broken sleep, no food and surges of adrenalin. She, too, had to struggle to formulate a plan feeling as if *her* head was stuffed with cotton. How would she explain Doc's disappearance?

About noon the following day, the bottom feeders were threaded through a bottleneck of reporters by Landeros and Tibaldi. News cameras shadowed them.

When Detective Landeros interviewed twenty-year-old Spens, she found her expressionless, disaffected, not fully credible and with a personality "like a straight razor." She had a cold, embittered demeanor. Dawn was guarded, superficially cooperative, yet secretly worried.

Meanwhile, McMaster heard of his friends' arrests as he drove aimlessly trying to formulate a plan. He watched the seconds, and his freedom, tick by. Like the neighbors on Casper he wondered if he could distance himself from the bully. And, like Dawn, he turned his back on Fry and proceeded to Homicide for damage control before police seized him. He never had the stomach for this kind of predicament and kicked himself for getting involved in the first place.

When a reporter later asked Frank why he assisted in the cover-up, he explained, "John and me had a past relationship. I had fear of the man. He's crazy. He's a...a *lunatic.* Anybody that tried to back away from him or, or, push him off to the side... It's just something... He'd do terrible things. He's just *nuts!*"

Along with Detective Madelyn Williams, Landeros

interviewed an uneasy McMaster. He tried to stall and bullshit with his rehearsed propaganda but soon felt differently. Williams caught him off guard immediately by divulging a few, accurate facts of his life, facts which McMaster preferred to keep hush-hush. She knew he was on probation and his legal name was Dale Frank McMaster. She held back what she didn't know, which caused him to guess frantically.

He cracked his knuckles. Beads of perspiration dotted his hairline. His eyes were on high beam. Detective Williams finally heard enough. With unrestrained laughter, she jovially declared, "You're one of the worse liars I've *ever* met!"

However, Landeros wasn't laughing. In fact, she leaned closer, looked serious as a heart attack and tapped his arm. "You know how I know you're a liar, Frank? It's this vein here, Frank. It twitches when you lie." He couldn't resist peeking nervously at his own perspiring arm.

And there was more. Landeros paraded the incriminating 8x10 glossies from Casper and read signed statements from witnesses. They detailed his buddy's bragging and that Fry and Spens left Detroit late on the 13th during heavy rain with garbage bags and a suitcase in the car registered to W. Alan Canty. Frank had no idea how often John shot off his mouth describing "body parts spread across five states." He was also unaware a confidential informant had contacted Homicide hours earlier with a tip that Al's body was "up north, near Petoskey."

The best was saved for last. Williams dropped a Polaroid of the car he helped torch a week prior.

"Recognize your handiwork, here Frank?"

Landeros chimed in, "Oh, another thing. Officers are outside your house this minute, waiting on warrants."

"No!" McMaster blurted.

Landeros dialed the phone. "May I speak with Detective Gerry Tibaldi?" Frank winced from hearing the familiar name. "Yes. That's correct. A bulldozer? Not a problem. We'll authorize it…. Oh, an hour at most. Sure, I'll put him on."

Detective Landeros (in 2015)
(Credit: Marlanna Landeros)

Polaroid of Al's car shown to me by police

Frank grudgingly reached for the receiver. His one-story house was his primary asset. A couple dozen tires, and lumber substituted for landscaping, but it was home.

"Look, McMaster. This is Detective Tibaldi of Detroit Homicide. Got a search warrant for your house here, signed by a judge. I'm gonna execute it. Know what that means, Frank? We'll be lookin' inside. If we don't find what we want, we're gonna use a bulldozer. It ain't gonna be pretty!"

Frank McMaster's home in near Petosky (Credit WJBK Detroit Fox affiliate)

Frank exclaimed, "My neighbor's got a key! Don't break in!"

"I'm comin' with bulldozers and cranes, Frank. I'm gonna find that body! Understand? I'm as stubborn as they come." Tibaldi slammed the receiver for emphasis.

Frank was ready to snitch but demanded immunity from prosecution—in writing. Landeros called the prosecutor and nodded to Frank. He gulped hard. It was time to rock and roll. Landeros obtained a detailed six-page statement of incriminating facts. Frank described the satchel, its location, the wallet in the log stove and car burning. As for John's motive, Frank wasn't so helpful. Fry fed him so much BS over the preceding days even *he* didn't know the truth. Officers up on five knew they needed a body. John was right about that.

Detective William "Tony" Brantley's home phone interrupted him. This was his day off, and he'd anticipated sipping a cold one while watching the Tigers triumph the Texas Rangers in what was projected to be a close game. The commander's office beckoned. *"Now?"* he asked. He dressed in a suit, tie and new shoes.

Detective Tony Brantley learned from Detective Bernard Brantley that he'd been redirected to a waterlogged area of rural Michigan, in the northwest tip of the Lower Peninsula, about a missing persons case. Detective Brantley and three others boarded the cramped twin-engine Beechcraft with their informant, McMaster, and flew 250 miles northwest to Emmet County under low clouds. The five men landed hours past dusk near secluded terrain owned by the University of Michigan Biologic Station, for studying ecosystems and where roadkill was deposited to breed mosquitoes for research.

The informant led them to a soggy plot of murky expanse, occupied by crickets, fog, insects and animal carcass stench. Thankfully, it was not raining. Tony Brantley took note it was near midnight as they set out, flashlights in hand. An officer from the Alanson Police Department joined them with a cadaver dog. McMaster escorted the men through the damp blackness, in what appeared to be circles, from 11: 30 p.m. until 1:00 a.m. Brantley grew increasingly tired, sweaty and irritable.

To make matters worse he'd ruined his new shoes, his suit was punctured from thorns, and the hungry, blood-sucking pests bit furiously. McMaster feared he would not find the shallow grave in the darkness which would negate his prosecution deal. He tried not to even think about Fry.

By early Sunday, July 21st it was still a warm sixty-one degrees. The humidity hovered at seventy-four percent. Calm winds from the south failed to relieve the mugginess, buzzing insects, haze, or discomfort. One detective wondered if their informant was stalling.

"Here! Over here!" McMaster abruptly bellowed through the gloom. He beckoned investigators to a stand of dead pines and scrub oaks twenty-five yards off-trail. The accomplice pointed to the shadowy burial spot. The search dog confirmed his recollection. There, Evidence Technician Richard Lee slid a chrome trowel into the moist earth. Approximately eighteen inches below ground a solid object was struck. The men gave one another a glance understood by all. The mud resisted but, with effort, the detectives extracted a saturated overnight bag. It had been a gift from Al to Dawn in better days. Brantley unzipped it without hesitation. Inside they found what they'd come for. The scent of decaying flesh instantly enticed additional parasites; whose tube-like mouthparts pierced their hosts' skin repeatedly. The men tried in vain to swat the menaces away as their welts reddened, itched and multiplied.

The first tightly-wrapped parcel was opened under closely positioned flashlights. Inside they found a pair of feet, size nine, cut around the ankles. The second package held a similarly wrapped colorless pair of men's hands severed above the wrist. Within the final bag, framed by dozens of flying insects, the flashlights illuminated the moist, detached, fractured head of Doc Canty - the man who deceived and gave generously and paid with his life.

They measured and photographed their gruesome discovery. Technicians prepared the satchel for delivery to the State Police Post in Pellston, where the segmented man was secured in a beverage cooler over ice. Soon afterward, detectives accompanied his chilled leftovers on a return flight to Detroit as daybreak hinted on the horizon. The Wayne County medical examiner's office received the evidence by early morning. This discovery essentially closed the case against John Carl Fry and Dawn Marie Spens.

The Detroit News prominently featured an update on page one.

### Police think they've got Canty's body.

> A mutilated body [part] believed to be missing Grosse Pointe Park Psychologist W. Alan Canty was found in Oakland County last night, a day after the fifty-one-year-old therapist's head, hands and feet were unearthed near Petoskey [Alanson] in northern Michigan... It was delivered to the medical examiner's office for identification and an autopsy to determine the cause of death... Two suspects, arrested on a west side street corner early Saturday, are being held for questioning.

Doc Miller's murder was unusual for Detroit in some ways. Homicides were usually committed with a firearm. Most victims were black. Most killings were linked to domestic violence or gangs and occurred in March. However, in other ways, Al's murder squarely fit the statistics. Drugs, money, and anger were factors. Both assailant and victim were male and casually known to one another. Both were between the ages of 25-54, and the homicide occurred on a weekend night. But, dismemberment killings were rare and when they did happen they were usually carried out in the victim's residence, not the perpetrator's. The disunion of the body parts was usually to conceal and transport the body more easily.

The evening news aired a brief interview with McMaster as he left Police Headquarters. He was asked to explain his involvement.

> He [Fry] said he had some incriminating evidence he needed to bury, that his girlfriend and him had been cashing bad checks, forging checks, using phony identification and he had stuff in bags he had to get rid of. [It contained] the head, the hands and the feet of Dr. Alan Canty.

This was no longer a missing persons case. The man I love became the man I loved. Nine days had passed since *Live Aid*. Nine oppressive days. The puzzle came together, and the time had come for the assailant, and his young collaborator, to test their bravado.

Spens and Fry making their first court appearance 7/22/1985
(Credit: Edwin C. Lombardo, The Detroit News)

The two from the Corridor had their initial appearance Monday, July 22, in 36th District Court, Frank Murphy Hall of Justice on a cloudy, warm morning, the kind so common for Midwest summers. The soon-to-be defendants looked typecast for their roles, still clothed in apparel worn from their arrest. Spens' ensemble was her usual "business attire" of a low-cut blue halter-top and skintight jeans. Fry bulged beneath his grey plaid shirt, opened to his sternum, with rolled up sleeves. His new skinhead look was reminiscent of his motorcycle days. TV crews hovered like fruit flies over Sangria.

The accused rose to hear allegations spoken by District Court Judge Isidore Torres. The court charged Fry with Murder in the First and Mutilation of a Dead Body, while Spens faced Accessory to Murder After the Fact and Mutilation of a Dead Body — an old law in Michigan to deter grave robbers. Both remained mute. Fry was held without bond, while Spens was unable to meet her one-hundred-thousand-dollar cash bond.

Print journalists launched into full battle with an eye toward the grandeur of page one. Following the formalities, local news coverage grew as virulent as an outbreak of whooping cough, causing the line between fact, speculation and error to bleed.

Following their arraignment, Spens made several collect calls to her old school friend, Dee, and urged a visit. When Dee arrived, she struggled to merge the fresh-faced, bright-eyed, high school senior she remembered with the thin, hollow-eyed, yellowish apparition full of track marks in a WCJ jumpsuit, held on felony charges. On top of it, Dawn was *flippant*. Dee was appalled when Dawn *laughed* about events that led to her arrest.

The mask had slipped. In that unguarded moment, Dawn's amusement revealed just what laid beneath. Dee saw no remorse, scruples or insight, just callous indifference to the suffering Dawn witnessed, the refrigerated body parts she helped transport, the fallout from Al's murder on others. This was the "straight razor" personality Landeros described and the "prima donna" McMaster complained about. The apparition before Dee paraded the frosty detachment Bando witnessed and the vapor of a friend Dee once knew.

Furthermore, as Dee tried to leave, she suddenly could not produce her visitor pass. A frantic half-hour later she obtained clearance to exit the stifling holding area. Dee never returned, despite repeated requests from Spens to do so.

Following the formalities, Magistrate C. Lorene Royster told the accused, "The conscience of the court is shocked." And she had heard much during her time on the bench.

# TWENTY-FOUR

# THE TOMB

"Good morning. This is Detective Landeros again. Sorry for calling this early but I'm coming by soon. We need you at Headquarters again. Your parents can come if you want."

I scrambled to alert Mom and Dad who stood ready in no time. It was Sunday, July 21st.

Bernard Brantley had also been summoned, too. We were haggard, wired and rode the vintage elevator in silence. After introductions, Inspector Hill moved a new pack of Kool cigarettes to the side.

Detective Gerald Tibaldi handed me a burned remnant retrieved from Frank's wood stove in upper Michigan the previous night and characteristically got to the point. "Recognize this?"

My fingers gingerly grasped the last, tangible remnants of Al's life as I stroked his familiar Seiko watch with the broken link in the band caused by unloading paving bricks. I nodded. He then handed me a bent, laminated cartoon that seemed out of place in the seriousness of that moment. It looked familiar yet wrong. Between scorched margins, some words lingered. "...*est places in the world is anywhere w*.." I grasped it as if it could reverse this nightmare. It was tangible proof of happier days, of the man I married, or the man I *thought* I'd married. *He loved me, didn't he? I was important to him, wasn't I? He carried this for eight years. Didn't that count for something?* I hesitated to hand it back. It was a reminder of why I once loved the man who loved to deceive.

Tibaldi immediately presented a third item, a Polaroid taken at night, of a burned car sitting on half-melted tires near railroad tracks. At first, I didn't recognize the charred, abandoned sedan and shook my head 'no,' but then it clicked. I unwillingly took it in. And pushed it away.

Detective Landeros moved closer. I did not want to hear more. *Why was she doing this? Stop!* I silently responded. With closed eyes, I fought the urge to put my hands over my ears. The siege was coming. My labored breathing disclosed that I anticipated more horror.

"We have body parts in the morgue."

I struggled to breathe, as if underwater. I was immobilized. Mom squeezed my hand. Couldn't the clock be rewound? The hourglass flipped over? I'd wanted adulthood so eagerly, and here it was, and I *hated* it!

I didn't want to accompany this compassionate woman, this hinge between life and death, normalcy and evil. I slowly shook my head no and stayed rooted in my seat while trying to make her go away. Make IT go away. She patiently, knowingly, opened the door to an unwanted future. It was another boundary I dared not cross, a world I knew nothing of and wished to run from. Like the Ghost of Christmas Future, Landeros pointed toward a fixed and unfixed end, a reminder we're all on a march toward death. I did not comprehend nor comply with her request. My mother gently pulled on my arm, which triggered me to stand robotically.

The old Wayne County Medical Examiner Bldg. It has since been torn down

Display case upstairs

(Credit: Detroit Free Press)

The short drive to 400 E. Lafayette and Brush near Greektown was a blur. Detective Landeros spoke calmly as she chaperoned us to the sinister building no one wanted to enter. The exterior of the triangular, two-story 1926 brick and granite structure was austere. There was more than a bit of irony in the traffic sign warning "Do Not Enter" prominently posted near the entrance. I wanted to comply.

The morgue was regarded by some as "majestic" and "reminiscent of an Egyptian mausoleum" since Egyptian themes were regarded as "dealing in all things of death." But its broad Craftsman-shaped columns framed two retrofitted, ugly aluminum doors more suited for a convenience store. We pulled alongside a curb in chards. Loose wires dangled purposelessly and vertically near the entrance, resembling a noose when they slowly swayed in the breeze. The nearby mailbox hovered over large, tangled weeds and even they looked near death.

I rocked in my seat with my right hand endlessly twisting my wedding ring. The thought of Al being kept inside was revolting. My guide, my interpreter, opened the patrol car door and offered her graceful hand, which I did not take. My legs were useless and heavy.

"You can do this," she said reassuringly. "You won't be alone, and you won't be here long."

My father quietly added, "We'll be with you. Let's go."

She paused and softly added, "We're positive it's him. There's no doubt in our minds. But we need your I.D. of him for court, and this will help you realize he's never coming home."

As we approached the worn doorsill, the morning sun penetrated the leafy summer trees which cast a cheerful, dotted "welcome mat" across our path in disparity with our purpose. Two reporters had assembled. *Predator!* They reduced us to a sideshow, a commodity with fleeting value, a mere headline, a rung in their ladder, a gloating point in their resume which they would file and forget, once we'd served our purpose. The four of us rushed past them like fish swimming downstream.

We ascended a few steps, then encountered echoes of voices down two hallways spanning out in a "v" shape. A large marble staircase was to our right. I then recalled a newspaper article which pictured a large display case on the second floor containing implements of death collected from suicides and homicides over the years. *Wasn't this place disturbing enough?*

Mom vividly recollected, decades later, the odor of

the morgue. "It was a blend of disinfectant, formaldehyde and rancid decomposition."

My parents were directed to a small anteroom. *They should've never been subjected to this! It isn't right.* Dad had his own battle underway with leukemia and intestinal cancer.

Detective Landeros calmly interrupted my preoccupation. As she pointed, she said, "You'll see a face behind this wall. Tell us if it's your husband. Your identification will help at trial. Just say 'yes' or 'no.' You must respond verbally. Do you understand? I'll be there with some other people."

I weakly nodded.

"Do you need a moment?"

I shook my head 'no.' This was my high-water mark of grit.

My father insisted again he accompany me. "It's for the trial, Dad."

I stood to walk the mere twenty feet, which looked like a football field. Officials waited, but momentum wouldn't be achieved. My legs felt numb. *How many families had endured this drill? Mothers identifying children? Husbands identifying wives? This was a building of loss. Endings. Sadness. Grief. A genuine house of horrors!*

Landeros placed a supportive arm under mine. My legs remained disobedient. Dad steadfastly stood on my right like a human crutch. I felt faint, sick, disoriented. My guardian angels slowly headed to a small, windowless, rectangular room with stark fluorescent lights above worn pinwheel tile. This chamber had no connection to the outside world, to laughter, vivid colors and joyful sounds of summer with people who had hope and trust and futures.

This arcane cavity was a vault, a cage, a bunker. I felt cooler and weaker with each footstep. We stopped. I tried not to breathe. The pungent odor inside that chamber was a suffocating mix of used kitty litter, rotten eggs and unwashed Styrofoam meat trays from the market carelessly left out overnight. Disinfectant did not neutralize the foulness of death, grief, or confusion. Al's body parts had been submerged inside a desolate, warm bog for a week before being exhumed.

My eyes closed reflexively. Detective Landeros leaned in and quietly said, "When you're ready."

I'd *never* be ready. How can a wife ever be prepared to gaze upon the bludgeoned, detached head of her spouse five feet away? Seconds passed like minutes. My eyes slowly opened and observed Al's contorted face, supported by a white sheet wrapped tightly around his severed neck. His eyeglasses were missing. His face was knotted, his eyes puffy and black, contrasting with light gray skin. Deep lacerations crisscrossed his head like a network of roads. His mouth was open and round with a swollen tongue that protruded to the right at an angle. A cavernous gash framed his badly swollen right eye where a section of scalp was missing. It was horrific. He was badly defaced. *What did he do to deserve this viciousness? What kind of monster did this?!*

A thousand questions littered my brain. The three-letter word everyone waited for was lodged in my throat. My stomach wanted to heave. My knees buckled again. Arms supported mine. I was a marionette. They waited patiently, but no words came. The procedure was repeated. I again faced the decomposing, torn mask of a face that used to smile at me, at a mouth that once upon a time offered encouragement and lies. I finally blurted, "Yes!"

I was hyper-focused yet disoriented. Rooted in the moment but I had floated into a far-off space. My surroundings had grown frighteningly distorted. I'd been yanked into a two-dimensional world, swallowed in improbability. My emotions were...how shall I explain? They were *blunted*. My head felt wrapped with invisible padding. *Is this what it felt like to be a robot?* My breath was on pause again. I was determined to stop the horror yet frozen in my actions. I could not reconcile the man I knew and once loved with the repulsive pulp of a face before us.

They abruptly detached me from the spot where the living greeted the dead. It was a blistering July morning, but I was clammy. *I want to get home, curl into a tight ball and shut out everyone.* We headed toward the exit, but the hurdle of bloodthirsty correspondents had grown. Their camera tripods resembled machine guns from World War II and were aimed at us. Landeros spun me around to face a rear exit just beyond a tunnel of a hallway then ordered me to lie down in the back of her patrol car.

Freshly back from the Wayne County Morgue on that humid day, we secured the garage, but gruesomeness, fear, and disbelief forced their way inside. What we witnessed could not have been my hard-working husband of nearly eleven years. It was the disintegrating mask of an alien, a mutation, a Frankenstein. Instantly I understood I'd never be the same.

Detective Landeros 1985
(Credit: Edwin Lombardo, The Detroit News)

We eased our way to the kitchen table but groped for words. At this moment, my parents didn't know how to help. I didn't know what was needed. We were in uncharted territory. Mom's blood-shot eyes were again frightened, though she tried to appear calm and reassuring. Dad clenched his jaw in protective anger at what had happened and what had yet to happen. We sat in awkward, unfamiliar silence for several moments, each deep in thought. We tried to absorb what we wanted to reject. "Thank you for staying with me," was all I could muster. It did not begin to convey how relieved it felt to be protected by their steadiness. They anchored me. Without them, I would have forcefully imploded.

"Why do you suppose his car was incinerated?" Mom quietly asked in a faraway voice directed at no one.

Her question floated over me. I could not relate to it. My mind remained riveted to the damage seen firsthand. She was forgiven. She did not witness his remains. Thankfully, she was spared.

"We'll go and tell Gladys personally," Dad offered. "No mother should be put through this."

I mechanically nodded.

Dad said this twice in ten minutes, to bring order to chaos. That was his strength, my father. Ever decisive and clear-headed with a knack for prioritizing. He paced slowly, arms crossed over his chest, eyes cast to the floor.

"Whatever monster did that was out of his *mind!*" he suddenly blurted.

Mom tossed him a cautious look, meant to ease up. However, he'd stood next to me, arm under mine, as officials displayed Al's leftovers. Dad knew of what he spoke. The killer could *only* have been a madman. My spouse was unarmed and innocent. Of that, I was sure. It was an unjustifiable homicide.

I hugged my parents tightly and thanked them repeatedly for relaying the appalling news to my mother-in-law.

My father phoned to deliver a heads-up. "Gladys, it's Lee. Yes. She's here with me. No, we haven't... What's that? Yes. We've come... I will. We've come from Police Headquarters and want to drive over. Yes, if possible (pause). Can you get your friend...ah, Eva, is it? Yes, *Edna*, there? (pause) See you soon."

Impatient to conceal myself in a long cleansing shower, I forced myself up the narrow, curling back staircase, left lights off and shut the window blinds. I felt detached from everyone and everything. The hot spray was an antidote for the contamination felt to my bones. No cleanser known to humanity could eradicate the odor, garish images and vile words running through my mind. My knees buckled again as I tucked myself into the wet, tile corner, and slid to the saturated floor. I cursed. I exploded at him. At the cannibalistic city which preyed on its own. A sense of shame and evil walled me in. *How did this depravity ensnarl my husband?* I wanted to slough off the topmost layer of skin to rid myself of the stains I felt, the shame experienced. I wanted to float into the dark drain along with the sudsy water. My body remained in a crumpled knot until the shower turned cool, forcing my evacuation.

I crawled into our now-vacant bed, wrapped in his robe. His pillow, still indented, had his scent. Al's slippers sat in the corner and a smiling, framed photo of us mocked me from his nightstand. I wanted to dream myself back to an earlier time; one with optimism, belief, and closeness. Instead, I pulled our covers over my head and tried to disappear. My fingers trembled. He didn't just break my heart; he broke our future, our bond, our promises. I experienced an eerie sense of floating and numbness.

Meanwhile, my parents sat stiffly near Gladys and her friend, Edna. How do you prepare to destroy the peace of mind of another? To tell an elderly, widowed mother her only child was murdered? To explain the sordid company he'd lured, that the police suspected he supplied them with money—a good deal of which was *hers*—for drugs, cars, food, and sex over a year and a half?

The aging friends sat upright in queasy anticipation. Their eyes were wide. They braced for the detonation.

"Gladys, there's no easy way to say this. I don't

know how to start," Dad began.

"Come out with it, Lee. *What's going on?* What happened to Bus?"

Mom wrapped her arm around Gladys. She could think of no words to say. Nor could she imagine losing her only son.

My Dad began. "It's, ah... Well, they think... They say Al's been...*killed*... He got involved with a prostitute on Cass, and they argued, and he got killed...on Saturday."

Mrs. Canty shut her eyes, inhaled and held her breath. Her complexion blanched, which gave her an eerie transparent quality. Her friend grabbed her hand. Both remained silent as they deflected and absorbed the wreckage.

"The police are doing everything they can. Here is their card."

Regardless of Al's actions, he was her only child, the namesake of her husband, their legacy. She carried him for nine difficult months. He was the curly blond boy who accompanied her to museums, crossed the stage with diplomas, and always remembered her birthday. He faithfully stopped by Sundays to run errands. She was elderly, alone and obviously distraught. She belatedly exhaled. "I'm glad his father isn't here for this."

As my parents left, Gladys reassured Edna there must be an explanation. Blackmail perhaps?

The coach lights on the carriage house were finally extinguished.

# TWENTY-FIVE

# THE BUZZ

*The Detroit News* printed more, again in section one, from the pen of Mike Martindale and Chauncey Bailey.

**Psychologist's double life traced**

For nearly two years, psychologist W. Alan Canty led a double life — complete with an alias.

Canty's Grosse Pointe Park acquaintances knew him as a quiet, hardworking professional who attended block parties and once suggested the neighbors get together more often...

At his Fisher Building office, he took time to help a garage attendant work up a paper for a psychology class...

Neighbors on Berkshire say Canty and his wife, Jan, also a practicing psychologist, were friendly and outgoing.

"He was planning a high school reunion next week and we offered to let him use our pool," said Gloria Gaitley, a neighbor.

The death notification was usually a one-time occurrence. The next of kin are advised, assisted in the identification of the corpse, then proceed to internment. In my situation, it happened sequentially with the discovery of body parts. In heavy eastbound traffic listening to WJZZ, an announcement interrupted the music.

"We have an update on the murder of psychologist Alan Canty. A badly decomposed leg was recovered in Auburn Hills along I-75 and J…"

I snapped it off, nearly careening toward the shoulder, cutting off another driver. My mind raced in opposing directions; piloted by disgust and anxiety. Anxiety won. Still behind the wheel, a panic attack burst forward. *Slow your breathing. Look at something in the distance.* My mouth was parched. I banged the steering wheel with futility. The wolf was not *at* our door, he'd been living *beside me!*

Police securing Al's leg and taking it to the morgue
(Credit: WJBK Detroit Fox Affiliate)

The "me before" was removed from danger. I foolishly didn't believe in boogie men. Peril touched *others*; people in risky lives, tourists carelessly out late in the wrong part of town, gamblers involved with high-stake bets. It affected criminals, gangs or families embroiled in domestic violence. It existed in movies, came with dangerous jobs or was reported on the news, but would never visit me *personally*. Why should it? I'd had my nose in a book for decades.

Detroit Police had followed me surreptitiously ever since they executed their search warrant on Casper. They were uncertain if all accomplices were caught and theorized I could be in danger. What they could not have understood, was I'd been in danger all along from the person who slept beside me disguised as my intimate partner.

The dreaded envelope arrived from the Michigan Department of Public Health. *How ironic, considering how far Al is from healthy.* It was not yet time to open the formal description of what we witnessed in that brightly lit chamber. It was set aside, pacing the bombardment.

*The Detroit News* for Wednesday, July 24 splashed the sordid mess across one-quarter of page one. Sleazy details accompanied an artist rendering of a couple seductively silhouetted behind a closed window. The drawing looked suitable for a cheap X-rated movie poster, the kind which shouted from Times Square. The column's authors were James McClear and Mike Martindale. Like others, it carried minor inaccuracies.

### Sordid tale's grisly end: 2 charged in slaying of therapist.

It began on Michigan Avenue two years ago, when psychologist W. Alan Canty picked up eighteen-year-old Dawn Spens. It ended eleven days ago in a southwest Detroit house with Dawn's boyfriend clubbing Canty to death and cutting up the body in a bathtub...

Police say Ms. Spens, a prostitute and alleged heroin addict, and Fry decided to capitalize on the fatal attraction she exerted over the respected Grosse Point practitioner, who was married and the son of a prominent Detroit couple.

"I am discounting these things," said Canty's mother, Gladys, seventy-eight, a former president of the Detroit Board of Education, after the lurid story was printed. "I know my son as my son. He was a beautiful human being. I love him dearly."

In the end, Canty, a brilliant student who followed in the footsteps of his late father, Alan Canty, a police psychologist, despaired of his double life and wanted out...

"Canty finally refused to turn over the money," Ms. Becker said she was told by Fry. Rebuffed, Fry "blew up and went to town with the baseball bat."

Three days later I opened the official envelope and slowly unfurled the sheet of ugliness. There it was, a one-page document, listing ugly facts bureaucratically, methodically, dispassionately. My husband's "Certificate of Death." serialized #0727833, listed his date of demise as 7/21/1985. The cause of death was a homicide from a "blunt impact to head" on an "unknown date" at an "unknown time." He was "beaten and killed in Wayne County, and his body dumped in Emmet County." There it was. Pure and simple. The permanent, abridged version of a nightmare that never had to happen.

# TWENTY-SIX

# BUSTED PLAY

It was a new week, an early hour and time for Inspector Hill to introduce himself to Fry up on nine. "I have to know, John. What brought you back from Petoskey?"

The detainee flippantly sneered, "I had some...*business* to take care of, *mon.*"

"I see," responded the lanky Inspector. "I'm glad we found you before you got to

your...*businesss.*"

Fry chuckled contemptuously. Given his attitude on African Americans, it must have been irksome, indeed, to have found himself answering to Hill. Who was the alpha now?

Inspector Hill early in the investigation. (Credit: WJBK Detroit Fox Affiliate)

Several phone calls interrupted their one-on-one. Some inquiries were from the media. Hill didn't rush. The captive was on his clock and unlikely going anywhere. Dawn again declined to make a statement. Hill stood. "There's someone I want to bring in." Her father awkwardly crossed onto Hill's turf and she glimpsed her sister waiting in her wheelchair in the bustling hallway. Hill reminded Spens this was a splendid time to make a statement but, still, she hesitated. Another knock announced Sergeant Brantley, Sergeant Williams, and Detective Landeros. The office barely contained them all.

Hill introduced them, in part, for effect. "Detective Landeros has something you should hear. Please, go ahead."

She read Frank McMaster's declaration aloud. Several gruesome 8 x 10s from Casper accompanied the detailed, incriminating narrative. Then there was the matter of statements by neighbors who witnessed her hasty departure on July 13, the Polaroid of the charred Buick, the pending laboratory results from the medical examiner and note from her residence with contact information of the deceased — proof of their association.

After show and tell Spens swallowed hard, rethought her weakened position and paused.

Four floors above the meeting, Fry did not realize storm clouds had rapidly formed around his recently shaved head and Dawn's promise to "not tell anyone, babe" had weakened.

Detroit Police Headquarters at 1300 Beaubian. Homicide was located on the 5th floor.

Entrance

By six o'clock on July 20th, Landeros had typed Dawn's statement. Spens' document would be cross-validated with other information, in part because law enforcement knew heroin and cocaine impaired short-term and delayed memory due to chemical changes in the brain.

Dawn reluctantly outlined the dynamics of her peculiar arrangement. She sprinkled in lies she swore were true. Old habits die hard. She fudged on the money and skirted a question concerning plans for fleeing. She insisted she was throwing up from dope "when Lucky struck Doc" but admitted seeing one swing of the bat and hearing three dull thuds. The prostitute conceded to witnessing his seizing body, blood spatter, her pimp perspiring and wide-eyed while holding a blood-soaked bat.

Landeros knew Dawn had been straight with her, though not fully. Landeros saw her as accustomed to deflecting blame, wiggling out of jams and entirely more connected than she admitted. But the more pressing question, the issue that mattered most was, would evidence of her involvement be enough for trial?

By late evening, a full picture emerged. The DPD had physical evidence. The medical lab was finalizing its report. Al's car was secured, Frank's statement filed, the hooker's confession written, Mobil gas card receipts gathered, information supplied by neighbors, Dot Wilson's statement typed, items pulled from Frank's stove, evidence from the warrant and the midnight snitch's tips intertwined with what they knew.

Landeros' field interviews turned up a common refrain. The locals liked Doc. Many felt Spens and Fry abused his generosity. Their neighbor, Juanita, told me decades later, "I liked your husband. He was kind, caring, intelligent and always had a nice word to say. He even helped me with my son. I was grateful."

Throughout Sunday, detectives communicated with the Prosecutor's Office and came to an agreement on the charges Fry and Spens would face. But if Nolan proposed a plea bargain in exchange for information on other crimes — such as child prostitution, cold cases or drug importation — and the prosecutor agreed, the charges would be reduced. He had reason to be hopeful, since half of all murder cases were resolved that way. There were benefits to everyone. The prosecutor would get closure on other unsolved cases and free up his calendar. Judge Sapala would be credited for reducing jail overcrowding and ease his calendar. A plea bargain would not only provide Fry and Spens with a reduced sentence, but allow earlier release, negate the need for witnesses to testify and essentially excuse them from their full culpability. Negotiated justice does not equate with justness.

# TWENTY-SEVEN

# THE MEMORIAL CIRCUS

"We'll do whatever you say. We just need to know what you want." The simple question drove home the title "widow." I hated the word. It sounded so formal, so...*forensic*. My mother gently brought up the memorial service over coffee and pancakes. My head was too heavy for my body, for this discussion. Everything felt surreal and effortful. Out of habit, I painted smiley faces in syrup and recalled that's what Dad did when we were kids, back when I did not know the recipe for mixed jive.

My parents exuded worry and fatigue. I did not wish to burden them further. I shrugged.

"Really, Mom, what I want is *nothing*. It'll be a sideshow."

"Well, think about Gladys, his relatives, his patients…"

I put down my fork, stared out the window at the lilac bush, now in full bloom, and halted, feeling squeezed again between what I *wanted* to do and what I *should* do.

"All that's important is that it's private. No strangers. Just small and simple." I saw this as an intensely reserved, solemn situation. Like our wedding, I didn't want a production. "Let his mom choose where and when. I don't care."

Friends from graduate school offered to fly in. I thanked them but implored them to stay. "If you feel you need to do something, please donate to an animal shelter. We love animals, but your call is really enough."

The accused awaited formal charges. I waited for a formal eulogy.

And it came on a steamy afternoon of July 28. The sun penetrated the haze and ramped up the discomfort on a day that already promised misery. By 10:00, my mother implored me to get ready. By choice, I arrived alone, at noon, to the two-story, white-columned Verheyden Funeral Home on Mack Avenue in Grosse Pointe Park. The service commenced at 2:00 p.m., but I needed the cool aloneness of the vacant sanctuary to steady myself. The flawless emerald lawn led to a peaceful, airy lobby with soft white double doors revealing a spacious, soothing room of light coral and crème. I paused to absorb the calmness. Dozens of bouquets dotted the room, but my preference would have been a donation to a worthy cause instead. I hoped they brought Mrs. Canty comfort but, to my mind, the flowers disguised Al's actions like fresh paint over crumbling wood. Why the pretense? None of the names on the tags looked familiar. *Spectators? Al's relatives? Patients?*

The white-haired undertaker interrupted my reading. I handed him a paving brick. "Please put this next to Al's urn when he is buried. And keep reporters *out*."

He nodded, then meekly added "Dr. Canty, understand we cannot control who parks outside. It's a public street.

"Right, but you control who steps *onto* your property. I don't want reporters inside."

He agreed without a hint of conviction.

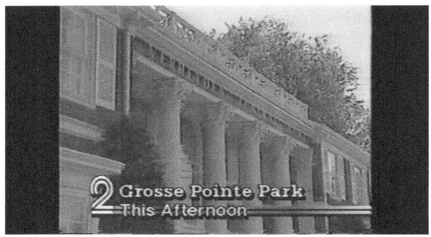

Verheyden Funeral Home as pictured on the evening news
following Al's service.
(Credit: WJBK Detroit Fox Affiliate)

The tropical humidity awaited as I retrieved a Tums from my car. Oversized TV news trucks swarmed, which validated the unoriginal notion "if it bleeds, it leads." The oppressive clamminess and heat matched my simmering anger. Their garish satellite dishes, microphones and wires were unwelcome, inappropriate and invasive. Reporters gazed at me while leaning on their vans as if they belonged, as if at a festival. I pointed them out to the undertaker and my friend's husband and implored them to prohibit them from entering.

To my dismay over three-hundred observers crammed the rose-scented room shortly before the service began, leaving some to stand near the vestibule. *We didn't even know three-hundred people!* If some were relatives on Al's side, I wouldn't have known them. Interlopers sprinkled in among the mourners and gradually turned the service into a spectacle.

The eulogy began with a stagnant 85 degrees outside and a dewpoint of 60. I sat near my sister, friends Celia and John in the same row as Mom and Dad. I wanted this over with, and it hadn't even started. Media brazenly pulled out notepads, gossiped, conjectured and deeply offended. A few smiled and chuckled as if this was entertainment for public consumption. All that was missing was popcorn. I overheard one mourner mutter to a reporter, "You'd think you had your fill, you bastards!"

*This is exactly why I didn't want a service! They're meddlers, peeping Toms, bloodsuckers, just like the defendants!* I wanted to flee but didn't want to give them something else to comment on.

To get through this I tried to imagine myself on the other side. *Why did I even agree to this sideshow?* I wanted to unknow my husband.

Segments of Dr. Mooney's eulogy faded in and out:

"As I look out, I assume you are thinking the same as me. When Jan called a week ago to ask if I'd give this eulogy, she asked in her typical gentle style if I needed time to think about it or did not feel comfortable, she would understand. My response was instant. "Yes. I would be honored and privileged." The only reservation was that I may fall apart emotionally. Jan assured me that would be all right.

"As the week progressed, many thoughts came to mind that are essential to be expressed today. Whatever pain of living Al suffered, his pain and suffering has ended in death. For us, it is now the pain of loss from his death.

"A mother has lost a son.

"A wife has lost a husband.

"Others have lost a friend, a therapist, a neighbor, a colleague. The profession has lost a competent, caring psychologist.

"Life has ended for Al Canty… Life goes on for those who survive."

The eulogy grew remote. Wasn't everyone trying to reconcile Dr. Mooney's words with Al's actions? Al-Buster-Miller-Canty-husband-trick-psychologist… Who *was* I married to? Did he not *get* it? Even a kid knows if you play in the dirt, you get dirty.

My thoughts were dragged to the gut-wrenching question I hesitated to consider. *What if he intended to provoke his assailant? What if he felt so backed into a corner, professionally, financially, legally, and maritally that he knew it was hopeless to salvage? He cleaned our offices the day before and gave away props from his Indianwood Project. He returned to tell me he loved me the day he disappeared, apologizing for an unclear reason. He then went to Casper empty-handed, in a downpour, knowing they were expecting money. He pushed Fry while he was angry and high. Was my elderly neighbor correct?*

*Was Al suicidal?*

Mom tried to picture my future but couldn't. She was angry, protective and apprehensive about returning back to Phoenix.

"As news of the tragedy of Al's death unfolded, I am sure all of us experienced shock; the jolting of 'no this can't be true.' As news

stories progressed, my thoughts became 'How could he? How

could they?"

My poor sister. With closed eyes, her shoulders silently absorbed her anguish. Her face, red with grief, was coated with tears that dripped off her chin. I wanted to comfort her, to leave with her. She spotted more reporters and cameramen through the window.

"Dad. *Look!*" she whispered urgently.

Dr. Mooney's words flowed through the now-stuffy parlor, and I found myself in an odd, silent debate. *Was it better to be the wife of a cheater or the widow of one?*

As Dr. Mooney ended his 30-minute eulogy, I eagerly rose to leave but was blocked by a broadcast reporter who thrust his industrial-size video camera and floodlight within inches of my face. My friend's husband immediately capped his hand over the intrusive, repugnant lens. *"Go! Get OUT!"*

I collapsed into my friend's lap—the same ally who'd been on this ugly journey from the outset. My defenses succumbed. *"No! No!"* I covered my head with my hands. Was *nothing* off limits? The inner scaffolding that kept me strong crumbled. In its place a black hole formed, sucking normalcy and predictability and patience. The morticians did nothing to block the intruders, despite explicit, repeated appeals. They undoubtedly benefited from the notoriety it afforded their business on the evening news.

As I sat feeling crushed in shame and sadness, it occurred to me that people in the news, consumers of the news and those who report it, seldom see things the same.

I ducked out another back door, switched cars with John and dashed home to sit alone, making sure no one followed on this sideways day. How could I get my life back, my privacy, my sleep? The police needed to leave. The media needed boundaries. The strangers who brought this suffering needed to *pay!*

As the memorial circus concluded nearby, I sat alone inside my silent, locked house filled with questions and photos and promises. The Siamese cats assembled in a row with curious expressions beaming from their dramatic blue eyes. I caught my bearings and attempted to decipher all the horror compressed into fifteen long, bewildering days. I'd abruptly stopped from an outlandish, wild roller coaster ride and fought the urge to drive aimlessly until the map turned blue. I was tired of prying eyes, judgments, speculation, questions, and snickers... The deeper, more painful question lingered. "Was it *all* a charade? Did Al only want me to *mentor*?"

The sun cast a beam across the maroon Persian rug in the quiet, muggy afternoon while my breathing slowed allowing me to study its curves, loops, and texture. Three chimes from the grandfather clock lulled me back, accompanied by the soothing aquarium bubbles. It was time. I slowly slid off my beautiful wedding band with a large amber stone and laid it on the glass coffee table. It whispered a thousand memories, scenarios, questions, and broken promises.

It was now painfully clear that Al's late days "at the office" was a grand pantomime of a hard-working husband. My illness and subsequent increase in post-doctoral work hours opened the door to spend time with his strumpet. No wonder he was "so understanding" about my overtime. The cluttered papers in his office likely concealed clues to his secrets and our financial woes, explained Al's sudden anger when he found them sorted. And, as for his psychotic stupor, it was fueled by the impossibility of managing two clashing worlds of his own creation. His fragmented sentences during the drive to Ann Arbor weren't meaningless after all, and his return to the gutter following his discharge sealed his fate. It even made sense, now, why he was "gone for lunch" in the middle of the day. His blank appointment book proved he discarded his practice. His sudden interest in his appearance even made sense. Less clear was the wad of dusty keys in our basement, did they belong to the previous owner? Were those late-night drunken calls from his killer? And who drove by in the old car the day I was weeding? Those three cigarette butts…

Was this the finish line or the finish of me?

Then I remembered from my studies that the average number of secrets kept by a person at any given time is thirteen. How did he track them all? The recollection of that tidbit increased my fatigue, pessimism and gloom.

My grief was conflicted and therefore unspoken. I could not utter the truth, to say aloud I felt relief mixed with sorrow. Society understood mourning only in narrow terms of sadness. The phrase "I'm sorry for your loss" felt inappropriate and superficial. I slipped deeper into the blackness.

Predictably, *The Detroit News* printed another installment of shame July 29. The article inaccurately described Tom Mooney — who delivered the eulogy — as Al's former supervisor. The author, Liz Twardon of the "police beat" quoted various passages of the service, revealing she was one of the trespassers. The title of her narrative should have been "Interlopers and friends bid farewell to Canty at memorial."

# TWENTY-EIGHT

# TAKING A STAND

For a county abundant with corpses, the scheduling of Case Number 85-75999 occurred in record time. A subpoena ordered me to appear at the Frank Murphy Hall of Justice, 36th District Court, Wayne County, Michigan, Criminal Division on Wednesday, July 31, at 9:00 a.m. Unfamiliar names appeared next to mine. Tamara Becker, Gary Neil, Keith Bjerke, John Bumstead, Michael Oliver, Cheryl (a.k.a. "Twiggy") Krizanovic and Dale (a.k.a. Frank) McMaster.

Michigan's 36th District Court on St. Antoine was one of the largest and busiest in the Midwest. Named after a native attorney who became an Associate Justice of the US Supreme Court, it was equipped to handle high misdemeanor and felony cases. This qualified.

I dressed with care in my best blue suit and heels but felt and looked ten years older. A shower and professional clothing did not camouflage insomnia and the invisible backpack of rocks which I felt I carried. A clash of emotions rattled me in preparation for court. No amount of cosmetic wizardry undid my puffy eyes or sour mood.

My father drove us to the Preliminary Hearing and struggled to find parking despite being early. Mrs. Canty declined to come. We faced a routine security search with an examination of our purses and pockets. Before Officer Landeros separated me from my parents, my mother firmly whispered, "Tell the truth. Tell them everything. Don't be afraid to be angry." She assumed I'd whitewash Al's actions. Ha! She misread me entirely.

Like the memorial, the room filled. Everyone underwent a secondary security search at the entrance to the courtroom. The concerned sat among the curious, the indictable among the innocent. Court officials led my apprehensive parents to a back anteroom to share benches with spectators and journalists. This upset me because, while they could hear and see the proceedings, it was only from a distance. My parents insisted to a bailiff they be allowed into the main courtroom, which they were, so long as it was not near the witness stand.

Again, Marylss Landeros aided me in facing the formality of this ominous morning. She perceptively whispered, "It's a chance to take back control, to face the defendants. You can do this."

*Damn right I could!*

Suddenly my guide ushered me in an about-face to a small office. The confident, lanky prosecuting attorney, Robert Agacinski, hastily introduced himself. At the last minute the defense attorney, Jay Nolan, joined us. He was a small, wiry, restless man with a sharp voice, given to wearing straw hats and striped suits in summer. He hiked court stairwells for exercise in winter.

The defense counsel motioned to stipulate what I would say — in effect gag me. I stood as tall as my 5' frame could reach and faced the bespectacled 6'2" prosecutor.

"No! *Absolutely not!* Put me on! This case belongs to *me!*" I'd rearranged my life to be there.

Judge Sapala denied Nolan's request.

Landeros escorted me back into the congested courtroom, with a muted air of victory, and guided me forward with the defense table to my left. This was the first time my eyes set on the people I'd only seen in the news. Thing One and Thing Two at the defense table were clip art for "pimp" and "prostitute." I needed to make a stand by *taking* the stand. I turned the congested corner and edged my way toward the bench in the crush of another media circus while my pulse throbbed in my ears. In the process, I deliberately placed two fingers of my left hand on the defense table, within inches of them, as if I needed to balance myself in the swarm. However, I had deliberately encroached into their personal space, outing them, exposing my palpable rage, my lack of shock and awe.

In navigating past them my eyes hastily glanced at their hands, knowing full well what they'd done. I'd seen John's handiwork firsthand. It was ugly, vicious and undoable. The murderer's fingers were thick, scarred, and invisibly stained with blood. Spens' hands had reluctantly caressed my husband's thighs and what lay between. She used them to accept cash and gifts, carry away body parts and plunge syringes of poison. But at that time, she rested them in her despoiled lap as if sitting in a church pew. Dawn's face was puffy, ashen and soulless.

I felt entitled to my time on the witness stand. I'd earned it! My annoyance was barely restrained.

My parents sat at attention. So did court reporter Matthew Dreger. After the swearing in a morbid hush fell over the spectators who'd assembled to eavesdrop on this smutty story that was not theirs. I did my best to ignore them and focus on the questions at hand.

Mr. Agacinski began:

Q: "How long were you married?"

While I responded I forced myself to look at Fry and Spens, to again intrude into their space. John was huge, like a crude Mr. Clean. He wore a wrinkled gray Western shirt over his tough, upholstered arms. His younger accomplice appeared sunken, ill, oddly detached, even bored. Her swollen ankles bulged above stretched, cheap shoes with tacky mesh toes. Her skin was a sickly grey-green. Dark circles accentuated the same dull eyes that witnessed Al's convulsions. *This? This was the company he sought? He drained our life savings for them?*

A: "Ah, nearly eleven years."

Q: "When was the last time you saw your husband?"

A sketch artist quietly drew to the left which irritated me—but it seemed *everything* did. The room beyond the defendants and attorneys was a blur. "Saturday morning of July 13."

Q: "Sometime after that were you asked to come to the Wayne County Morgue?"

A: I bristled at that question. "Yes," I quietly answered as I looked down.

Q: "Were you asked to make an identification of a person at the morgue?"

A: "Yes," I replied as flashes of the gore made by the man sitting forty feet away were awakened. I swallowed hard. The hands in my lap curled into tight, perspiring fists.

Q: "Did you give anyone permission to bury the body or perform an autopsy or dismember the body in any way?"

A: "No," I firmly answered, "I did not," as I looked directly at the defendants where John intensely studied his bland table. Dawn was on the nod.

What I was not asked about was my loss of faith in people, my rage, my inability to confront my husband about his shameful behavior. The officers of the court did not want to hear about sleepless nights, the emptiness, the fear of lying in my own bed while I listened for car doors or muted voices outside.

Mr. Nolan quietly stood and rapidly asserted, "I have no questions for this witness, your honor."

*Why is that, Mr. Defense Attorney? You cannot wait to get me out of here, can you? You want to pretend I don't exist!*

Agacinski rose to say something but reversed course and sat back down. I glared at Nolan. Once again, I was ushered through a rear exit and over to Greek Town by my family, though food and company did not interest me whatsoever. The only thing I wanted was justice, the Wild West kind.

# TWENTY-NINE

# UNTANGLING THE WEB

Others on the subpoena testified. They wore clothing appropriate for lawn work, not a day in court. The men were shaggy. Most females revealed garish tattoos which underscored their hardness. Practically all displayed inarticulate, crude speech and most needed a shower, barber, dentist, and grammarian. *This* was the company Al chose? It was a mystery to everyone, including the accused.

The court called John's pal, Dale Frank McMaster, next. In part, his testimony to the prosecuting attorney's questions was as follows.

Q: Was the satchel opened in your presence?

A: Yes, it was.

Q: What did you see inside?

A: Plastic bags.

Q: Could you see inside the bags?

A: No.

Q: Were the police officers present then?

A: Yes.

Q: At any time, when you were with the police, did you look inside the plastic bag?

A: Yes. They took parts out, part of a dead body and started taking pictures.

Q: Did you see that yourself?

A: Yes, I did.

Q: What body parts did you recognize or see?

A: Just the head of Alan Canty.

Q: What happened after that, if anything?

A: We went grocery shopping.

Q: Who did?

A: John, Dawn, and myself and my girlfriend.

Q: You had just helped John Fry bury the identifiable body parts of a body…

A: …yes

Q: …and you went grocery shopping?

A: Yes, why not?

Following Frank's testimony Frank McMaster's girlfriend, Cheryl Jean Krizanovic (Fry's former girlfriend) was called to testify.

Q: You indicated Dawn said she cleaned up the mess, referring to the situation here in Detroit?

A: Yes.

Q: Did she tell you when the mess was cleaned up? I don't mean by that the date she told you.

A: Not specifically.

Q: Did she tell you what the mess was?

A: Blood.

Next, Assistant Medical Examiner Marilee Frazer was called to testify as to her autopsy findings. Her credentials were stipulated to—not questioned—and she was sworn in. Again, Prosecutor Agacinski took the lead. In part, her testimony consisted of the following.

Q: What, if anything, did you observe in making that external examination?

A: Initially, on external examination, there were two lacerations on the right side of the head in the region of the right temple, each three-quarter of an inch and one-half inch above the right ear, there was semi-circular abrasions, one inch below the right ear which measured one-eighth of an inch in width by one-quarter inch in length.

The deceased also had a bruise or a contusion over the center of the forehead and that was…there was extensive bone destruction underneath. There were abrasions over the bridge of the nose. The individual had bilateral periorbital contusions, more commonly called black eyes and there was extensive damage to the tissue inside the eye conjunctive, more extensive on the right than the left.

There was a three-inch-by-two-inch bruise over the left cheek. The left corner of his mouth was swollen and discolored, and the inside surface of the lip and gum were hemorrhagic or bloody.

Q: Could you determine if all these injuries were inflicted while the body was alive?

A: Yes, they were.

Q: How many separate injuries did you observe to the head?

A: I would render an opinion there were at least four separate blows, maybe more.

Q: What kind of injuries were life-threatening?

A: The initial finding was the presence of extensive

skull fractures on the left and right sides of the head, essentially the whole front of the skull in the front of the ears was just fractured in multiple connecting fractures; kind of like an egg being cracked. Further examination of the brain revealed contusions on the right side and the front of the brain underneath the impact site.

I know he was alive when he sustained his impacts because if he hadn't been, I wouldn't see the reaction in the brain and in the skull underneath that I did.

The fifth witness called was Detective Landeros.

Q: What, if anything, did you see in the bathroom?

A: There were bloodstains throughout the bathroom.

Q: Besides the bathroom, did you notice evidence of bloodstains elsewhere in the house?

A: There were bloodstains in a small bedroom, too. It was on a sheet or something and there were bloodstains which appeared to be in a master bedroom that had a dresser. There were bloodstains in the living room, I think in front of a window, and more in the kitchen.

Following the testimony of these and others, Judge Sapala ruled that Fry faced first-degree murder, premeditated. Spens was charged with accessory after the fact. Both faced a count of mutilation of a dead body. Sapala read Spens' statement in his chambers and admitted it into evidence. "Therefore, Mr. Fry and Ms. Spens, you will be bound over to stand trial in Detroit Recorder's Court as you are now charged."

So, rather than flee to the west coast to slug Zombies and inject Black Tar, both were remanded back to the custody of the stuffy Wayne County Jail. Whatever plans they discussed, whatever cover story they invented, their arraignment curbed it, and their next appearance was scheduled for August 7, 1985, at 9:00 a.m. Both were asked how they pled.

"Not guilty," replied Fry.

"Not guilty," replied Spens.

# THIRTY

# THE MOURNING AFTER

Al was buried twice within three months. Both internments took place amid trees and scandal without family. He was placed into the warm earth again on September 19, 1985. Al's permanent resting place was near a broad pond in the northern section of Elmwood's Cemetery near Lafayette and East Grand Blvd. As an open criminal matter, an earlier burial was impossible, and family was not notified beforehand. The graveyard was just nine miles northeast from his last moments alive. His mother selected a spot alongside his father, where the three of us had stood the preceding year.

The cemetery was the oldest continually non-religious cemetery in Detroit. The National Register of Historic Places added the name in 1982. Dozens of people interred at Elmwood had streets named after them, and he always loved Detroit's history. Buried there were at least twenty-seven mayors, eleven U.S. senators, six governors, cabinet ministers, and ambassadors. Ironically, one grave contained the remains of Lewis Cass, the man who established the Corridor and the Springwells neighborhood where the Casper house was. That was accomplished in the previous, civilized century.

*THIRTY-ONE*

# BOIL DOWN

The conclusion of the prelim presented a lag time before the December trial. Summer yielded to autumn again, noticeable in brisk evenings and earlier dusk, then yellowed saplings and increased rain. Al had been gone nearly two months. It seemed like an eternity.

"Mom, can you and Dad help with a yard sale before you leave? I want to get rid of as much as possible."

In truth, a vacant cottage tucked deep into a forest halfway around the world would've sufficed. I felt like a wounded animal who wanted to flee into the wilderness to escape the pack as far as possible. Books, paintings, furniture, clothes, jewelry, dishes… I asked Dad to sell, take or give away car parts, tools and surplus paving bricks. I wanted nothing to do with any of it. Mom put her foot down when I hauled the Persian rug outside.

We drew a sizeable crowd both days with perfect weather. Each item was embedded with bittersweet memories. Some belongings were stolen but I didn't much care because in the last hour everything was marked "free" to ensure the tables were picked clean. The thefts only validated my current opinion of strangers anyway.

More obstacles... As if on cue, the Siamese cats took sick. They seldom ate, didn't move much and one had matted fur. The on-call veterinarian speculated.

"They're old. I don't know what it is. I'll run tests but let's keep them for the night."

"But all three at the same time? Maybe it's contagious?"

"Could be, but their temperatures are normal, they're up to date on shots and their exams show nothing so far. Has there been big changes at your house, you know, construction, a new pet maybe?"

"Why?" I stalled.

"Well, pets are sensitive to change and when they're as old as these three musketeers it doesn't take much... What I'm saying is, it can lead to food refusal or compromise their immune system or accentuate an existing illness just like in elderly people."

"Oh. They haven't seemed hungry and, yes, there has been some...ah, changes. A busy garage sale because my husband... Well, it's...complicated..."

Mercifully, the veterinarian interjected, "Oh, a divorce...I see. Yes. That's enough to stress them. They sense the tension and his absence. Let's see what I can find out. Call tomorrow after 10:00. We'll go from there."

By morning, I learned one had died over night, and another needed continued hospitalization and did not seem to respond to treatment. I'd neglected them the past several weeks. The inattention, coupled with Al's absence, packing, their age... Had they not been overlooked maybe they'd all be alive. If I could rewind the clock, I'd do things differently. In fact, there was a *lot* I'd do differently.

The challenge of unwanted, intruding stares persisted. Some friends avoided me. I didn't blame them. I wasn't up for a movie or a day at the lake. My hairdresser asked me to suspend my appointments "until things quieted down" because she "didn't want the distraction" in her salon. I'd become a nuisance.

And easily annoyed. How dare couples smile as they walked hand in hand. Why did people watch murder for entertainment? Couldn't the grocery stores sell smaller loaves of bread? Not one sympathy card reflected conflicted feelings. I admit I began to *look* for things to be angry about and was terse with people who did not deserve it.

*The person who promises to catch you if you fall*
*sometimes pushes you off your feet*
---Unknown

Triggers for flashbacks developed. In contrast with my life-long love of baseball, it now conjured up gruesome visions. Thunderstorms grated my last nerve. Places and individuals that reminded me of us, as a couple, were sidestepped. When I was indoors, I wanted to be outside. When I was alone, I wanted my friend. Yet in her company, I wanted solitude. I even rudely left her home in the middle of an overnight visit without so much as leaving a note. It was selfish and impulsive. I was inconsolable, maimed, without direction. My only solace was sleep.

Around this time, I wrote the following to the Detroit Free Press.

Until a few weeks ago I had no firm opinion about the competence of the Detroit Police Department. However, the recent murder of my husband, W. Alan Canty, changed that considerably. I cannot emphasize enough how professional and empathetic the officers of the homicide division were to my family and me during the grueling events of recent weeks.

Everyone from the office staff to Inspector Hill went out of their way to assist my family. Each time I returned to the fifth floor of Police Headquarters, I was treated as if my husband's disappearance and subsequent murder was the only problem the staff had on their minds. The question I'm left to resolve is, how can Inspector Hill and Officer Landeros continue to function as caring, considerate human beings when they are perpetually involved with the ugliest side of human nature?

Police Chief William Hart has reason to be proud of the Homicide Division. I realize most Detroiters will never come into contact with Inspector Hill and his staff and therefore have no basis for a personal opinion. It is my hope this letter will change that just a bit.

I wrote this because detectives charged with the investigation, and Detective Landeros in particular, had preserved my fragile sanity. Negative press sells. I wanted to bring balance.

By this time, I needed, *wanted*, to return to work full-time. Bills would not pay themselves, and they had mounted. I never knew a paid day off. For another, I'd been trying to establish my practice, a career over a decade in the making. My caseload could not sit on idle.

Equally pulling at me was the need to escape my "beautiful prison," the phone, memories, the "lookey-theres" and the boxes waiting for relocation. Like high school graduation, an uncertain abyss awaited before me.

But, before returning to the eighth floor of the Fisher Building, some groundwork needed to be laid. First, the security team was asked to block reporters. Their intrusiveness would be a problem for other tenants as well. The next call was to the leasing agent to request a smaller office on another floor in exchange for our double suite, which reduced overhead, as it was not possible to immediately get out of the lease altogether.

Subsequently, I met with Dr. Rutledge who assessed whether I was ready to return to work steadily. I trusted that man with my life and knew he would leave no stone unturned. We met weekly for case supervision for a couple months, to be doubly assured. He, in turn, asked me to get medically cleared. I did. Dr. Hillenberg was concerned about my lack of appetite, weight loss, and insomnia. He prescribed 0.25 milligrams of Xanax—a minimal dose. My hand accepted the prescription with no intention of filling it since I had a philosophical aversion to sedatives. I'd seen much abuse of drugs in my career and wasn't about to go down that road. But Dr. Rutledge convinced me to use them as prescribed at least for a week. With the very first dose, I slept a solid fifteen hours. The world looked clearer when I awoke, and I was less irritable and clumsy.

We agreed I could not see Al's patients. While the income was welcomed, I lacked the energy for twenty additional people, and the dynamics would be muddled. So, I located a nearby competent therapist for them to transfer to if they wished. Next, I petitioned Probate Court for an order allowing me — as a personal representative — to destroy Al's meager psychology records for all the years he worked. They could fall into the wrong hands, and I did not want responsibility for his work product, nor the extra work involved in responding to requests for them in the future. Judge Szymanski so ordered this, effective February 26, 1986.

A deep breath. Al's office, like his closet, had been avoided but the move to a smaller space was approaching and I had to face this. I reluctantly stepped inside our beautiful-just-completed suite where the faint scent of paint, coffee and pipe tobacco falsely promised he would pop out with his awkward grin. His office walls held remnants of a wasted career. Al's leather-bound books, slate table, African art, and framed psychology license were mute reminders of a life that once held meaning and integrity; a life traded for a greedy underage drug-abusing whore and her Neanderthal pimp.

As I sat there alone in the quiet, surrounded by my dream of a joint practice I felt anything but fulfillment. It was not at all how I imagined. The space was beautiful. My certificates were hung. Business cards printed. My name on the door. But my heart felt heavy.   My head ached. I wanted to choke Al on the ashes leftover from the dreams he burned!

It felt as inappropriate to comb through his office this time as it was necessary. Circumstances converted me to "custodian" of a psychology practice I once felt intimidated to enter many years and promises and lies ago.

I discovered six unused phones in a large shopping bag that needed to be returned to Michigan Bell, as he'd been paying monthly rent on them for no reason whatsoever. Some books were left behind, and others relocated to my new space, as well as a couple of pieces of art. Most were given away.

My eyes again fell upon his familiar black appointment book. Although I glanced at it the frantic morning Celia and I searched for him, this evening I studied it from his oversized slate blue leather chair. A more careful review distressed me more than words could convey. He'd entered practically nothing for several weeks, precisely like his appointment book at home, and some names appeared strangely made-up, hastily scribbled, as if to conceal his absence from himself. He entered other names two or three times a day. No wonder the answering service said things had been quiet. It confirmed my worst fears. *He not only turned his back on us, but he'd also turned his back on his profession!* The disservice to the patients who'd trusted him was impossible to measure. This discovery angered me more than anything the media, undertaker or neighbors stirred up. He did this deliberately, selfishly and repeatedly.

*Before you choose a counselor,*
*watch him with his neighbor's children*
--- Sioux Nation

Just as I thought it impossible to become more confused and exasperated, two money orders surfaced from his cluttered table, each for $250 with my forged signature! Al paid rent on some place I'd never set foot in. Casper perhaps?

These discoveries, combined with weeks of frustration, my crushed aspirations and fatigue, triggered a rage I'd not experienced since the preliminary. His spiral appointment book was hurled against the wall with such force it seemed capable of leaving an imprint. I shoved his heavy leather chair over and yelled obscenities at the familiar, charcoal portrait of a pensive man from Northville State Hospital who observed the spectacle unfold from a distant wall. Adrenaline surged through me. I *so* wished I could scream within millimeters of Buster's face! *He left me with this mess! He had plenty of warning and time to backtrack. He was a victim and perpetrator! What was there not to be angry about?!*

I'm glad my rant was after business hours. I wasn't acting professionally myself. The whole situation was just... *inconceivable.* I was tired of deception and unanswered questions layered amid fraud and disgrace and complications. Thankfully, dead men tell no more lies.

# THIRTY-TWO

# FACING FACTS

Eventually, it was time to face the rest of whatever the media had conjured up, as it was essential to know what my patients knew. Turns out, anyone in the tri-county area was privy to our address, names of restaurants we'd frequented, make, color and model of our cars, where my childhood home was and where we married. They'd displayed a photo of me entering the morgue and another inside the memorial. There was gory coverage of the crime scene, with blood-smeared walls and the very bathtub where Al was butchered. I watched silhouetted interviews of anonymous hookers claiming valuable inside information; their five minutes of fame.

Simply put, it was worse than imagined and robbed me of safe harbor. But anger was swiftly eclipsed by fear. "Oh my gosh! It's *him!*" My heart accelerated as I recognized the stranger being interviewed for the evening news. It was the same man who stopped out front the day

I pulled dandelions to ask if Al was home. The man who had spoken to me was informant Frank McMaster.

Nothing alarmed me *then*, but knowing his connection to the sordid mess, to Fry… If Frank saw me and where we lived; if Fry had our address; if they'd seen photos of the house interior… The cigarettes I'd found in the backyard… The hang-ups… My lizard brain was in overdrive.

The worry for my safety and protection of my patients consumed me. I would be *damned* if they'd pay the price for this mess! I prioritized. There was my security system. My brother convinced me to purchase a handgun. I did. I learned to use my revolver at a target range run by former police. Though never comfortable sleeping near it, it was better than having chalk lines drawn around me. Turned out, my aim was satisfactory. The practice sheets which hung on my delicately flowered guestroom walls reminded me, "Never brandish a weapon unless you can follow through using it." It calmed me to step away from feeling like prey, yet…*me* aiming a *revolver*?

Therapists conducting psychotherapy in Western cultures are taught to think carefully about interjecting personal information into someone's session. Self-disclosure is risky. Recanting words impossible. Phrasing has to be delicate. Timing is crucial. Self-disclosure must be beneficial for the client, not undertaken to meet the needs of the therapist. Nevertheless, in my practice, the *media* made that delicate decision for me, leaving me with the fallout! The journalism code of ethics warned of the "limitation of harm." Didn't they even know the ethics of their *own* profession? Nothing in my training prepared me to handle that complication. It was harmful enough that the media invited the community into my private life, but their actions compromised my work, too! *Ugh!*

The following week each patient was telephoned, to explain my return to a fuller schedule. Each person was invited for one appointment, free of charge, to decide if they wanted to continue where we left off or obtain a referral. Either way, they would be assisted. If I were in their shoes, I assured them I'd bring questions. It was my job to hear them, but if I felt the question was inappropriate, I reserved the right to decline an answer. They were also assured the security team would keep media out of the building, and escort them if they so wanted.

The security team did escort persistent camera operators and reporters out of the Fisher Building because they disrespected boundaries. But one slipped through the net and sat in the waiting room in a flowered maternity dress and flat shoes. She carried a small purse, no briefcase, tape recorder, I.D. badge or scruples. This woman presented herself as a former colleague of Al's "wanting to extend condolences." It seemed odd. I had no relationship with her and never heard her name. She referred to Al as "Alan" which signaled she either knew him from childhood or not at all. Within moments the conversation grew curiously personal.

"Do you plan on selling your house? Will you be at the upcoming trial?"

I replied, "That's an odd way to extend condolences."

The security team was notified, and she was escorted out—minus answers to her questions. I was in no mood to be polite or extend the benefit of a doubt to anyone who was unfamiliar. Those days were *over!*

After my last appointment, I sent a letter to the University of Michigan records department to request them to destroy Al's hospitalization records or include my letter with them, so they did not fall into the hands of prying journalists posing as God-knows-who. Al's death certificate was attached, along with a copy of the paid hospital bill.

Damage control was front and center.

Insofar as my patients were concerned, they were remarkable. When invited to ask questions—within the parameters defined above—they usually asked two. "Are you planning on moving?" and "How are you doing?" They were genuinely concerned. Not *one* was inappropriate. If they felt judgmental, they did not show it. If they had intrusive questions, they did not ask them. If they experienced doubt about the mental health field, they would not have come. Of all the patients on my caseload, only one did not return. In short, the patients in my practice were more considerate and mature in their responses than the police at the substation, some neighbors, most strangers, my hairdresser, the undertaker and all the reporters I'd met along this ugly journey.

Once work was regularly underway, I looked forward to it. I moved into my smaller office which became my "holding environment;" a refuge from stolen glances, the media, and sad memories. My new surroundings held reminders of fulfillment and stability. Very little was associated with Al. No boxes of belongings to sort through. No scent of tobacco. I found comfort in the rituals of my work. At least one corner of my life was predictable.

More roadblocks. Within the first dozen days of

September, I received notices of unpaid taxes from 1984, overdue answering service charges and unpaid office rent totaling thirteen-thousand-four-hundred-eighty-three dollars — over thirty-three-thousand in today's dollars. Around Al's fifty-second birthday, I received a check from Social Security for his death benefit. The grand payout was one-hundred-twelve-dollars.

With money incredibly tight, I returned those phones to Michigan Bell along with the bill. The clerk's eyes flew wide. "It's *him*! It's *you*!" she bellowed to her coworker, jabbing a finger toward my frazzled head.

The coworker abandoned her customer and blared, "Oh! You're that *widow*!"

I was instantly exasperated. "That's right. I'm not the whore. I'm a celebrity. *Now take them off the damn bill!*"

With debts mounting I finally asked Mrs. Canty if Al had life insurance. To the best of my knowledge, she would've had the only copy of that document if it existed at all. "He had none," was her reply.

As chilly evenings descended in earnest, my parents returned to Phoenix. It was a quiet trip to Detroit Metro. Eventually, they peeled themselves from my embrace and were swallowed by the waiting jet. I wanted to reach out like a five-year-old on the first day of kindergarten. Oh, how I wanted to follow. Nothing would have been more comforting than lounging in their sunny home, a thousand miles from this hard, unforgiving, gray place, this place that boasted slogans like *Come back to Detroit. We missed you the first time* — with a drawing of a handgun.

I struggled to see the impressionistic-appearing road on the way back from Detroit Metro, as moisture lined my lower lids and dribbled over my cheeks. It felt

303

incredibly alone to be surrounded by the rubble of a mess and living on empty. No living relatives were within many neighboring states. Friends and neighbors could only be intruded upon so much. Besides, I'd become irritable, reclusive, wary. I'd changed my home phone number so often I had to write it down to remember it. The only place peace could be found was at work or with Dr. Rutledge.

Simple things grew irritating. How could Halloween be a holiday if it celebrated graves, and death? With all the murders in the city, why didn't the public shift their attention to someone who needed it?

My parents landed in Phoenix with a heaviness. They feared for my safety, the upcoming trial, and my future. They welcomed the sapphire blue skies and rustling palms of Arizona, but these failed to lift their spirits. This mess did not fit their picture of retirement or the life they'd known. Mom later told me that leaving me behind was the hardest thing she'd ever done. They became collateral damage…

Their neighbor, Toni, who once worked at the Roostertail Nightclub on Jefferson Avenue, breathlessly called them after speaking with her son who still lived in Detroit. He knew his mother was friends with my parents. Before Mom and Dad could even unpack, Toni was banging at their door craving an update. My parents were in no mood. From then on neighbors subjected my parents to ongoing invasiveness. People who never said hello before now expected them to disclose personal details of what happened. As a result, Mom and Dad remained indoors a lot and bypassed the community pool for an entire year. Neighbors and acquaintances in Arizona and Michigan unthinkingly added to the misery of our family, along with the media. All we wanted was our privacy, time to heal, to have friends as buffers, not bullhorns.

Gladys Canty was struggling, too. She was alone, elderly and frail. She lost her husband eleven years earlier and her only child to a zero of a man. One night she experienced a… "dream." She was in that hazy twilight between sleep and wakefulness and saw Buster sitting at the antique typewriter he'd bought her years earlier. He distinctly said, "Oh, Ma, it wasn't that bad." She believed the apparition. It comforted her. I hasten to add she was disinclined to such visions. It reminded me of the night I glanced into the mirror in Al's home office and simply "knew" he was dead. How are these to be explained?

Understandably, Mrs. Canty had difficulty comprehending the actions of her only child. The book *Pollyanna* had always been her guidebook, and she turned to it again. "He will be remembered for all the people he helped." "He worked too hard." "He was generous."

And I had difficulty comprehending her. I believed Al would be remembered for discrediting his professional ethics and marriage vows. He worked hard at deception. He was generous to the point of giving Fry and Spens the lifetime savings of two families so they could shoot poison into their arms, sit in squalor and mock their benefactor.

Al was a hypocrite—a lie in action.

My husband left a legacy of indecency. *Let's call it what it is*, I'd think to myself when Mrs. Canty waxed with vindication and nostalgia. In the decreasing contacts with Gladys, I grew weary of her denials and distortions, yet resisted adding to her heartache by telling her so. It was best I kept my distance.

Home became my unwanted, beautiful prison. I

withdrew to the room with yellow floral wallpaper and targets, without the comfort of my parents nearby. I neglected my garden, closed off our bedroom and never again set foot in Al's home office.

During that time, one welcomed call came from an old post-doctoral colleague on the east coast, a psychologist and talented musician, Matt Alexander. He said something off-handedly, which consoled me over the next difficult year. He warmly, quietly and simply commented, "Well, life is an adventure, you know?"

Hmm, an *adventure*... That implied this could lead somewhere. Maybe one day I'd be in another place, on the other side. I clung to those words.

Written confirmation of my husband's burial with the paving brick arrived on September 20, 1985, from J. Robert Stutton, general manager of Elmwood.

That same month Gladys sent me a $25 check inside a Happy Anniversary card. This anniversary, our eleventh, was...*happy*? Something to *commemorate*? Was. She. *Kidding*? I refused to join the Canty window display! Pollyanna was not *my* role model! I ripped her upsetting mail into confetti, jammed it into a new envelope and hastily printed, "I will not celebrate a wedding to a whore monger," across the outside in red felt marker for all the mail handlers to read. Not surprisingly, this was our last verbal communication.

Murder doesn't just kill the victim, it kills families.

# THIRTY-THREE

# LIFE DOWNSTREAM

"Was it possible?" Had I been exposed to the recently identified HIV virus? Some people, even in the medical center, speculated the new, frightening infection was spread through sneezing, kissing or contact with perspiration on the playing field. My fears intensified by the highly publicized deaths of celebrities. Splashed across the front page were stories of actor Rock Hudson, musician Ricky Wilson of the B-52s, supermodel Gia Carangi, designer Perry Ellis, attorney Roy Cohn, actor Stephen Stucker, designer Chester Weinberg, entrepreneur Steve Rubell, designer Willie Smith, pro football player for the Washington Redskins, Jerry Smith, Formula One racer Mike Beuttler and two unnamed priests. They had perished along with almost thirteen-thousand Americans. How many more were ill with it? Who was yet to be diagnosed?

The CDC stated that unsafe sex practices,

contaminated blood supplies, and IV drug use were known to transmit the virus. They believed the highest risk groups were IV-using prostitutes and men who frequented them. No vaccine or meaningful treatment was available nor on the horizon. HIV was a death sentence. Period.

Only a few months earlier the FDA licensed the ELISA blood test to identify antibodies. I reluctantly, clumsily asked my physician's office for it. Momentary silence met my request. The nurse who drew the blood was double-gloved, with a surgical facemask and paper gown over her clothing. It was frightening. And humiliating. I wanted to scream, "I'm *not* a drug user! I'm *not* a prostitute!"

It seemed the results took forever. "Your blood shows no evidence of HIV circulating at present," Dr. Hillenberg reassured. "That's the good news. But there's an incubation period. So, let's repeat the test next year and the year after. If by seven years, there's no evidence of HIV, you're clear. Beyond that, remember the test is new and imperfect. About seventeen of one hundred blood samples will be false positives, and there are bound to be false negatives, too."

That meant this threat would loom until 1992. *How much more could those three steal from me?* If prostitution was "a victimless crime" why was I here?!

But life was not all bleak. A couple who lived nearby extended a heartfelt invitation for a peaceful dinner in their private backyard garden. To make it special, they arranged our gathering under a large, candle-lit trellis at their restful, Mediterranean-style home.

It was a dry evening with soft breezes and, for early October, unusually mild. Their kerosene patio heater kept us cozy. Alongside my plate was a key to their back door, attached to a lush purple ribbon. They encouraged me to use their peaceful guest room whenever desired. No questions asked. No socializing required. They wanted me to treat it like a hotel room.

Their offer was soothing and cherished. Over several weeks, I periodically took them up on their generous suggestion and slipped in and out of their exquisite home under the cover of darkness. It felt indulgent to crawl into a safe bed away from sad reminders, searchlights, a sidearm and boxes. The room had a high dome-shaped ceiling and I found myself repeatedly looking up at it. It was so peaceful there. Between the frightening financial problems, HIV scare, death of my cats, media blitz, worry over Fry's accomplices, upcoming trial and demands of work, there had been little time to plan, reflect, exhale. But not there.

Was Arizona no longer an option now that prying eyes extended there, too? The idea of simply…disappearing would not be silenced. The shadows of dropping leaves across their nighttime walls felt somber yet soothing, and one night as they tumbled, I decided to legally change my name as another step toward taking back control. *Why not?*

A warm letter arrived from Albert Ellis, Ph.D. — the man Al and I had traveled to Manhattan to meet in better days. He expressed his condolences. It, too, was comforting.

Back home on a Sunday at three in the morning in late October, my body jolted awake to ear-splitting squawks as I covered my ears trying to get my bearings. My home security system urgently demanded attention! I lurched from my bed in the darkness. The monitoring company called simultaneously. "Did you set off the alarm?"

"Ah, no…! Maybe it's false?"

The voice on the other end wanted my code word but my brain locked. I could not even recall my address in the pandemonium. I reached for my nearby desk, but my foot became painfully twisted in the covers, causing me to stumble.

"Where are you located?"

"Ah, second floor, back side, ah, the north side? Back, north side." I gave her the code.

"Stay on the phone. Lock the door to your bedroom. We're sending police."

*Not more police!*

I firmly, quietly locked both entrances into the guestroom and pressed my back to the dark wall directly behind the secured doorway to the main hall. The t-shaped hallway outside was dim. *Which stairway is he coming up?* The phone was gripped tightly in my left hand, my Lady Smith in my right, as the pounding tambourine in my chest accelerated. My eyes studied the faint stripe of light below the door to detect any shadow of movement. I'd long ago memorized the squeaky spots on the second floor and listened intently.

Was this connected to the defendants' friends? That stupid emergency photo album I regretted making? Seconds dragged. I ran through firing range instructions. *Keep the revolver pointed at their mid-section, put your index finger right there. Keep breathing.* The unseen lifeline finally pierced my concentration and directed me to hang up and slowly walk downstairs to waiting police. With an abundance of caution, I tiptoed into the still hallway and paused. A police bullhorn blasted orders to come to the front door. Blinding floodlights deluged the downstairs, carving sharp, sweeping shadows in the darkened house, reminiscent of the lightning the night Al went missing.

The revolver was set aside, and I cautiously stepped toward two waiting patrolmen. They'd discovered an unlocked door between the house and screen porch—from a real estate agent—had set off a sensor. Anyone could've gotten inside.

I had to put an end to living with apprehension, or the apprehension would put an end to me.

# THIRTY-FOUR

# THE BEAUTIFUL PRISON

In early winter, my fingers floated over the beautiful, thick plaster as I studied its complex bubbles of texture. The carpet was dense and clean, brass sconces softly dotted the living room walls and windows were encased in small leaded panes. The 1928 estate with seven gables, two chimneys, hand-carved stonework, and copper trim, rested on a deep, manicured corner lot of a sleepy intersection just two blocks north of Lake Saint Clair. The home we once shared masqueraded as a sanctuary to the uninformed, the unrestrained, the unafraid. But they were wrong. *Dead wrong.*

Over the fall, I'd developed a habit of watching the grandfather clock's rhythmical brass pendulum. It felt soothing, perhaps because it measured the distance from my spouse, from the violence. Chimes echoed in the massive entryway. A self-imposed quarantine from the outside world persisted since the arraignment back in July.

Days were spent marking time, marking regrets.

Although the Tudor lacked guards and razor wire, it felt like a prison, nonetheless. I'd not been free to come and go unnoticed. Persistent reporters intruded, though less frequently over time. Visitors were unwelcome. After my parents left and dusk arrived early, closer attention was paid to deadbolts and yard lights and pedestrians. My new normal consisted of scanning the perimeter through heavy window blinds to reassure myself of my inaccessibility. The security system monitored first-floor activity which provided additional, invisible fortification from the broader, uncertain world. Its tiny red and green lights blinked, and thus assured me the electronic sentry was watching and waiting when I could not. Hopefully, there would be no more false alarms. The phone was a menace but thankfully rang less from neglect and changes in the number. Half the Tudor rooms were vacant and echoed and were seldom entered.

Back in July, police cruisers drifted by at late hours deploying small, piercing searchlights to the darkened hollows of our landscaping, sometimes causing an errant beam to blanch interior rooms in a menacing arc. This always halted me dead in my tracks. Thankfully, they'd left. But the parade of the curious still sporadically drove by, paused, pointed, and sometimes took snapshots like vultures cleaning a skeleton. Confusion and defenselessness flooded the large, lifeless interior of my "prison" and each cell in my body. After dark, muffled sounds of car doors or voices immediately alerted me to a possible provocation.

Rearview of the Berkshire House 1986. So much snow to shovel.

The house always seemed too massive to be homey, even when shared with Al and our cats. I never shared his enthusiasm for the sprawling place. What couple needed six bedrooms, six bathrooms, two staircases, two fireplaces, and a carriage house? Despite its imposing size, it offered minimal closet space and a cramped "serving kitchen." The numerous drafty windows were single pane, no match for frozen Michigan winters. Anyone could see the electrical wiring was perilously out of date and that outlets were scarce. The steep, shingled roof should have been swapped with a new one years earlier and the oversized, original steam furnace, tucked in the recesses of the five-room basement, protested heating the three-thousand-nine-hundred-square-foot home. The boiler, with its knobs, glass tubes, and brass gauges belonged on the Titanic yet, admittedly, kept the radiators clattering and Jack Frost at bay. The Tudor on Berkshire Road, though stately, was impractical, imposing and just plain pretentious. It was a hollow reminder of an illusion.

The surrounding community was nothing like the place of my birth. The neighborhood of my childhood was so densely populated it required no effort to overhear harsh words shouted between neighbors to the south and the late hour they dragged their bottle-laden trash to the curb for pickup. The three-generation family who shared our north property line spoke little English but understood perfectly when I begged for homemade pasta in summer. "Please? *Pleeeease?!*" Ah...a steaming bowl of lumpy fragrant heaven, all red and white and gooey on front cement steps. On a lucky day, they also handed over "ali d'angelo" (angel wings) — a flakey pastry dusted in confectionary sugar. Not even the finest restaurants surpassed what came out of their modest kitchen. And their dog was brilliant. He understood commands in Italian!

Kids in the affluent suburb south of Mack Avenue in Grosse Pointe Park, the neighborhood for the well-heeled, would never know the perfect thrill of gliding on imperfect front-yard skating rinks nor wrapping one's nose in the fresh scent of damp laundry flapping lazily under warm summer skies hung in the backyard. No, the children of this stately community were not envied.

At the title signing in 1974, the realtor proudly exclaimed, "You're not just buying a *home!* You're buying a *lifestyle.*"

Pressed into my handshake, he deposited an expensive orb pendant watch of genuine silver and crystal, but it felt more like a stage pass than a welcome gift and reinforced my newcomer status. Al smiled proudly. This was just one unnoticed clue of our differences.

At the time we moved in I considered the L-shaped

Tudor an impressive study hall, an extension of the university, a place for reading and paperwork and refueling between classes. I had little interest in it one way or the other and never felt belonging to it or the unearned privileges that came with the address. But now, shackled to it a decade later, it seemed...*cavernous*. A sinister motionlessness engulfed the dozen massive rooms rendering it more a mausoleum than a homey shelter.

No inquiries from buyers came despite the months on the market at a bargain price. I could not abandon it. I couldn't relax there. I could not afford it. I never wanted it. And I could not seem to sell it. As a fall-out to Al's murder, real estate laws in Michigan mandated a "hidden defect" disclosure to potential buyers that reduced its value. Insult to injury... How could I escape, redefine my life and put this behind me?

This new "normal" also consisted of dwelling on Al's last moments, mulling over his final words to me and wondering what went on in the mind of his killer. *What makes a human behave so inhumanely? Was he brain damaged? High out of his mind? Appalled at the viciousness of his own attack or did he feel smugly superior after reducing another to a mound of brokenness?*

In anticipation of the day when my surroundings could be abandoned, most contents had been liquidated. What remained was on idle. The basement, with the second fireplace and rickety wine cellar, was freshly painted. This dwelling was constructed during prohibition, so how it even *had* a wine cellar was puzzling. Not only did my husband have riddles, so did our house.

Al's modest closet still preserved the scent of sweet pipe tobacco and Irish Spring soap. His brass, rectangular home office clock obediently, and much too cheerfully, enumerated the hours since we parted. He did not perish because he had to. He perished because his decisions made it inevitable. There was no making it right.

From the mahogany window seat in the sunken library I occasionally studied the deteriorating weather and remaining leaves. It would soon snow. Leftover leaves resembled goldfish wriggling for freedom from delicate, frosty branch tips. I wasn't the only one who wanted to escape this place; this stunning, awful, silent place.

With the passage of time and seasons, it became clear my husband had layers, agendas and ulterior motives. He wore a mask. He was a storyteller, a thespian, a hypocrite. I fell in love with the window display, ignorant it was pinned together with omissions and deceit and avoidance. His lies finally caught up to me.

During my period of disengagement, I pondered how it was I continued to trust when trust was undeserved, to remain when all that remained was a shell of a marriage. I once believed I was a good judge of character, life was fair and hard work brought rewards. But doubt overtook belief. The library window seat became my favorite place to cocoon. It was reliably warm and hidden from prying eyes and couples who effortlessly, contentedly, annoyingly walked hand in hand. From this perch, the colorless late afternoon sky behind the massive bare branches of the 120-year-old elm stared back as I tried to assemble the puzzle that brought me to this place in this way, at this time. It was all so disgraceful, wasteful, and irreversible.

Living room from the foyer and front stairway

The irony was I'd been studying human behavior intensely in graduate school yet didn't see the pathology under my own roof. *I should have known. How could the clues have been misread?* The steamed-up window glass and frosty backyard were as blank as explanations for my failings.

I felt, inept, tired and undeniably angry.

As early dusk closed in, the now vacant, long living room beckoned and I made a small fire inside the substantial, stone hearth. I studied the remarkable stucco cornice atop the walls of a squirrel chasing a bird chasing an acorn. Around and around they went.

While lying on the slate blue carpet shielded in a fluffy, cotton quilt, my thoughts drifted to my parents' marriage. They demonstrated solidarity, trust, integrity. When they disagreed, my siblings and I anticipated the conclusion of their spat with eagerness since their few arguments ended alike. After the silent treatment one cracked a joke, the other reluctantly smiled and — *whoosh* — tension evaporated. There was one especially long standoff, concerning what I didn't know, where Mom initiated the truce by sewing giant, red felt hearts on Dad's worn, favorite, light blue work pants. My father rushed in, looked exasperated, arms wide and implored, "What have you *done*?!" We pointed and erupted into laughter. Mom explained, "Just wanted the world to know I love you." He shook his head trying to conceal a grin and quietly asked that her public display of affection be removed. That memory brought a smile. Those lessons and others taught us marriage involved forgiveness and teamwork; spouses had a common destiny, a shared vision of their intermingled lives and that harm came from *outside* the family. Trust was implicit. I was a believer — well, once upon a time.

I poked the sizzling logs cradled in the cast iron grate and admitted openly I once loved the squinting, smiling man behind the tortoiseshell eyeglasses posing in the framed photograph atop the mantle. I now feared he posed throughout our marriage. But love wears blinders, does it not?

The crackling dry wood beckoned me close, encouraged me to study its grid of grayish charred squares that, when they dropped, revealed red-hot embers beneath. Being so warm was pleasing. The intricate ceiling was tinted orange by the glow of the small popping fire, but the radiance and pirouetting shadows above and behind me only magnified the empty darkness beyond the stucco arch of the sizable living room. I felt even smaller and more alone—even insignificant, as if fading away.

How was it even an experienced team of specialists did not crack Al's code of deception during his six-week psychiatric hospitalization? No one saw through his defenses. I silently asked the mute photo, *who were you? Don't you remember the early years when we laughed and made pledges to one another?* I left myself open to exploitation, humiliation, defamation. I didn't see it, but what blind person could? In time the fire, like us, was reduced to coals.

Minutes later an additional piece of the puzzle to Al's past fell into place. One factor, common to all three psychiatric hospitalizations, was that he was not in charge. That is, he was not choreographing his life at that point in time. When his first wife left him, when he'd been drafted into the Army and when Fry had him pinned into a corner… All three situations rendered him out of control and beyond the rescue from his parents. He could not negotiate, pontificate nor eradicate the situation away.

And something else clicked. The psychiatric hospital where his father took him called The Haven was once a private home to the Shinnick family. It resembled the home that surrounded me. *Is that why he insisted on purchasing this home in particular?*

It's often said there are two sides to every story, and sometimes, two sides to a person. My husband revealed one to those who loved him and another to those who exploited and destroyed him.

Daylight grew shorter, and a punishing winter defeated the vivid autumn oranges and reds. Snow conquered freezing rain. The darkness had won.

Shielded under layers of quilts in my upstairs

hideaway I admitted that not once did I consider Al would bring danger to our home, but we were no longer us. He was not him. I was no longer me. The man in the photo was a stand-in, an actor, a deceiver, a cad. Our marriage was a fraud. Yet, I proposed to him. So, what did that make me?

The complicated questions, tight budget and perspiration-laced nightmares in the pale-yellow room waited every night. Ah, the nightmares... Malevolent dreams punctured my much-needed sleep. One haunted me repeatedly.

*I arrived home late, but the lights would not come on. I heard Al snickering down the long, darkened hallway. I entered his home office where he was undressed. He was burning a bag of money and photographs.*

*Someone stood in the shadows behind him, off to the corner. I asked him what he was doing. He heard me but said nothing. It started to rain hard inside the house and a flood quickly built.*

Gasping for air, I jolted awake and surveyed my darkened bedroom again. It was unnerving and confusing. I felt helpless to stop the repetitious visions. On those nights I could picture my own grave.

In the corner, my eyes set upon the pile of newspapers accumulated over the months. Edgar Alan Poe could have effortlessly authored the articles, since mystery and the macabre were his craft. Questions of death and lost love permeated his writings, along with murder, obsession, guilt, torment, and sorrow. The Detroit newsprint illustrated the selfish intent behind all three of them, exposed in sordid episodes over months for all to see and speculate and judge. One reporter commented, "Even by Detroit standards, his slaying was one of the more bizarre and grisly cases." It would become his unwritten epitaph.

However, one luxury waited each evening. My warm electric blanket comforted like an embrace of a loved one on chilly nights. It was soft and yielding and reliable. The substitute would just have to do.

It was best we never became parents, since I could barely take care of *me*. At heavy times such as these, my thoughts floated back to my father's mother. I idolized her. If only she were here. Nothing could harm me when wrapped in her arms or handmade quilts. Nothing. Although she passed away from cancer when my sister and I were young, the memory of her gentle face, easy smile and kindness remained vivid.

At thirty-four years old nothing prepared me to cope with the menacing realities that trapped me this night and nights to come. I'd become so spotted with bruises from clumsiness brought on by fatigue one physician ironically asked, "Are you in a safe relationship?" Aloneness was foreign. So was the disgrace. And so much anger. *How does one prepare for something they cannot sense approaching?*

# THIRTY-FIVE

# EXIT STRATEGIES

The accused were caged, anticipating separate trials throughout the fall and early winter of 1986. Spens characteristically blamed others and wrote her pimp sugary notes adorned with hearts. She volunteered love for the beast whom she would later claim—under oath—forced her cooperation in carrying body parts. "You're one helluva good man," Spens gushed. Over objections from her father and attorney, she persisted at writing her former pimp behind bars. One intercepted message stated, "As soon as possible I want us to get married and have a baby."

But, her helluva good man had other ideas. On the evening of September 11th Fry successfully paid a guard one thousand-dollars to smuggle in a .25 caliber automatic pistol, by collaborating with inmates Lamont Sapp and Damon Cutts who were being held for homicide. Fry also received two saw blades and intimidated a correction official into swapping clothes, then slid onto the catwalk.

Not entirely original, but effective. He held guards and Detroit Police off for nearly four hours before surrendering again around 9:30 that evening after Sapp, a member of the Eight Mile Sconi's Street Gang, was discovered on a stairway. Sapp's nineteen-year-old girlfriend had parked her Ford Tempo on nearby Beaubien as a getaway car. Freedom was close, but not in the cards. Subsequently, a charge of attempted escape was added to his rap sheet. The tax-weary citizens of Wayne County would be footing the legal bill for those trials as well. Fry's antics were a public embarrassment to Administrator Warren Evans who admitted there were problems with security at the jail and with officer complicity in Fry's planned escape.

On October 1, 1986, in an Evidentiary Hearing before Judge Sapala, Spens tried to recant her confession taken by Detective Landeros in July. The accused asserted she provided it under the false promise she could go home, and it was forced. Under questioning by Prosecutor Agacinski, Spens' testified, in part, as follows.

Q: Why did you give that statement?

A: I was scared.

Q: Of what?

A: They told me I was going to prison for the rest of my life.

Q: Who, specifically, told you that?

A: Everybody. Every police officer I talked to told me.

Q: Williams?

A: Yes.

Q: Landeros?

A: Yes

Q: Hill?

A: Yes.

Q: Brantley?

A: Yes

Judge Sapala didn't buy it. "The court finds this defendant is lacking credibility. Virtually everything she said is farfetched and fantasies. Motion denied."

Dawn surreptitiously vented her frustration on her wanna-be fiancé. "I really don't know much of anything anymore. I do love you. I know I always will... I know one day we will [embrace again] but, it just seems so far off right now..." She failed to see that he was not her knight in shining armor. He was just a felon with a drug habit and no work ethic.

The tunnel that links the (Old) Wayne County Jail to the courts
(Credit: Detroit Free Press Archives)

# THIRTY-SIX

# WAITING FOR TRUTH

Thanksgiving passed without my family, but I was not without thanks. I had them at a distance, my education, friends, health and was not homeless. As bleak as things seemed, they could have been worse.

The impatient media was on idle. Numerous calls from various television hosts — through their agents — arrived with a request to sit under hot lights and be picked apart. Most invitations were local, but not all. One came from *Oprah*. All were declined or ignored. What I'd been through, and what I had *yet* to go through, shook the foundation of my belief system. *Me? Speak with clarity, with coherency, on Al's life and death? I had countless unanswered questions myself! Was I even safe? Did they capture everyone? Did anyone in the Corridor spread rumors that "the Doc" stashed bundles of cash or jewels or weapons or God-knows-what in Grosse Pointe?* Moreover, I did not wish to stir things up for my patients and family. Never did I feel I owed strangers any explanations. And, as far as the tabloids went, didn't they invade my privacy, complicate my cases, make my parents' retirement miserable and turned the memorial into a circus?

Life was on hold. Al left so many things behind — not the least of which was us. As I lay in the darkened room, I noticed my heart was still beating, still fighting. I made it through another day. While the world slept, I took another walk down memory lane, recalling our intimate talks in restaurants with candles reflecting in his glasses and his smile reassuring me of his love and future years together. I remembered how it felt to share my dreams, the day he surprised me with the new typewriter and how kind he'd been to my family. There was a vivid memory of holding him as he sobbed after the death of his father and how we stayed up most of that night facing the grief together. But now the ceiling and I had staring contests. I usually won. It was so confusing to try and merge the pleasant memories with the ghastly ones, his happy face with the one at the morgue. I was not only mourning the end of Al's life but life as it used to be.

An old English nursery rhyme states:
*As I was walking up the stair,*
*I met a man who was not there.*
*He was not there again today.*
*Oh, how I wish he'd go away.*
Al was nowhere. And everywhere.

# THIRTY-SEVEN

# FROM THE FRYING PAN TO THE FIRE

It was fitting that trial 85-04487 commenced on a dreary, frozen morning; December 2nd. New snow quickly darkened and ultimately resembled shiny rocks along the curb. Pedestrian traffic competed with the vehicles.

The defendants' trials were separate and concurrent. John Fry elected a jury trial while Dawn Spens chose a bench trial. Judge Michael Sapala presided over both.

The media primped for an encore, always ready to air more dirty linen and snare a headline. As with the Preliminary, Prosecutor Agacinski served for the State and Nolan for the Defense.

It was alleged Fry had knowledge of unrelated homicides in and around Michigan, which triggered rumors he would be murdered in court to silence him. Undoubtedly, his closet *was* full of skeletons. Some speculated he might plea-bargain for a reduced sentence in exchange for such testimony. Many believed Sapala would go light on Spens.

I did not wish to share oxygen with those two again, to be part of a media frenzy, to listen to salacious testimony. Instead I attended the *Evolution of Psychotherapy* conference in Phoenix. The hiatus was what I needed, despite the unusual two-inch snowfall in Arizona that December. No reporters, back exits, interviews or involvement with prostitutes, pimps, drug addicts, thieves or detectives. Besides, nothing in that stuffy courtroom would un-ring the bell. No matter the verdict, I'd still be a widow in an unwanted house with nightmares, a mountain of debt and an unclear future. Court cannot bring closure. It merely cages the outlaws and serves as an ending to the public who fail to understand that there is no ending.

The trial opened with a trio of motions. This became a common refrain throughout the proceedings. The next formality was jury selection. The prosecution and defense counsels proceeded with voir dire of several women, among them: Lillian Kennedy, Edna Moore, Carol Simon, Stella Hayes, Shirley McKee, Marguerite Stitt, Sabrina Shockley, Donna Kase, Deborah Barnes, and Edith Williams. Not all were called to serve. Twelve females were impaneled.

Nolan assumed women jurists would be unsympathetic to the deceased for his flagrant infidelity, thereby offering leniency toward his defendant. Wasn't this premise simplistic? First, "Doc Miller" wasn't on trial. Second, wouldn't women be inflamed *against* a defendant who controlled young women in the sex trade for his profit?

Judge Sapala ordered a screening of everyone entering his courtroom for Fry's trial with a hand-held metal detector in addition to the routine search at the courthouse entrance.

The defense argument was admittedly unusual, if not desperate. Nolan planned to show Fry murdered "Doc Miller" in a rage, not cold blood, "out of love for Dawn" and for his "manhood, not money." Fry's statements of "wanting to kill the Doc" would be minimized as blowing off steam. The defense strongly believed Sapala would not hand down a first-degree murder verdict with mandatory life.

The pimp arrived in a loaned, brown, tweed suit, no doubt at the urging of his attorney. His beard and hair were conservatively trimmed. He could pass for an attorney, or at least a law-abiding citizen, in his new costume. Lucky did a decent job of dialing down the thug image and concealing his track marks, "tatts" and street life.

Though generally on his best behavior and expressionless, Fry occasionally smirked and rolled his eyes as testimony unfolded. Nolan tried to show Fry's bragging that he'd "kill that fuckin' doctor," and repeated warnings to distribute the body "across five different states" as mere spouting off. If it was meaningless, John was a deluder. In other words, Fry's peculiar defense was he was a bullshitter who murdered a defenseless victim out of love for his "fifty-dollar whore" — whom he thought of leaving.

With jury selection completed on Monday, December 2, 1985, the trial commenced the following morning.

The prosecution called their first witness, Frank McMaster, at 10:00 a.m. Close to a third of the way through his testimony, the following exchange unfolded.

Q: After you buried the bag, what happened?

A: We got in the car and went back to the house.

Q: Did you have any further conversation [with John]?

A: Not really.

Q: What happened when you returned to the house?

A: John spoke to Dawn and said, 'It's taken care of.'

Q: Did Dawn say anything?

A: She turned around and dropped her head.

Q: Then what happened?

A: We went grocery shopping.

Q: Who did?

A: John, Dawn, and myself and my girlfriend.

Q: You had just helped John Fry bury the identifiable parts of a body...

A: Yes.

Q: ...and you went grocery shopping?"

A: Yes, why not?

The next witness was Fry's Aunt Dorothy Wilson. She described the midnight conversation from July 14.

Q: What was the first thing said when you picked up the phone that evening?

A: I said 'hello' and John told me he had 'done it again.'

Q: Those were his first words? 'I done it again'?

A: I said, 'How did you do it?' and he said, 'With a baseball bat.' I said, 'Why?' 'Because he didn't pay.'

Ms. Wilson's statements concluded day one proceedings. The trial resumed Wednesday, December 4 at 9:30 a.m.

The second day consisted of establishing a timeline of events from several witnesses—friends of the defendants—and the destruction of the Buick. The case adjourned until Monday.

The second witness to testify on December 9 was Officer Johnson of the Detroit Police Department. The line of questioning focused on the defendants' arrest between 11:00 p.m. and midnight on July 20th, 1985. Again, Agacinski spoke first.

Q: What did you see when you got to the area [of Heyden and Schoolcraft Roads]?

A: I saw the gentleman going door to door knocking on houses.

Q: Mr. Fry?

A: Yes.

Q: What did you notice when you saw him?

A: We parked our vehicle three, four doors away. He'd been three houses from where we first seen him. We walked up and asked him to identify himself.

Q: Did he?

A: He gave us a name. I don't recall the name he gave us, but he had a picture ID and stated he was the name he'd given us, but it wasn't John Fry.

Q: Do you remember what kind of ID it was?

A: A State ID.

Q: What happened next?

A: I told him he fit the description of a perpetrator wanted in connection with a homicide and placed him under arrest.

Q: Who was your partner at the time?

A: Sergeant William Deck.

After recess, Detective Tony Brantley, of the Homicide Section in the Special Assignment Squad, was sworn in to testify about the search warrant for the Casper house. Next up was Gerald Tibaldi, also from Homicide. Agacinski questioned him about the execution of the search warrant for Frank McMaster's residence.

Q: What, if anything, did you discover?

A: We took samples of clothing of what we thought had blood, some charred pieces of letters or papers in the wood burner, and a couple unregistered guns; things like that.

Q: Did you do other work while up north?

A: We conducted a search of a wooded area near Pallister [Petoskey], Michigan.

Q: Was anything discovered?

A: Yes, sir. We discovered a leather satchel.

Q: Did this bag have to be dug up?

A: Yes.

Q: What, if anything, was inside it?

A: There were two hands, two feet and a head.

Q: Were other items recovered by you?

A: There was a small, laminated piece of paper that appeared to be a cartoon with some print that came out of the fireplace.

Q: Was there some point in time that a watch came to your attention?

A: Yes, sir.

Q: Tell us about that.

A: It was before I went to Petoskey, Michigan—we talked to a person who stated he received a watch from

John Fry for twenty-five-dollars. That was at a home off Vernor and Junction in Detroit.

Q: Is that [the residence] of Jimmie Carter?

A: Yes.

Q: Was the watch identified by Doctor Canty's wife, if you know?

A: Yes, it was.

Q: How about the laminated paper you found in the fireplace, was that shown to Doctor Canty's wife?

A: Yes, while she was at Homicide.

Q: Did she recognize that?

A: She stated she gave it to her husband and had a special meaning to her.

The prosecutor called Dr. Marilee Frazer, Assistant Medical Examiner, to the witness stand next. In part, she testified to the following.

Q: Did you have some indication of how the parts came to be severed, the body parts, Doctor Frazer? I mean, what was the cause of severance?

A: I can't cite the specific instrument, but would say with medical certainty, it was a sharp cutting instrument, mostly likely a saw.

Q: How can you make that determination?

A: Well, on the right side of the neck I found small cuts insufficient for a knife cut, and the cut through the neck tissue was clean. It was made with a sharp instrument. There are few knives that will cut through this tissue.

Q: Why like more a saw than a knife?

A: Most knives wouldn't go through this bone.

Q: Did you also perform an internal examination of the head and skull—look for further injuries of the head?

A: Yes

Q: What did they reveal?

A: As we always do, we cut the scalp, examined the skull and the underlying brain. In this case, the individual had multiple fractures of the skull in the area between the two ears. This individual had bruises or contusions over the surface of the brain.

Q: What does that indicate to you?

A: Because of the direct location of the bruises under the impact side, it means these bruises were caused by blows, not falls, and he sustained bruises while alive at the time he received the blows. In addition, he also had hemorrhages inside of the eye. That would be caused by a direct force, not leaking blood from broken bones.

Q: What kind of force would have to be employed to produce the skull fractures and the hemorrhaging you observed?

A: He had multiple skull fractures, at least ten separate intersecting fracture lines from the area between the ears to the front of the head. So it was multiple, extensive blows to cause all that fracturing. It was like the shell of an egg cracking.

Q: Examining the feet or the leg that you were presented with, did they reveal anything remarkable other than they were dismembered?

A: The leg I received was very decomposed, much more so than the feet or head.

Following the testimony of Dr. Frazer, Defense Counsel, in the absence of the jury, attempted to enter a guilty plea in exchange for limits put on Fry's testimony. Specifically, Nolan motioned that the prosecuting attorney could not ask Fry about weapons used post-mortem. He dismissed the need for testimony regarding the murder saying, "It was just to bring in the gore. I hoped to head him (prosecutor) off at the pass." The request was denied with Sapala saying to agree to such a motion would "limit cross-examination."

Detective Landeros was sworn in next. Mid-way through her testimony, she made the following statements during the cross-examination by Nolan, regarding Spens.

Q: How did she look then [at the time you took her statement]?

A: This is just an observation, but she looked more pleasant; I don't want to use the word happier.

Q: Did she cry during the time you talked to her?

A: No, sir. I don't think she did.

Predictably, the Detroit News ran another story on December 4, by James A. McClear.

### Canty murder trial opens

...Agacinski charged that Fry was living off the money Canty provided Miss Spens and Fry "exploded" when the doctor tried to end it. Agacinski said for days before Canty's death Fry boasted he would kill the doctor, "cut him up and bury the parts in five states..."

"Our contention is that he [Fry] was acting under great stress," said Nolan [defense counsel].

Miss Spens' attorney, Robert L. Ziolkowski, will argue his client was "psychologically controlled" by Fry and incapable of disobeying his orders."

On Tuesday, December 10, Fry's trial resumed but a

medical emergency the preceding night caused an alternate juror to be sworn in.

The last witness to testify was the Defendant, John Carl Fry. Segments of his testimony were as follows. Agacinski asked:

Q: You killed Doctor Canty?

A: Yes, I did.

Q: You dismembered the body?

A: Yes I did.

Q: What prior record, prior convictions have you had in the last ten years?

A: I was convicted in 1978 of attempted B and E; 1975 of conspiracy to pass or possess counterfeit money.

Q: What were you doing when you met W. Alan Canty?

A: Selling weed. Living off the proceeds of a prostitute.

Q: There has been testimony that your friends and neighbors overheard you say, about the doctor and the money, 'I am going to kick his ass, take him out, kill him.' Did you say those words?

A: Over a two-year period of time, I'm sure I have.

Q: Under what circumstances were you making those utterances?

A: It would be...we grew to expect a certain amount of money every day. It was like clockwork. If a day arose the money didn't come, which it did occasionally, we still had the same habit to feed. We were sick.

Q: When you came home around 7:00 what did you see Dawn do on the night in question [July 13]?

A: I got pissed! She was doing cocaine. Injecting it. I turned to Al and said, 'I discussed this in the last month, and it's been three weeks since we left the clinic. You're supposed to be helping me with this because Dawn doesn't have much willpower with drugs.' He said point blank, 'Fuck you. I don't have to justify anything I do to you.' He shoved me like he was walking out.

Q: What did you think?

A: I went out! It's just as he said, 'fuck you.' That's the way he made me feel. There was no concern for her, no concern for what we were trying to do. I was pissed!

Q: What did you do?

A: Well, there was a stool behind me. When he shoved me, I stumbled over it and saw the baseball bat, grabbed it and hit him.

Q: How many times?

A: Once, maybe twice.

Q: You weren't on dope at the time?

A: Yes, sir.

Q: How did that happen? I thought you and Dawn made a promise at 3:00 not to use any more cocaine.

A: We talked about that, yes.

Q: You broke your promise?

A: No.

Q: You weren't high at the time?

A: It depends on how you look at being high.

At 9:42 a.m. the jury began their deliberation on Wednesday, December 11, 1985.

The jury had two outcomes to consider. Did Fry kill in a fit of rage (second-degree murder)? Or, did he plan to murder Al (premeditated murder)? The difference was substantial concerning the penalty. The former could carry a twenty-year sentence with parole, whereas the latter meant natural life, no chance of parole except by a gubernatorial pardon.

Jury deliberation took less than three hours. Since they did not wish to be viewed as hasty, the twelve jurors actually waited in silence for a while before rendering their verdict. The women whom the defense presumed would be sympathetic to the gigolo-pimp were not. As one juror said on camera, of their second vote, "Murder One... Murder One... Murder One."

Afterward, the defense counsel quipped the situation was an "infernal triangle." Nolan postured for the media outside court following Fry's conviction to say, "If he had called the police immediately and said, 'I killed this person,' instead of doing the ridiculous thing he did (to dispose of the body), he would only be here on manslaughter charges."

Only?

In an interview the day Fry was found guilty on all counts, the jury foreman spoke for the majority outdoors on the blustery entrance ramp remarking, "The evidence was overwhelming." Asked what had the strongest impact, she responded "His [Fry's] testimony and the witnesses. We knew what he'd done and, ah... But it *was* gory...yes."

A second, younger, juror interjected, "In our hearts and minds we decided it was a planned murder."

On that day history was made, of sorts. Fry finally faced twelve women who were not addicted or intimidated. They did not want or need Fry's protective services. They were not convinced he was one "helluva good man" nor that he was "acting out of great stress" as Nolan asserted. Instead, they saw Fry for what he was — an angry, hedonistic two-year-old addict who was accustomed to lying, bashing and defrauding to get his needs met.

After Fry's trial, Ray Danford briefly spoke on camera outside the courthouse about his old friend. "Al liked that tough guy image but never was. He had a beautiful wife, and he was messing around down there... I'm thinking it was a waste of time, but that was the way he operated. Alan always had to have something on the side, some intrigue. He did it for that reason. He couldn't just stay home and do his practice. He needed something going on."

# THIRTY-EIGHT

# DARKNESS GREETS DAWN

Dawn's separate bench hearing of December 12 did not require extra security, draw a standing-room crowd nor a media circus.

One spectator, Roy, studied the floor and listened intently. What went through his mind? Was he dusting off old memories to piece together his daughter's pathway to this moment? Whom did he blame? What did he wish for? Why did he not take the stand? Did he see a vulnerable, young daughter unduly influenced by a barbarian pimp and drugs, or an unreachable, angry, lost cause who rebuffed him when he offered to pull her up from the sewer? Did he blame himself for the domestic violence inflicted, for shooing his daughters outside without an explanation, leaving them supervised and feeling like a burden?

Dawn's mother did not show at all. Neither did the mother of the deceased.

Sapala had appointed Robert Ziolkowski as Dawn's defense counsel.

The valedictorian tried to clean up her frayed image also. Her working girl wardrobe had been swapped for a cheap clingy purple dress. Her numerous brown track marks, revealed beneath her nylons, confirmed her involvement with the life. Her perm had partially grown out, and she'd gained twenty pounds. For good measure, she secured her fuzzy hair with a delicate, small black bow, the kind reserved for elementary school girls. She did not show the aloofness noted by the detectives during earlier arrests and, instead, looked as reserved and pensive as a Modigliani painting. Spens' defense was she followed orders from her pimp under duress—she did not possess free will. She wanted the court to believe she was a passive, unwilling and therefore innocent young woman simply caught up in the web of her evil boyfriend. Her long-honed skill of deflecting blame was now imperative.

Landeros was the lead witness for the prosecution. Agacinski directed her to read Spens' eleven-page statement, transcribed at 6:35 the evening of July 20.

Dawn's statement corroborated what the court already knew. Excerpts from it follow.

> I have known Doctor Alan Canty for two years. In November 1985 I knew him as Doctor Alan Miller. I called him Al. We met when I was in front of the White Grove Restaurant on Second and Charlotte in Detroit. He pulled up in a 1982 or 1981 black Buick. He asked if I was a working girl. He took my phone number and said he'd call later and did. The first couple

months I saw Al twice a week then every day or almost every day.

When Al came over Saturday, July 13th, 1985, it was almost noon. He stayed for a half hour to give me forty-dollars. Al said he was coming back to give me more. I said, "Good. I need it."

Al came back about 6:45. A few minutes later, me and him went to Uthes [Street] to get some snow coke. John and me split it. We were in the bedroom, and Al watched us get high. I got sick off it, so I went into the bathroom to throw up.

I heard John and Al arguing. I guessed it was about money. I heard Al say, "I don't have to justify anything I do to you." Al touched John. He didn't move John or nothing, but John reached for the baseball bat and hit Al in the head. Al fell on the floor and his glasses flew off.

I said, "Don't hit Al," but John was swing[ing] again. I ran outside and heard a second hitting sound. I stood outside and John came and said, "Go make money." But I went back into the house and Al was laying in the bathtub with his feet in the air.

I asked, "What the fuck did you do?"

John said, "What does it look like?"

John told me to make sure Al was dead, to use the stethoscope and check Al[s] heart. I did but couldn't tell 'cause my heart was pounding. I knew Al was dead. I then turned two dates for thirty-dollars. I did them in their cars.

I then sat at City Coney Island on Springwell and Vernor. John came with Al's watch and his Buick. We went to Uthes to trade it for coke. We got twenty-five-dollars' worth for the watch.

We got back to the house and did the coke. When I went into the bathroom, I didn't see Al in the bathtub no more. I saw blood.

I asked John, "What the fuck are we gonna do?" He suggested going north to Frank McMaster. John said, "Start packing."

John pulled Al's car around to the alley. I heard John going from the basement to upstairs. John said, "Clean the bathroom." I poured bleach in the bathtub twice to get blood out.

John removed some bedroom carpet. I helped John move the clothes to Al's car. John said to take the overnight suitcase, with the body parts, out of the freezer. I got it and he put it in the trunk.

We left Detroit around 1:00 in the morning and drove to Alanson. We took I-75 to Frank's. I was sleeping most of the way. John woke me up and asked me to drive. He was tired. We stopped at a rest area approximately two hours away from Frank's. I drove the rest of the way, except for the last twenty minutes because I didn't know the way.

We got to Frank's Sunday, July 14th around six in the morning. John and Frank went outside and talked and left. They were gone for an hour. I fell asleep. John came and sat next to me and said not to worry. Frank said, "You don't have to worry about them finding nothin. You couldn't tell the ground was overturned even."

On Monday, July 15 we drove to Gary Neill's house on Morrell. We parked Al's car across the street in the vacant lot and went to Gary's apartment. He said he heard Doc was missing. He said the State Police and feds were at our house looking for us about checks.

John didn't know what he was going to do with the car, so we went to Gary's. The guy they wanted to sell it to wouldn't take it but wanted the tires.

Frank got gas in a can on Livernois. John drove Al's car, and Frank lit the car on fire. Frank came and got into his car with us and Frank drove to his house. But I know Frank got a ticket by a state trooper on I-75 in the morning between 2:00-3:00.

We got back to Frank's around 5:00 a.m. Nothing happened Tuesday or Wednesday except I got a money order from my mother. I gave Frank half of the fifty-dollars. Me, John and Cheryl walked to the store on Thursday, July 11 to get a pop but we ended up getting a newspaper. When we got back to Cheryl and Frank's we read it, and learned I was wanted for questioning and John too. [This date is inaccurate. Al was alive on July 11th. The Detroit News printed their photographs on July 20.]

John made arrangements for us to get a ride [back to Detroit] from a black guy who lives by Schoolcraft. John went to talk to the guy who drove us to John's aunt's house on Heyden. That's where I got arrested.

After Landeros read Dawn's statement into the record, Ziolkowski motioned for acquittal "on the basis the prosecution has not proven the elements in Count 1 as it applied to Miss Spens. There is an insufficient factual basis on the evidence to justify proceedings further on that count."

The prosecutor countered by pointing out that the statute included simply *transporting* as one of the possible acts for the crime of mutilation and everyone was an accessory before or after the fact. Ziolkowski had no rebuttal.

Sapala denied Ziolkowski's acquittal motion.

Spens took the stand on her behalf. She insisted Fry intimidated her, forced her cooperation and she could not deny him. Ziolkowski hired psychologist Michael F. Abramsky, from Birmingham, Michigan, to support the "he made me do it" defense.

Ziolkowski began with the psychologist.

Q: So, Doctor, given her, what you believed to be her background and drug dependency, would you expect she would stand up to someone like Fry?

A: No. From the indications I got, she wasn't even standing up for herself, which is very unusual. Most people I see try to present themselves in the best light possible. I found her very passive.

Q: Based on that, do you believe Dawn Spens was under duress at the time of this incident?

A: Well, from the psychological point of view, she saw no alternatives. I don't think there was a discussion of alternatives or any thought in her mind she could do anything else. There seemed no alternative. She had to carry out these acts. They were never questioned.

In rendering the court's opinion on December 17, at 1: 40 p.m., Judge Sapala said, in part:

I think Doctor Abramsky is correct in describing Miss Spens as highly dependent, who found a safe haven in John Fry. I believe ultimately Miss Spens acted out of motives other than fear of death or suffering grievous bodily harm. I find insufficient evidence of duress as defined by Michigan law.

Sapala's summation was:

Because of questions raised in this case, by the law and review of the facts, we find the Defendant not guilty in Count II, and for reasons aforesaid, we find the Defendant guilty in County III of accessory after the fact to the crime of murder.

Sapala announced sentencing for Spens would take place January 2, 1986.

In a parting comment, Sapala added, "We're left to determine the fact of this shameful and disgusting episode via an odd, bizarre parade of dope addicts, prostitutes, thieves, and admitted lawbreakers... Whether it was Spens, Fry, Neill, McMaster, Krizanovic, Becker, Bumstead, Ramieres, Flores or W. Alan Canty, Ph.D., we see only gratification of individual appetites."

I couldn't have said it better myself.

# THIRTY-NINE

# JUDGMENT DAY

Judge Sapala's clerk called the afternoon of December 19 to ask for my sentence recommendations for Fry. Taken aback, I requested an hour to think it over. There were many things to consider. I wanted to be able to live with the outcome and do what was fair to the taxpayers of Wayne County as well as people walking around on the street.

After considering several options, I requested the maximum penalty for John, reasoning he was the mastermind, the one who wielded the bat, mutilated Al's body, predicted he'd "distribute him across five states, *mon*" and ordered others around. He was older, with a longer criminal record and bragged about his actions. Damaged goods.

Prior to sentencing, Fry said, in his characteristically disarranged manner, "Throughout this trial, I've been betrayed as a cold individual. I have regrets about the way things happened. I regret for Dr. Canty and his family.

Anytime an individual's memory is sold, it's a shame to humanity. My main regret is to Dawn Spens. She was subjected to jail and possible prison. Anyways, I ask for mercy, not for myself but for Miss Spens."

John was age forty at the time of his conviction.

Fry's only comment after the verdict was directed toward his attorney. "See you in January," referring to his second trial for attempted jailbreak. Sapala sentenced this "helluva good man" to natural life with no chance of parole. The streets of Detroit had just ridden itself of another obnoxious pothole.

Ray Danford spoke on camera outdoors after Fry's sentencing.

> It's capital murder. Fry should be off
> the street. It [Al's involvement] wasn't even
> a sexual attraction. It was… He just liked a
> young girl by his side.

Immediately following Spens' conviction, her cousins spoke on camera. Lenore Kosalsky commented, "I feel sorry for her. We feel bad."

Ken Kosalsky added, "It's a good example of what drugs can do."

The reporter asked if family would help her. Ken continued, "I hope so. Somebody has to."

Spens also awaited sentencing over the holidays.

As for Spens, I asked Judge Sapala for intensive, inpatient drug treatment, a shorter prison sentence than John, vocational training and volunteer service. She was a lot of unscrupulous things, but guilty of mutilation, of dismemberment? Not as I saw it. Guilty of accessory after the fact? Absolutely.

I did not want taxpayers paying for the care of both

defendants for twenty or more years. We spend more on the criminal justice system than our educational system, which seemed a crime in and of itself.

Judge Sapala explained, "I think she is redeemable... What happened with her is a result of her bizarre association with Fry. Sure, in a sense, she's a victim of him. He's a user — of people. He's one of the great users of all time. He is absolutely a casebook study of a sociopath. He is totally self-absorbed in the pursuit of self-aggrandizement and dope, dope, dope. At least I want to give her a chance."

Sapala asked Dawn if she wished to make a statement.

"I would like to say I am sorry to Dr. Canty's family and my family for all the pain they've suffered. But I am a victim, too. I would like another chance to live in society without getting into trouble."

The high school valedictorian was granted three-years' probation and ten months in the Wayne County Jail. With credit for time served, she was halfway home. The public voiced a sharp, immediate criticism with Sapala's slap on the wrist.

351

Spens was a victim? She sidestepped the multitude of *choices* she made. She *chose* drugs from childhood, despite being surrounded by peers who did not. Dawn *chose* to quit school despite being voted valedictorian. She *chose* to move downtown despite a host of other communities open to her. She *chose* prostitution despite being employed. She *chose* Fry over Donnie. She *chose* to rebuke drug rehab despite medically facilitated offers. Dawn *chose* to continue prostituting, despite her father coming to take her home to the suburbs. Spens *chose* to accept cash and gifts from Al even after knowing his true identity and marital status. Last, and not least, Spens *chose* to return to the scene of Al's murder and participate in the cover-up, despite having left unaccompanied while the assault was in progress.

Childhood is handed to us, like a deck of cards. The way we *play* it is free will. Even those who assert they're victims, that they believe in fate, look before crossing a street. Spens' request for a second chance, in fact, illustrated she also believed in the power of choice.

> *Our lives are fashioned by our choices.*
> *First, we make our choices.*
> *Then our choices make us.*
> ---Anne Frank

Spens' sentence was more typical for grand theft or a DUI. Dawn's request to enter Brentwood Rehabilitation, a Canadian drug treatment facility, following her release from jail was denied because Canadian officials pointed out they didn't want felons from the U.S. She was worried about entering a Detroit-based program out of fear of becoming associated with "the dopers and hookers" — her peers. She was transferred from the Wayne County Jail to Dawn Farms Rehab, forty-five minutes west of Detroit in Ypsilanti, Michigan. She regained her freedom March 19, 1986, at the age of twenty-one.

# FORTY

# NO DAYBREAK

It was inevitable. The earlier gush of support dwindled to a trickle. Our would-have-been eleventh wedding anniversary slid by and a new year was underway. It could only be better than the last.

*Officer Landeros beckons me into the Medical Examiner Building then departs. I stand in the booth ready to identify Al's remains. It's brighter than sunlight on the beach. My hands are cuffed behind my back, and I'm told to place my feet over the blue, painted shoeprints on the cement floor. A reporter stands by with notepad and camera. The medical examiner smiles. The lights go out. The medical examiner shines a flashlight on Al's battered head. He turns to speak. Words are not possible. He gurgles and chokes. I try to ask him questions but* am told, "Be quiet."

The nightmare caused me to bolt upright in bed, with perspiration dotting my forehead and neck from the fruitless struggle. I didn't know how to move on but was determined not to become damaged from the trio's licentiousness.

A third, recurring nightmare punctured my much-needed sleep.

*I'm free-falling from the sky. An autumn storm is brewing, and wet, yellow leaves are scattered below. The ground approaches quickly. Al is working on the driveway. I'm tumbling directly toward him. At the last second, Al lifts his face up, smiling.*

Throughout the winter of 1985-86, it was necessary to lower my thermostat, despite freezing temperatures and drafty windows, to save pennies, while draperies were drawn tight. The mountain of papers Al accumulated had been sorted and the majority eliminated. The two-story carriage house was just about empty, except for Chili Pepper. Was homelessness in my future? Just when no more solutions were to be found, an insurance settlement of eight-thousand, nine-hundred-dollars and four cents arrived for the incinerated new Buick.

My feet darted to the stack of unpaid bills. Organized by date, I started to tug myself from the quicksand of red ink. To mail out a payment, I arched my arm toward the shelf in Al's home office closet where our address book was kept. Grasping it, I plopped it down but discovered I'd retrieved our small wedding album instead. It was an unexpected time capsule that crashed into my evening. I inspected each photo with the curiosity of a museum curator for clues of duplicity. If only there was a super spectrographic test to probe his character before we said, "I do." It was impossible to connect with the young woman smiling back from the 5x7s. She did not know she was speeding toward a dead man's curve without a guardrail with her husband at the wheel.

At this point, I aimed for good *hours*—having abandoned the goal of a good *day*. Funds were so low I skipped lunch and conserved electricity by hanging damp laundry near the basement boiler. To conserve my own energy, I wore two pairs of socks. Light bulbs were switched to a lower wattage or avoided, the dishwasher and dryer turned off and errands combined to hoard gas. One night frozen pipes developed in an unused upstairs bathroom but after applying a hair dryer to the pipes and turning up the heat in the house they oozed a rust-colored slush. The careful budgeting reminded me of earlier days in my downtown studio apartment. Never could I have imagined that those accounting skills would be needed a decade later.

It was about this time my sister sent me some family photos from December. In each one I was off to the side, not looking at anyone. My face was drawn, downcast and preoccupied. I looked spectral. None of us were smiling.

In late February, three rough-appearing boys around age thirteen with a younger girl asked to shovel the driveway for a low price. I agreed. I was weary of it. The following morning, they returned demanding more money "because we didn't charge ya 'nough yesterday."

Their tone was provocative. My mood was sour, and fatigue magnified it. "No. Say what you mean and mean what you say. We had an agreement. Live up to it.

I'll pay you more if you want the job next time it snows." That evening, after dusk, there was glass from smashed light bulbs and my light fixtures littering the driveway, steps, and porch.

A new night terror began.

*It's late afternoon in a jungle. The heat and humidity are oppressive. Insects swarm. It's softly raining. Rumbling thunder increases. I'm standing alone peering through thick foliage from a hillside. A feeling of danger is palpable. At the bottom of the hill, I see a weak man inside a bamboo cage. He's trapped, withering, starving. He feebly claws at the cage. Uniformed guards stand by, a man and a woman. They have weapons. He is no match for his captors. I want to help, and he knows I'm nearby, but the situation is futile.*

In a strange, unexpected twist at this time, my attorney informed me of an error in my mother-in-law's house deed. As it was, half the proceeds of the sale of her house—or all of it if she passed away—would become mine. Mrs. Canty requested me to sign off on it—through her attorney—and bestow full rights of ownership to her. I didn't object. Mr. Korachis relayed, in a subsequent phone call, she was not willing to pay the necessary attorney fees to alter her own deed. "Then forget it. It's of no importance to me." A few weeks later, she reversed course and her documents were signed.

At the end of March in 1986, I finally felt ready to visit Al's headstone. I hoped it would help me heal. However, as I prepared that morning the radio announced an assault and robbery of an elderly widow at Elmwood had occurred the previous afternoon as she stood alone at her spouse's gravestone. The news report stopped me dead in my tracks.

In late 1987, Dr. Rutledge called unexpectedly. "Can you drop by? I know it's short notice." Always delighted to visit my steadfast mentor, I rearranged my plans to make it happen. Months had elapsed since we last spoke and there was always a lot to toss around. The following morning, we sat in his cluttered office that smelled of Old Spice and old books. As usual, a sense of calm overtook me. He held his calls. That was different.

After some pleasantries, he paused and turned serious. I long ago memorized his face, mannerisms, gaze. We were always candid. He merited the respect and trust reserved for my own father. He gazed down, tears lining his thoughtful, observant eyes, and said quietly, "I wanted you to hear this from me. It's best done in person." After a weary pause, and barely maintaining his composure, he continued. "I am dying. I'm considering closing the fellowship program and moving to Florida. I want my wife surrounded by our family when I leave her."

Thoughts would not process. Disbelief shielded the full impact of this additional loss. I was grief-stricken and shaking. He had contributed so much to so many. This was unfair and much too premature!

Dr. Rutledge was battling radiation-induced leukemia from delayed exposure working as an Army Chaplain during the bombing of Hiroshima. Oddly, my father had his own fight with leukemia underway. Waves of heartache welled up. I could not meet his eyes. "If I could, I would trade years of my life to extend yours," I finally said aloud to the floor.

Tears welled in his eyes, and he nodded. "I'm glad I was there when you needed me, but this is what fate has planned." We sat in unfamiliar silence, just as I had with my parents the morning we returned from the morgue. My heart was aching. He leaned forward and politely asked, "Would you, could you, consider co-directing the fellowship program to keep it going?"

I uncomfortably groped for words for what felt like an hour. "Dr. Rutledge, I am flattered to be considered. It's an honor, but I must respectfully decline. I'm sure you can find others, but no one can fill your shoes. *No one.* Like you, I'm planning on moving away from here also."

It burdened me greatly to deny his only request, but he preferred honesty and doing what was best for my future. He nodded with acceptance and offered a reassuring hug for the first and last time. Eventually, I said an aching goodbye to a man I revered and learned much from. He bore witness to the best and worst days of my life. He never stopped believing in me or challenging me. We knew we would never speak again in person. He handed me a framed blue and white print from his wall I'd always favored. "I know you admire this but would never ask. Please take it." It depicted a small Mount Fugi in the distance behind the crushing arc of a giant surge. The *Great Wave off Kanagawa* has hung on my wall since.

# FORTY-ONE

# BOOMERANG

Miracles happened. "Tell them I accept." Two springs following Al's hospitalization and six months after the verdicts, new owners for the Tudor materialized. Freedom was finally at hand. The buyers, from England, felt the house reminded them of home. *Wonderful. Take it.* They received a markdown because of the "hidden defect" clause. That is, Michigan's real estate law required informing a purchaser of any violent crime connected with the residence or its owners, in case they were superstitious—even if the wrongdoing did not happen on the property. If ignored, the purchase could be revoked.

On my first day house hunting, I wanted the first place shown me, though my realtor insisted we search further. We did, but I disliked everything else.

The last afternoon at the Tudor, in late June, I surveyed its barren interior, all of which held bittersweet memories. The never-occupied nursery off the master bedroom, the khaki-colored tile my father and I laid on the back porch, the stained-glass kitchen ceiling fixture Dad made... The only item turned up was a small, wooden toy monkey Al kept since childhood. I left it behind. I did not look back. I had to look forward.

My new home was a narrow, garage-less, porch-less 1928 brownstone tucked beneath large elms, within walking distance to stores. Was this the adventure my friend previously mentioned? I drew a long breath, unpacked and became accustomed to the sounds and feel of my new residence and living alone. I thought of it as my safe house.

Just as life softly drifted toward an overdue calm, an unexpected and unwelcomed phone message by a Mr. Lowell Cauffiel intruded.

The Grosse Pointe News reported back in March that this journalist had signed a contract to write a book to chronicle my husband's death, tentatively titled *Siren* — alluding to the illicit sex angle. He'd planned to interview all major participants. The media sucker-punched me before, and I wasn't inviting a return engagement. It was members of the media who paraded silhouetted call girls on the evening news, who elbowed their way into my office waiting room, who shoved the camera in my face at the memorial and the gaggle that preempted us outside the morgue. *Voyeurs! Parasites!*

Was there an escape hatch? I met again with my attorney, Mr. Korachis. To my surprise, he *promoted* cooperation. "*What?!* They've brought nothing but suffering. They don't even get their facts straight! Al was no 'authority on autism,' and some reporter said Dawn was charged with murder, not Fry. Besides, the media's carelessness complicated my caseload! How would you feel if they did that to you?"

Mr. Korachis politely nodded.

"They never gave my patients a *thought!*" My ears reddened. He waited. "One evening newscast displayed a photo of Al and me while the voice-over said, 'Al Canty has been rumored to keep company with this local prostitute!' And you're telling me to *trust him*? To *cooperate*? *NO!*"

Mr. Korachis answered in his systematic manner, "First, there is an amendment protecting the freedom of the press, right?"

I sat taller, stiffer. "But what about *my* ri..."

"Look, if you contribute to it, the book will be accurate. Do understand it'll be written with or without you."

"Why should I care about its accuracy? It's not my publication or my problem. The public made up their minds and returned to their business. I have no energy to be concerned about someone else's pet project."

He tactfully glanced at his watch.

"Besides, people I do care about won't be persuaded by anything some *journalist* writes!" My words echoed in his downtown office. I hadn't realized my voice had become so loud.

He calmly replied, "I can't stop it. A lot of what's out there is a matter of public record—the court transcript, news articles, arrest records and so on."

I gritted my teeth (a habit formed in the last year). "I'll sit this out. No thanks."

Mr. Korachis waited until I'd smoothed my feathers. His elbows rested on his busy desk. "There's a more personal reason to cooperate with him."

"Oh? What would *that* be?" I asked with more sarcasm than intended.

"This author will help answer your questions. The police didn't have time. You repeatedly said you don't understand what happened. Law enforcement solved the case and moved on. Think of this as a…free *service*. Cauffiel has probably taken a leave from other work to devote his full attention to it. Understand, he *will* write it. Can you *think* about that?"

I exhaled deeply and studied his ruby red cufflinks at the end of crisp, white sleeves for what felt like an eternity. "It just seems…invasive, opportunistic. He has no right."

"Yes, legally, he *does*. That's my point."

I stretched my back. "What about *ethically*?"

"Jan, I'm a lawyer, not a priest. You came for my legal opinion. I say go for it."

I wrung my hands with a year's worth of frustration and looked toward the high ceiling of his second-floor office. "*If* the interview goes forward, I'd like some conditions."

"Such as?"

"Well, like review the parts I'm in, to minimize my involvement, before it goes to print."

"He'd probably agree, as long as you don't extend into areas that have little to do with you. You can't ask him to omit or change facts."

"I know. I *get* that. But I want an insignificant role *if* I even agree."

"Well, tell him that. You can't stop him, so hear him out. That's my advice but do what you feel is right."

I left brooding. Everything in me wanted to deny him, but I reluctantly admitted it would be helpful to have questions answered. It seemed each decision shadowing me had far-reaching consequences.

In anticipation of another contact, I researched this writer. What stories had Cauffiel written? Were they sensationalized? What motivated him? Had he blurred opinion and fact? Did he skimp on research? Unfortunately, he was highly regarded in his field. Still, I didn't budge. Why would a man want to be weighed down by a load that wasn't his to carry? I believed peace of mind came from minding your own business. But I also believed that moving on meant I first needed to learn the ugly truth and I wasn't about to get that from Gladys, the police or Al's headstone.

# FORTY-TWO

# UNLATCHED

In late autumn, crisp breezes hoisted swirling leaves like red and orange butterflies. They accumulated along curbs and under outstretched branches, resembling colorful skirts around tree trunks. My feet hurried to get inside in search of warm fleece. The back door to my cozy brownstone was poorly illuminated and, as usual, finding the keyhole at night was a challenge. I reminded myself again to leave a light on near the rear entrance window.

Stepping inside with my back to the wall while pausing on the landing, I locked the door. Suddenly there was a soft tap in the middle of my back while I stood in the darkness. I froze with terror and listened intently. My mind raced through a couple of ugly scenarios while the old grip of fear flooded my body and mind. There was no sound except my quickened breathing.

I then abruptly darted forward into the kitchen only to hear the handle of my broom—which had apparently loosened from its hook—fall to the floor behind me. I exhaled and felt foolish. I was so tired of living on the edge, assuming the worst, waiting for the other shoe to drop.

Several months later, on July 13, the first anniversary of Al's death, the Detroit News published a lengthy blow-by-blow. Cauffiel authored it. The article glared back over my breakfast, smack dab on the cover of the weekend section. *"Masquerade: The Strange Life and Death of W. Alan Canty."* I felt stalked 24/7/365. Where was my safety zone? I'd developed symptoms of what had been called "media terror"—re-traumatization from media glare following a crime. I was comforted knowing I'd moved from the beautiful prison, legally changed my name and phone, learned how to use a sidearm and lived nearer to other people, yet his publication still plunged a wedge into my cloistered world. I was snagged between the right of the media to inform the public and my right to privacy.

> *Al knocks on the door. He surprises me with tickets to New York City for Valentine's Day. He is smiling. It's snowing lightly but feels warm. I ask him if anyone else is coming. He answers by handing me tomorrow's newspaper and walks toward his car.*

It happened again in August of 1987. Detroit Monthly featured a cover story revealing excerpts of Cauffiel's book which was underway. Page one: *"Masquerade: His double life and shocking death became the crime story of the decade. Now for the first time, the truth behind psychologist W. Alan Canty's seduction, compulsion, and murder."*

Again, the author called me at work and indicated his book was moving forward. I curtly told him it was not a priority in my world. The following week he again requested an interview, explaining it would be a great opportunity. "For whom?" I asked. He sounded professional and non-defensive. Memories of my meeting with my attorney returned. With prolonged foot-dragging, I agreed to one interview, if only to make him go away.

We awkwardly introduced ourselves after my last appointment in my office. Lowell's questions pinged like a pinball in search of a target. I was tight, on guard and full of doubt. But before long, I peppered the author with questions of my own. As I did, bits and pieces popped in and out of my head like frames of old home movies. Morgue. Cigarettes. McDonald's bag. Hospitalization. Graduation. Phone calls late in the night from a drugged lunatic with a Southern drawl and murderous agenda.

Lowell delivered answers. They were grim, but I wanted the truth. We spent the following six months in intense, collaborative discussion—trying together to piece the story of a storytelling spouse into a coherent narrative.

There was an eeriness behind the book itself. It turned out the racecar Al owned—which he referred to as the Miller Racecar—was previously owned by the author's father. Lowell rode in the old vehicle that had been in my carriage house when he was a child.

Old Miller Race Car with Al in driver's seat. He was working on it in our driveway one humid afternoon.

When Lowell described his interview with Dawn he said, "She seduced me exactly as she seduced Alan, and probably had no idea she was doing it. Or maybe she did. She was a portrait of pathos. I wrote her in jail saying I was willing to help her get out of 'the life' by getting into drug treatment, and when I started interviewing her, I realized she was working me like a trick. I fell for it hook, line and sinker, and saw how Alan could have been manipulated by her."

Fry made a different impression. "John is excellent at feigning remorse. His is the ultimate, Machiavellian, psychopathic personality. He knows what's practical is practical, and he sees and does everything in terms of himself. He's not connected inside; unaffected by things that affect normal people. He figured maybe I could help him with his appeal and, besides, he likes the attention. In prison, he's a star." Lowell found Lucky to be "entertaining, charming, almost convincing and quite bright."

As I feared, in mid-1988, the news covered the upcoming release of Cauffiel's book on the evening broadcast. News anchor, Dana Eubanks, said, "This book 'Masquerade' promises a terrifying exploration of how little we know about people we trust. Author Cauffiel says it's about appearances."

Talk shows boosted *Masquerade* which escalated insensitive questions by people not in a need to know. It was so familiar, so draining. How many more times would someone ask, "How could you not know?" This always implied to me that obvious clues existed and, had they been in my shoes, they would have certainly seen them. Subtext "shame on you, fool."

> *It is an iron rule of history*
> *that what looks inevitable in hindsight*
> *was far from obvious at the time.*
> ---Yuval Noah Harari

*Al... I'm calling for Al..."* After the press picked up the story about *Masquerade,* three eerie messages flustered me after work on my home answering machine over a two-week period. Coincidence? The intrusions all came around four in the afternoon from a female or young male, speaking in a hurried, whispered voice. I handed over the audiotape to my attorney for safekeeping. Another change of phone number and installation of a security system. *Who uttered those words? Why would they harass me? How had the caller obtained my latest unlisted phone number?*

During another early morning meeting with Lowell, he hesitated, seemed unusually restrained, and asked, "Did the police tell you...? Did they explain...?" He uncharacteristically picked his words carefully and momentarily broke eye contact. "Ah, I know, from the police, that Dawn wasn't the first, the very first...um, prostitute Alan solicited." His words filled the air like pungent fumes. "Alan's fingerprints were taken for a solicitation conviction from February 28, 1983. They used that record, his fingerprints, for a positive i.d. hours before you came to the morgue."

No wonder Detective Landeros was confident it was him.

The floor beneath me opened up. At this moment I felt shredded by Al's lies and by Lowell's truths. How could I have been so unwise? So trusting? So...*irrelevant?*

Officer Bando, likewise, told me later of an enlightening, disturbing, validating discussion with a twenty-year-old hooker named Sheila Blanton also in 1983. She told Bando of a Dr. Canty who offered to set her up in an apartment when she was nineteen so she could straighten out her life. She died from an overdose the day after she disclosed this to Bando, who learned of her death the same week as Al's murder.

A pattern emerged. Carla McGuire—Al's student at Henry Ford Community College—was twenty-three when Al was thirty-six and married to Maggie. When we dated, Al was forty, and I was twenty-two. Al was forty-nine when Sheila was nineteen. Al was fifty when Dawn was nineteen. Buster was drawn very to young women without resources, likely sensing their vulnerability in the way other men catch the blade thin aroma of a woman's perfume. *Was it a coincidence that we (at those ages) all had long chestnut hair parted in the middle, without college, living on our own and lacking sophistication? Had this cardboard cutout of a husband been a sex buyer throughout our marriage? Was this his old 'go to'? His default?*

Like a distraught homeowner salvaging rubble from their incinerated dwelling, I needed *something* to redeem from our ten-year marriage. Was it *all* a hoax? I was the last to be clued in.

The pattern undeniably pointed to more indiscretions the further my training proceeded. Al needed to be front row and center. The Authority. Big Daddy. A Talking Head.

Lucky dominated through intimidation, Dawn by her physicality and Al by what he gave monetarily.

# FORTY-THREE

# AL'S REARVIEW

Was it predictable? My loyalty misplaced? Much too late I was on a mission to learn more about my husband's developmental and dating history. What piloted him toward his grisly end? Tidbits were assembled from former classmates, home movies, mementos, photographs, news clippings, high school yearbooks, greeting cards, police reports and the book that came out after his slaying. With greater clarity, it seemed Al was reared in a window display. One side, the public side, glistened with strategically placed lights and props all positioned to give the most attractive impact while the backside was held together with tension, denials, and secrets. Even the extended family could not peek there. Unfortunately, the rearview was never the preview.

Al's earliest years took form under sheltering cascades of mature elms on Chalmers Boulevard in a quiet area of eastern Detroit within an immaculate, roomy, two-story white Dutch colonial. The neighborhood was nicknamed "Little Venice" for its boat canals, custom, two-story homes, and recreational water vehicles. The front side, the public side, had majestic Roman columns as a backdrop to a rose garden carefully tended by his hard-working mother, Gladys. The curb appeal was peaceful and orderly.

Inside was not.

An only child, Al was dubbed "Buster" (or "Bus") from the 1903 Buster Brown comic strip. His mother, Gladys, bought the identical breed of dog and outfitted her son as Buster Brown on his first day of kindergarten, complete with blunt-cut blond hair cascading to his collar. He met his classmates wearing an ensemble of a wide, wool hat, large bandana, and shiny Buster Brown shoes. The onlookers pointed at his vintage clothes, reducing him to an outcast his first day of school. The name "Buster" (or "Bus") stuck, and commonly used by his mother during burgeoning disagreement or worry.

Although Al was named after his father, they did not want confusion between them, so they placed a "W" in front of their son's name. Many guessed it stood for "William," "Warren" or "Wayne," but Al's private joke was it stood for "Whatever-you-think."

My lumbering father-in-law was viewed as the only "doctor" among the parents of Al's friends. They also saw him as serious, self-absorbed and odd. Al Senior once volunteered to demonstrate hypnotism at his son's party. Many felt it had a tinge of "sleaze" to it but did not protest.

*If I had one day*
*when I didn't have to be all confused*
*and I didn't have to feel that I was ashamed of everything.*
*if I felt that I belonged someplace...*
—Dean's character, Jim Stark in *Rebel Without a Cause*

Al Senior—formerly employed in Detroit's traffic court—did not demonstrate pride in his namesake. A former coworker, Doris DeDecker, recalled when Al Senior, "took Al junior into the office and yelled and *yelled*. I mean it was horrible. It's not the sort of temper you expect to see between father and son, especially at a business place. There were no holds barred. I mean, he blasted this kid and called him lots of names, including 'stupid.' It was shocking. He never spoke of him with any pride, with love. The only references I ever heard were that he wished his son was doing something else; he wished he was smarter. If he got that kind of thing at the office, imagine what he got at home."

Al predictably developed into a socially awkward teen and regarded by some as a "mama's boy" for the pampering, generous allowances and nicknames Gladys bestowed upon him, to which he responded with an invitation to fight—a clear indicator this was on point. Buster performed in high school theater and fiddled with cars but was not especially popular or gifted mechanically, athletically or academically. Al spent weeks memorizing clumsy pickup lines. In fact, he approached life as theater, waiting in the wings to go on stage anticipating sought-after applause and admiration. Meanwhile, he often sat alone at parties, sometimes reading a book.

Al liked to tempt fate. Why not? Afterall, his parents

negated the consequences of bad decisions by pulling him out of jams. He once bragged to me he drove down a one-way street in the wrong direction in front of a patrol car, deliberately, brazenly, leisurely. He then opened his window and quipped, "My dad is Al Canty, Senior. Know him? He teaches at the Academy." Abracadabra.

Al in the driveway of his parents' home on Chalmers Drive

What made this bizarre was that Al's father launched his career by devising a profile of high-risk drivers who caused the most accidents back in the mid-1930s. Several states put his model to use which various insurance companies refined and adopted to tailor insurance premiums. A publication from 1953—when his son would have been 23—referred to Al Canty, Senior as a "traffic psychotechnologist." He wrote that problem drivers "may not merely be thoughtless or careless; they may actually be insane and have a personality maladjustment" with "contempt for social and legal conventions." Which side of the fence was he on?

A judge finally halted Al Senior's rescues, and the young problem driver served five days in county jail, the very place that later housed Spens and Fry. This consequence was likely too little and a lot too late because traffic offenses went unabated. Al Senior understood, theoretically, of the importance of obeying laws and briefly taught criminology at Wayne State University in the 1950s. This was another glimpse of life behind the public store window. In any event, Al never learned to respect danger because he didn't face the penalties for behaving dangerously. Instead, he flirted with it.

Al's developmental history did not prepare him for dating (nor adulthood) which is why he would recruit a buddy to help him land a date or rely on clumsy props and pick-up lines.

Al was close to Skip Russell who introduced him to Ray Danford, and both remained his loyal friends until the end.

The Canty family was regarded among his peers as having excessive money and deficient restrictions. Friends saw him as pampered, though seldom mentioned it. Females in the group liked Al, but not romantically. One described him as a "quiet nerd" who was "stiff" and "awkward." He earned a reputation for lacking social graces, by actions such as cleaning his ear at a party, sitting alone near the loud music, wiping the contents on the lapel of his new suit. He was known as the last to laugh. An old high school friend told me years later their group regarded him as "fascinated with deceit." It popped up in discussions at Al's initiation. He took a youthful pride in the shallow scams he pulled off.

Al identified with James Dean. The famous actor earned a degree in drama, over protests from Dean's father, drove exhilarating racecars, was viewed as sexy and became internationally famous for glamorizing the disenfranchised. One of Dean's enduring films, *Rebel Without a Cause,* centered on a restless, upper-middle-class teen (Jim Stark) who felt marginalized and misunderstood. After getting into trouble, Jim's appearance-conscious parents rescued him by relocating to get a fresh start which, of course, cushioned him from the consequences of his misdeeds. Dean's character was anxious to fit in and eager for honest communication with his parents, along with their own admission of pretense, of two-facedness. The title for this movie was adapted from psychiatrist Robert Lindner's book, *Rebel Without a Cause: The Story of a Criminal Psychopath* which Al later displayed prominently on his office shelves.

Al admitted to his old high school friend Ray that he identified with the film because it showed hypocrisy in families where negative emotions, were forbidden and denied—especially publicly. Al took notice that Dean's character was an outsider, a rebel without an obvious reason. Al predicted he would own a red Porsche, identical to Dean's, and later did. He also purchased a red jacket like Dean's in *Rebel* and learned how to dangle his cigarettes, posing as he did. Like Dean, Al drove recklessly and had a Siamese cat much liked the one Dean owned, named Marcus, which was a gift from Elizabeth Taylor. Was it a coincidence we later had three? Neither men were especially tall; both smoked heavily, owned horn-rimmed glasses and consumed hefty quantities of coffee with a contemplative look.

Al's adolescent attraction to the performing arts was likely augmented by his father's longstanding involvement in amateur theater. Al Senior was a proud member of the *Players,* an exclusive, all-male theater group who met in a prominent building on East Jefferson Avenue bearing the same name. They held "frolics" (plays) in the Shakespearean tradition. The Players' enjoyed late-night drinking revelries in their men's only pub following the productions and were expected to wear black tie and evening attire. Before becoming a new member, the applicant needed endorsement by two current members. Women were allowed to work in the office and applaud.

Al admired the Players' stately two-story brick structure, constructed in 1925, in the regal style of a sixteenth-century English Renaissance hall. Its massive rooms were crowned with dark, heavy beams arching over thick, wooden plank flooring with three twenty-foot leaded, arched windows. The tinted light seemed to emanate from an earlier century. The main hall displayed six Art Deco tapestries while the east end housed ten aristocratic stone sculptures dramatically illuminated by large iron chandeliers. The centerpiece of the entire structure, the stage, was four stories tall and faced a distant balcony with separate fireplace. It was all capped by a thick orange-tiled roof. The Players Club was, and remains, opulent, imposing and restricted.

In speaking with others who knew Al well, I learned years later that my spouse had a pattern of arranging things "just so." In high school, he created a homemade theater project merely to lure the homecoming queen to star in it. A short time later, he participated in his senior play, *The Royal Family,* originally an acclaimed

Broadway production, about an eccentric family faced with a decision to follow a conventional, domestic existence or erratic, adventurous life in the theater.

Al took an interest in fellow cast member, Betty Noble. They dated, but she found him controlling, critical, stubborn and overly invested in appearances. He behaved as if they were always on stage, instructing her into a fashionable and higher-status girlfriend wherein he would correct her grammar, suggest imposing words and recommend different clothing. He even advised postural changes and alternate hairstyles. He expected her to edit and type his term papers.

While Al was away at Hillsdale College, Betty put an end to their dating. He returned with a lump on his arm, claiming cancer, and begged for reconsideration. She stood firm. The following week she received a telegram, supposedly from the Mayo Clinic, alleging he was dying. Betty showed the plaintive message to her father who, in turn, contacted Al Senior to get his son to back off. It was done.

Al's conduct with Betty eerily paralleled his longstanding fascination with the outdated play *Pygmalion* by Bernard Shaw. The theme involved an English professor, Henry Higgins, who bet Colonel Pickering that in only a few months he would transform the uneducated, cockney-speaking, bedraggled Eliza Doolittle to pass for a mannerly duchess with flawless diction at an ambassador's garden party. Higgins succeeded but grew bored with his project.

Al also had a reputation for lying for no reason other than to see if he could get away with it, much like Buster Brown. Donna told me when Al was nineteen, he brought his mother's new diamond ring — a Christmas gift from his father — into Donna's car and insisted she try it on, first claiming he bought it for his date. It was one example of why his peers saw him as different, on the margins, sneaky, yet likable.

Al's pals would remember him for his elaborate schemes, one of which involved another love interest who did not reciprocate. Rather than let it go he rented a room across the hall from her family and befriended them to keep tabs on her. Eventually, he was the only guy her parents allowed her to date. After he succeeded, he hastily abandoned her. No challenge left. Job done. He bragged about this charade to his male friends, never showing embarrassment or regret. His goal was to outwit and walk away with a chuckle, earning him a reputation among his classmates as being "book smart and life stupid."

He was also known to have a particular preference for women he dated. Most had long, brown hair parted in the middle, were younger, without resources nor a college education and impressed with Al's position in life. Al underestimated his first wife entirely. Maggie Goodwin appeared to be a struggling single mother during graduate school when they married. However, she seamlessly blossomed in her career. They had ongoing tension over money in their marriage, which ended several years later.

I became aware Al's father shared an office in the Fisher Building with his son at one time but not that his name was on the lease. The elder Canty's space contained a large desk, locked credenza, and daybed. The solid entrance door (without lettering to explain the room's purpose) was another facet of the mystery behind the public window display.

# PART THREE

## RECOVERY

# FORTY-FOUR

# CONNECTING THE DOTS

Detroiters scratched their heads. Theories were created, traded and debated as the shameful story surfaced across airwaves and print press. How could this improbable melodrama have launched—let alone *persist*— for eighteen secretive months? The primary individuals involved appeared as unlikely chums as toddlers learning to skydive. The differences between them were painfully obvious, but this begged the more provocative question. How were they *similar*?

Al, John, and Dawn all lusted for deceit. They shared a compulsory attraction for ploys, a hidden agenda. They mastered plausible, glib explanations, like actors on a stage. They passed themselves off as "conventional folk" when useful, keeping their façade in check. Their alliance deceived the wider community and contained internal deceit, too. As a teen, Al created elaborate lies to obtain and keep dates. He had an alias, lied about the year of his

382

divorce and so much more.

Interestingly, Dawn's first impression of Al was he seemed to "wear a mask." Detective Landeros found lies sprinkled among the truths of Dawn's formal statement. Spens pleaded for money from her mother to escape Detroit following a rape that never happened. She watched with detachment as Fry fleeced Al for inflated bail money following her seventh arrest. As for Fry, he had spouted so many falsehoods to McMaster that even his accomplice didn't understand the motive behind my husband's murder. Fry went as far as *planning* to deceive, which is why he carried various identifications. Logic was often in the eye of the logician.

Second, they were so focused on immediate gratification, they did not weigh consequences. They lived in the moment. *They were survival machines.* Common sense was elbowed aside by a persistent, heady feeling of invincibility. *They were reward-driven risk-takers.* It's not that they were incapable of *seeing* ramifications, but they so urgently sought immediate rewards that consequences were dismissed like shooing off flies at a picnic. They lived life deliberately speeding on the center line. When Al used his birthday money to cruise the red-light district, when he handed over the photo album of our house, when he pried up paving bricks from abandoned inner city streets, he did not consider the consequences because Al focused on immediate gratification. And, why not? He was rescued from facing the consequences. Dawn continued to inject dangerous levels of drugs before she healed from previous hospitalizations. She repeatedly climbed into semi-trucks in an industrial part of the city close to expressway entrance ramps leading to who-knows-where. Fry doubtfully considered the probability of contracting Hepatitis C from his carelessness and impulsively telephoned the aunt he intended on murdering, giving her time to flee. Life was a role of the dice. What mattered was now, the next minute, con, or high.

Third, all three were skilled at exploitation. They had, as it were, a "vulnerability radar." Al sought the company of young women who lacked funds and formal education. He played the role of rescuer. Dawn feigned helplessness with sex buyers to line her pockets. When Cauffiel interviewed her behind bars, she "worked him like a trick." And John pimped young, vulnerable women to feed his addictions. All three learned there was never a shortage of targets ripe for the taking.

Last, they feigned emotions. They could be likable and agreeable when it met their needs, but words were just word deep. They were as disconnected emotionally from conversations as an interpreter. When Al greeted me at Detroit Metro, following my return from Arizona, he pantomimed the role of happy husband. Dawn play-acted lust no matter how unappealing her trick. And, as for John, he was as well behaved in court as his attorney. Lowell found him "entertaining, charming, almost convincing." The trio were social chameleons. They all sang the lyrics without the capacity to feel the melody.

Besides parallels in their behavior, some historical facts of their lives lined up, too. All had been institutionalized one or more times (and all had taken their turns in the Wayne County Jail). Early in life, Al and Dawn were psychiatrically hospitalized. This was a clear indication of their difficulty harmonizing with society and their need for external structure to contain their impulses.

Second, all had verbally abusive fathers who evaded the consequences of their tirades. None of their mothers interceded on their behalf.

Third, they all had addictions. Al loved caffeine, nicotine, and adrenalin. Spens and her "helluva good man" consumed street drugs at an electrifying rate. Time was measured by scams and grams.

A fourth similarity was their exposure to criminality early in their lives in a manner that normalized it. Dawn was encouraged to correspond with a felon as a teen and witnessed—if not experienced—domestic violence. Al's father regularly provided animated stories of criminals over dinner and John was severely, repeatedly brutalized by his father with full awareness of family members.

But there was much that Al's parents did right. The usual struggles of troubled families—alcoholism, violence, job loss, infidelity, poverty, divorce, or incarceration—were absent in the Canty household, so why the unhealthy urges in their son?

No single fact, theory or anecdote could explain the complex dynamics of Al's personality, nor anyone else's. What is helpful is to step back and see the forest for the trees. One clue may lie in my in-law's parenting style. They raised Buster as "authoritarian parents," with rigid adherence to their rules long past their usefulness. They failed to make the leap from what was best for them, to what was best for each person. Al was cast into the role of high-functioning puppet. Authoritarian parents cling to strategies from toddlerhood, falling back on control, shame, disapproval, and rescue, while underutilizing humor, affection, reasoning, and trial-and-error learning. *A confident, independent child is threatening.* The Canty's wanted to orchestrate many behaviors of Al, and later of me. To the degree possible they wanted to manage who he socialized with, where he'd go to school, what he'd major in, who he'd marry, what he'd do for a living. They wrote and provided a script and woe unto him if he violated it. My husband described his mother as "the ultimate passive aggressor"—indirectly hostile and controlling. Open disagreements were forbidden. I certainly never saw them.

The children of authoritarian parents "know their place" and are not treated as autonomous adults. So, Al did not function as one. Mrs. Canty suggested we not occupy the master bedroom, recommending a smaller one. She addressed Al as "Buster" and fashioned her own, juvenile nickname for me. One Christmas Gladys gave me a sweater from the children's department—which I discovered when I returned it, as I'm allergic to wool. When Gladys gave him five-hundred-dollars for his 50th birthday, she commented he "was a big boy now." His parents unintentionally embarrassed him when he was nineteen while hosting a surprise birthday party. They invited Buster's friends, decorating the house in a fall theme, with streamers, cartoonish matching paper plates and ice cream slices with turkeys molded into them, more suitable for a boy in elementary school. Buster was teased about this later, rendering him an outcast again. And for "keeping his place" he was "rewarded" with tuition, fancy meals, and rescues, which was how he treated me early in our marriage and why we grew apart when I was no longer "in my place." As long as I was admiring and in need of his resources we were balanced.

My in-laws were invested in commanding, not understanding. There is a parallel between authoritarian parents and a driver's education car where the instructor overuses their controls. Thus, the learner is not afforded full trial-and-error learning which undermines self-confidence, and necessary skills. Ever present to make decisions and avert danger, the instructor guides through directives and rescues. The takeaway lesson is the child believes there is little personal stake in the outcome because it's neutralized, no concern about natural consequences, because they are cushioned from them. This is similar to the "affluenza" defense of Ethan Couch.

The Cantys, like all parents, treated Al as an extension of themselves. They rewarded behavior which paralleled their own and punished that which didn't, and at times, to excess. Most of this was unconscious, but that did not lessen the impact. Their need for control produced a son who struggled with self-control. Their attempts to potty train him at a few months illustrated their need for control. Children reared by authoritarian parents are socially awkward and burdened with self-doubt. They sense their lack of life skills which their peers possess. Errors are a kick in the gut, not a teaching moment. Al obtained self-esteem through external affirmation — something he constantly sought. He wanted badly to be part of the fold, to have honest communication with his parents and forge his own identity, but never succeeded at that. No wonder Al identified with Dean's *Rebel Without a Cause*.

Besides parenting style, another clue was the Canty's over-concern with public opinion, much like the parents in *Rebel*. Al viewed his parents as hypercritical. Mrs. Canty withheld valuable information even during Al's psychiatric hospitalization. She sent me a Happy

Anniversary card after his blatant infidelity and murder. It was only through Lowell's book I learned of his first brief "stint" in jail. Gladys maintained a blackmail theory until she died, despite a landslide of information to the contrary. She never attended legal proceedings that would challenge her views. Al Senior was hell-bent on his son earning a Ph.D. — perhaps because he did not have a legitimate one. Children in homes where image is central, grew up disinclined to tell the truth. Where there is secrecy, there is fear of discovery and hypocrisy. However, through mentoring and gift-giving, Al temporarily filled his "emotional holes." He was looked up to, affirmed. No wonder Al over-identified with Higgins in *Pygmalion*.

***The key to leading a double life is having been forced to live one as a child.***

The hypocrisy and secrets which he grew up with paved the way for him to conceal the truth of our finances and marriage. Appearances trumped reality. He did not want me going through his papers and was unfaithful at least by the third year of our marriage. Al was so skilled at keeping secrets, even his treating staff at the University of Michigan hospital failed to understand what was behind the mask. (I often wondered if anyone asked *them* how they could not know.) Al took delight in describing the entire charade to his old friend Ray, not grasping Ray's lack of amusement at his double life.

Even the hang-ups, car theft, disapproval from Ray, hospitalization, knife to his rib cage, debt, disagreements at home, jeopardizing his psychology license, ridicule from Spens and repeated requests for money from his mother, even with all those warnings, he could not, or would not, admit he courted disaster. He play-acted dutiful son, faithful husband, hardworking therapist and busy physician. He tempted fate, like smoking near a "spontaneously combustible" sign.

My husband's behavior could not be explained as a temporary response to stress, a lapse of judgment. Even calling it a midlife crisis severely underestimated the pervasiveness of his fixation. These *lifelong* patterns were *marbleized* into his personality. Al sought admiration and a guaranteed audience. These moorings held us together until the "storm" of my growing independence pulled us apart. He then substituted Dawn and John and undermined their attempts at independence to ensure having an audience, of being needed even to the point of supplying illegal drugs. Had Dawn invested the money he gave her into education, business or other self-betterment goals, had she "grown up on him," he would've left skid marks.

But this was not the entire story. What of my part in this sordid drama? Everyone had a role of some kind.

The "before me" searched for my future. I lacked clear goals and a "map" of how to get from A to B. The era in which I grew up with infused with sexism. Each flame that sparked inside me was met with drizzle in school. My brother's and school counselor's attempts to put me in my place increased my determination. "I will show you!" was my byline. But how?

Even on the brink of high school graduation, I could not engage my parents in a useful discussion of future careers, and the only college grads I knew were my teachers whom I did not admire. The few people I met who had been out of the country were former military. The conventional community I grew up in was mostly high school educated, middle income and not especially driven to explore other continents, delay marriage or postpone a family. My female neighbors did not work outside the home or relocate to another state. They most certainly did not attend graduate school or live alone in the inner city.

The view from my little studio apartment around 1972 across from the Fisher Building (which was torn down to make way for the New Center Building).

So, by age eighteen I knew more of what I *didn't* want for my life, than what I did. My parents made it clear once we left the cocoon we were on our own. This was likely based on their wish to delay our emancipation, but also because they genuinely couldn't afford to support any of us with an apartment, car, tuition or other expenses associated with independent living. I was never offered help from anyone about securing a scholarship and never saw myself as "college material." I sought independence but groped in fog. Al was the first to enthusiastically support my dreams of college, and beyond. Considering the parallels between Eliza Doolittle and me was painful but undoubtedly accurate. But where would my path have led, were it not for Al's belief in me?

I left home with trust and belief in marriage, never questioning the comings and goings of family members. Harm originating *inside* the household never crossed my mind. My parents drove home the need to respect others and take responsibility. I wrongly assumed Al shared these values.

I failed to take at least one valuable lesson from my parents. They cautioned never to overvalue someone because of education, money or power. They asked, more than once, "Would you want to live without garbage collection, stocked store shelves or mail delivery? All jobs have value. Just do your work, whatever it is, do it honestly. We need everyone." Had I looked beyond Al's education and pseudo-stability I may have been less awestruck, more aware of the dynamics of our relationship and his family. We started as coworkers and drifted back to those roles. Over time, I could not provide him with the admiration, naiveté and guaranteed audience he needed. In turn, he could not offer me honesty, fidelity, interdependence or vulnerability.

The fact that Al was nearly twenty years older, and I was often away at class, undoubtedly influenced the outcome of our life. I had little investment in our house and neighborhood. We did not even furnish the living room until I started my private practice. I allowed Al to worry about finances initially, though wanted a change over time. I was sold on the "sizzle," never evaluating the steak. Had I been older, had he not shown enthusiasm for my aspirations, had we been home together more... Well, who is to say?

# FORTY-FIVE

# RED ZONE

I'm often asked, "How did you get through it?" Without a doubt, it was because of my parents. Thankfully, I was never beaten with an ax handle. At no time did my mother encourage me to write letters to a felon and I was never sent to school in an outfit from a previous century. Never would they negate the natural consequences of illegal behavior. My father would not even think about battering my mother. Quite the contrary. I never doubted their devotion to one another, nor our belonging to our bigger "tribe" of relatives whom we valued.

My favorite picture of my parents (around 1979)

The more decades I have spent as a psychologist, the more I appreciate how I was raised. Our parents modeled integrity, trust, perseverance, empathy, discipline, and love. They were not our friends, rescuers, abusers or enablers. Were they perfect? No. But they promoted and exhibited self-reliance and gratitude. Were they fair? Pretty much. Strict? Very. Predictable? Absolutely. They were involved in our endeavors and attempted to reason with us as we aged. Both could admit when they were wrong and did not hesitate to congratulate us on a job well done. Both had a sense of humor. With maturity, we earned increased freedom and gained self-confidence. They encouraged individuality. We were not raised to think we were a nuisance, invincible or entitled. They never accepted excuses or procrastination in carrying out an order. In fact, there were no empty warnings, no second "requests." They underscored the importance of treating others as we would want to be treated, regardless of their position in life and of paying it forward. At the end of the day, we answered to ourselves. That, they pointed out repeatedly, was more significant than answering them, a friend, even a court of law. We learned early our life would be the summation of our decisions and those decisions impacted others. No one was an island. One's integrity was the measure of worth. Our purpose in life was to leave the world better than we found it. The route didn't matter. The magnitude could be small. Everything was on the table. That goal could be accomplished through art, mechanics, teaching or parenting, but it was the least we could do.

Our parents backed up their words with action. One time I hid in the drapes around age five to eavesdrop on their adult conversation, unaware my feet stuck out. My father sat me down in the next room and said, "These people are guests in this house and must be respected and made to feel welcome. You go in there and apologize to them — *now*." On another occasion my brother rode his bike across the lawns of two neighbors creating an obvious muddy strip. My father marched him over to each house and not only made him apologize but committed him to cutting their lawns for the next month without pay. If he did a lousy job or failed to show up every Saturday, the "service" would be extended another month.

But the door swung both ways and they would back us up when an adult disrespected us. There was an incident where my high school band instructor demoted me from first chair to last chair because I forgot to bring a red pencil for marking up the music. He spoke sharply in the process and I felt like quitting. (I'd worked my way up to that position over one and a half years). My mom, just a hint over five feet tall, came to school the next afternoon and ordered the foot-taller teacher to "sit down and listen to me as if I was your judge and jury." He stupidly tried to ignore her. That was... ineffective. He never treated me unfairly again. Without me consciously knowing it, she was showing me how to be assertive in an era where women were supposed to know their place.

Because of my parents, I believed effort could make tomorrow better. I recoiled at self-pity, cruelty, laziness, and indifference to suffering. Growing up in Detroit reinforced the necessity of resilience, independence, even grit. Neither that annoying school counselor nor the unholy triangle was enough to crush me. Not by a long shot.

*She became the kind of woman*
*that when her feet hit the floor in the morning*
*the devil said, "Oh crap, she's up!"*
-----unknown

My parents taught me adversity not only built character, it *revealed* it. What adversity revealed with respect to Fry is that he never matured emotionally beyond toddlerhood—he was fundamentally immature, egocentric and selfish. Fry lacked patience, generosity, insight and foresight, just like any two-year-old. And, like them, he had meltdowns when things got tough, was unresponsive to reasoning and incapable of self-care. Demonstrations of empathy were limited to small children. Like most toddlers, Fry regarded kindness as a weakness to exploit with threats and by instilling a sense of obligation. He was stuck psychologically in the "terrible twos."

As for Spens, adversity led her to exploit others, first Carlton, then Fry and finally my spouse. Judge Sapala and Dr. Abramsky held the opinion that she was highly dependent. Her attorney put forth the "he made me do it" defense. But this so-called "dependency" was an affectation, a role, a means to exploit. When faced with adversity, she manipulated others to keep herself afloat because self-preservation was always her goal. She was a fearless risk-taker who used charm to influence. Like Fry, Spens regarded gentleness as a weakness to exploit. She also played on people's caretaker instincts and took full advantage through hard luck stories, guilt trips and instilling a sense of duty to her. Skills of manipulation and blame were used to get what she wanted, along with playing people off each other. She pushed one person until they were depleted and moved onto the next. And rather than be stressed by chaos, she thrived on it. At the end of the day, how did she answer to herself? How would she describe her integrity, her probity, her support of other women?

And when Al faced adversity, he regressed into a needy teenager in search of financial rescue and a young, approving female, not unlike Professor Higgins.

Learning trauma in the classroom was one thing. *Experiencing* it was another. My parents correctly cautioned books don't teach everything. The first trauma lesson was Al's death. The second was media exploitation. The third was losing my sense of safety. The fourth was identifying his head in the morgue. I could recite chapter and verse about the diagnosis, treatment, risk factors, comorbidity and prognosis of PTSD, as could any first-year psychology student. My insomnia, irritability, jumpiness, avoidance, fatigue, and nightmares were inevitable, a normal reaction to an abnormal event. Training as a psychologist did offer benefits. I "got" the fact that nightmares were part of healing and nothing to fear. I'd seen progress in persons with trauma over time. I never lost sight of people in every corner of the earth with much more suffering than mine. All one needed to do was pick up a history book or watch any news app on any day to find it. The most vulnerable — our children, mentally challenged and the frail elderly — were not even spared. The early support I received from friends, Detective Landeros, Dr. Rutledge, Dr. Hillenberg and family had undoubtedly been critical. In short, I did not overturn this mess alone. It took a *team* to do that. I was fortunate to have had them.

But there was a downside to being a psychologist,

too. Some expected more than could be delivered. "You're resilient. You'll get through it," or "You're *trained* for this kind of thing. You'll be *fiiiine*." I kept my nightmares, money worries, sleepless nights in a 3900-square-foot unwanted prison to myself, projecting an image of being "on the mend." Yet, I was one of the lucky ones. I had my education, health, supportive family and future of some kind. I never wanted pity. I was not open to unsolicited advice. I lived in a society, and worked in a profession, that valued stoicism, self-reliance, and the ability to overcome. I allowed my personality, profession and societal norms to add pressure, but drowning my sorrows in alcohol, blaming others or not meeting obligations was never an option. I did feel dazed and alone in the rubble. I couldn't go back to my old life but wasn't sure how to move forward either. My husband's murder and its fallout affected who I was, who I would become.

Over time, some individuals dropped their guard and allowed gallows humor to fly. A store clerk joked, "He got upset and lost his head." An intoxicated man at a neighbor's bar-b-que, whom I did not know, remarked, "I hear it was a home run." *Ugh*. These remarks were not amusing. *Ever*. They were dismissive, offensive and unforgivable.

Sometimes I wanted to grab particular individuals by their lapels, yank them close and ask, "Do you hear what comes out of your mouth? Do I *seem* amused? Describe *your* spouse's fractured, detached head. What ran through *your* mind when you saw the thick fingers of the monster who bludgeoned *your* loved one into a pile of pulp?"

To cope, I focused on work. It helped. I was also

pleased someone invented door locks, window blinds, prison cells, and .38 revolvers.

In the larger picture, though, something uncomfortable, undefinable was missing. A component of me felt...numb, as if I carried some unseen ailment, which could not be understood. I was a jigsaw puzzle with a missing piece or two. What had I overlooked? I began to feel *I* lived a double life. My public face of confidence belied how I felt when the lights went out.

There was an unwanted transformation in me. I developed an immediate, over-reactive stance against micromanagement. Decades later, it still reminds me of the helplessness I felt when Nolan tried to block me from the witness stand and the invasion of reporters at the funeral. It accounts for my choice of hobbies and job where I function independently.

In time, I understood trauma was not purely emotional or psychological. It's an all-encompassing *visceral* reaction. It involved my mind, body, and soul.

Part of what led to this understanding was an article in *Networker* entitled *The Biology of Fear* that explained how trauma transforms us right down to the cellular level—sometimes permanently. Blood flow changes brain processes, which interferes with normal cortex (brain) regulation. Evidence in black and white. It was real, identifiable, even measurable.

The second half of this light bulb was the re-reading of a worn publication—oddly, salvaged from Al's office—entitled *Man's Search for Meaning* by Victor Frankl, M.D. published in 1959. Dr. Frankl was an Austrian neurologist, psychiatrist and Holocaust survivor. Some passages meaningful to me were these:

- Suffering ceases to be suffering when it finds meaning.
- Everything can be taken but one: the last of the human freedoms — to
    choose an attitude.
- Those who have a 'why' to live, can bear with any 'how.'

Frankl's words humbled me. "Find value in this experience. *Your job is to identify the why.* When you do, it will feed your soul." That was what was missing. John, Dawn and Al robbed me of many things, but not my ability to *interpret* what happened in a way that was meaningful. My friend, Matt, was right. This was an unexpected adventure. This diplomatic man endured the worst humanity could offer. His suffering was immeasurable. Surely if *Frankl* could survive, I could also.

In Frankl's own words:

We stumbled on in darkness, over stones and puddles, along the road running through the [concentration] camp. The accompanying guards kept shouting and driving us with butts of their rifles...

That brought thoughts of my own wife to mind. And as we stumbled on for miles, slipping on icy spots, supporting each other time and again, nothing was said, but we both know: each was thinking of his wife. Occasionally I looked at the sky, where stars were fading, and the pink light of the morning was beginning to spread behind a dark bank of clouds. But my mind clung to my wife's image, imagining it with uncanny acuteness. I heard her answering me, saw her smile, her frank and encouraging look. Real or not, her look then was more luminous than the sun which was beginning to rise.

All trauma survivors are thrust into an unwelcome pilgrimage. Undoubtedly, more was at work the night I glanced into the mirror of Al's office and instantly "knew" beyond *any* doubt he was dead. The same could be said when Mrs. Canty's "dream" depicted Al telling her "it wasn't that bad" and Victor Frankl's seeing his wife's image in the sunrise. Psychology refers to these unusual occurrences as "anomalous experiences" which most commonly happens during times of intense stress; a kind of sixth sense. They are not culture-bound, experienced in one particular age group, one gender or educational level and often presented as indistinguishable, unshakable perceptions to the person having them.

Our primitive, reptilian brain doesn't have much capacity to reason. It thrives on retrieving bites of sound, smell, sights and raw emotion. If the lizard brain is working right, it assists the thinking, rational side, not clobber it. It's hard-wired to reduce tension, seek safety, avoid risk and fit in. But when it goes awry it is a speeding train without a conductor; or an autoimmune disease attacking the body without cause.

I had to let go of the outrage, the fear, and harness my lizard brain. After all, most fears *never* materialized. Fry and his pals never broke into the house. He and Dawn were not exonerated. I was never homeless. I never gave into my rage. I could still work with clarity. My friends never doubted me.

At some indefinite time, after sinking in self-pity, seething with anger and awakening from repetitive nightmares I had, as it were, a change of heart. Victor Frankl helped, as did the passing of time. So did my father's teaching that setbacks were opportunities for a comeback, and my mother's kindness. I pondered the why of what happened and recognized *I* did not pay the ultimate price because I still had a future. My choice became blatantly simple: *"breakdown or break away?"* It grew into a mantra. It had been there all along, just under the surface, ready to be embraced. I'd had my fill of feeling half dead, powerless and resentful. The choice was really no choice at all. Cry "uncle" or grab back power? Continue to be the nail or learn how to hammer? I refused to fall into the rabbit hole with the rest of them, another casualty of self-indulgence.

The time came when I exhaled and felt calm. The lizard brain dozed. The steps to my future were tentative, but at least I had one. The shadow receded. Like a heart monitor that began to register a beat, a comeback began. Eighteen months after that fateful, stormy night, sleep returned more regularly, and I found occasional humor and comfort in the presence of friends. I forced myself to pay attention to what was *unaffected* by his homicide and what was *right* in my world. Life would never be the same, but I no longer wanted that.

I came to understand, *genuinely* comprehend, the despondency and isolation of another and connect in ways never imagined. Words could not accurately express the abyss. Classrooms only approximated an understanding. This was an additional internship in learning about loss, betrayal and misplaced trust. I fixated on redirecting my sorrow, anger, and uncertainty into becoming a better psychologist, friend, and daughter, to learn more about the experience of other so-called homicide survivors. Suffering ceased to be suffering when I found its meaning.

When I meet someone, who has lost a loved one through violence, or who went missing, we exchange knowing glances. We understand what is not said. We experience this *viscerally*. Landeros was my tutor. That's the purpose behind this book. It is aimed at another weary pilgrim on the journey no one wants or expects to take. Victor Frankl was right. *This is survivable.*

This ordeal separated what mattered from what did not with such clarity; it is second-nature to ask, "Will this matter in five years?" If not, I try to drop it. I do not take the passing of years for granted. This may account for my tendency to take on more than can realistically be accomplished. A firearm, baseball bat, or explosion can snatch life unexpectedly. Time is a precious gift guaranteed *no one*. While I would never want to relive the strain of those months, nor wish it upon anyone, I survived. Others will, too.

Not only did particular *beliefs* aid me, but *actions* did, too. I got busy. I wrote a manuscript for a children's Christmas book and traveled to Kenya twice to join others in constructing a school. I joined a gym. Ten years ago, I completed my fourth triathlon. I volunteered with raptors and with the Red Cross during Katrina. Sleep became a higher priority. I accompanied my friend, Rita, to rural India to assist in a medical clinic. Several years ago, I began an autobiographical book collection of people who survived adversity. Their obstacles varied but were formidable. I reflected on them and felt there was a story inside me, too. Those narratives gave me the courage to step up and tell it. This assisted in putting Al's homicide into a wider perspective. My interests in photography, travel, and hiking were easily intermixed and led to volunteering on three continents and traveling to five. I adopted several "toss-away" dogs over the years and wept mightily as they grew frail and passed away. I taught undergraduate then graduate school for over two decades and now plan retirement as there is a decline in my health.

So, here it is, some thirty years later. Long stretches of time pass where I do not reflect on the strain of those years. My cynicism has weakened. I selectively trust but still enjoy being alone. My nightmares and hypervigilance have shriveled. Yet, my attention remains riveted when the news reports another missing person. As I write this today, a news bulletin appeared of a missing Detroit-area woman, age twenty by the name of Brenna Machus. Another vicious man with a FTW mentality abducted her from her job. Another family's nightmare has begun. Will they reunite with their precious daughter at the dreaded medical examiner building as so many have done before them?

We have an undeclared civil war in this country. Each murder has its own explanation, fallout, burial and vacancy at the dinner table, an endless procession of sadness, loss and legal entanglement. While the murder rate has declined in the United States since 1993, it is still repugnantly high, with a homicide occurring every thirty-three minutes — about the time it takes to drink a cup of coffee — and a thirty-three percent chance of getting away with it.

And, whereas Americans are fascinated by murders

and those who commit them, the same cannot be said about those left to grieve. Since the mid-sixties hundreds of publications and dozens of movies focus on those responsible for the mayhem, particularly serial killers and mass murderers, while only a handful of books and almost no movies show murder from the co-victim's perspective. Academia doesn't fare much better, as there are few scholarly studies pertaining to the impact of homicide on the bereaved. Podcasts are mirroring this trend.

Why is this? Perhaps we share a collective worry for our safety and murderers are powerful figures, so readers can vicariously share that power, rather than stand in the shoes of the powerless mourner. And, in the spirit of full disclosure, it may also happen because many survivors of homicide flee the limelight, as I did, when the news came knocking.

It is important to remember that the murderer leaves their own loved ones in the shadows, too. Relatives are ill-prepared for their undesirable legacy. The families of those who commit havoc are often unheard, marginalized, misunderstood and suffer in silence as the spotlight skims their faces. They labor to reconcile the person they love with the person in the news. A few, like Sue Klebold—mother of Columbine shooter who took his own life—go public and share their struggle.

Mrs. Klebold explained, "I know I will live with this tragedy, with these multiple tragedies, for the rest of my life. I know in the minds of many what I lost can't compare to what the other families lost. I know my struggle doesn't make theirs any easier. I know there are even some who think I don't have the right to any pain, but only to a life of permanent penance."

A few are faced with the difficult choice of cooperating with law enforcement or concealing information they alone possess. Such was the choice of David Kaczynski concerning his brother, Ted (the Unabomber), Bill Babbitt, brother of Manny (who murdered a seventy-eight-year-old woman in the middle of the night that he did not know) and Jeff Williams (over his son's killing of three fellow students in March of 2001 in Santee, California using Jeff's long-barreled .22 caliber revolver and forty bullets). Afterwards Mr. Williams was sued for negligence by the parents of the deceased. It's as if the relatives of the assailant are serving their own life sentence and a death of their own identity.

Parents, children, siblings, cousins, spouses, grandparents and lovers all experience stigma over the fallout of a crime they had no part in when the murderer is someone they love. A frequent refrain is being swallowed in shame, disbelief, guilt, even blame. Some are ostracized from neighbors, fellow worshipers and coworkers causing some to move away or contemplate suicide. Like other co-victims of violence, these walking wounded often turn to one another for help which is why there is an underground support community for relatives of serial killers. A few write books, such as *Shattered Silence* by Melissa Moore, and others advocate for improvements in access to mental health treatment. There is now a podcast entitled *An Unwanted Legacy* that explores the lives of children whose fathers were serial killers. The usual questions faced are: Could you have stopped it? Are you at fault? Does the apple fall far from your family tree? How could you not see it coming?

So, what, if anything, can we learn from science

about life after trauma? No doubt about it. Survivors pay the price—spiritually, physically, financially, socially, maritally and vocationally, especially when the victim is a child.

But there is a somewhat-debated concept in psychology called "Post Traumatic Growth" or "PTG." The basic premise is that trauma may trigger so-called "transformative change." What does that look like?

For one thing, trauma survivors may develop new understandings of *themselves* (i.e. "I have more grit than I thought" or "I didn't know I had the strength to pull that motorcycle off the rider.") They also see *their world* differently (i.e. "I cannot assume violence only impacts other people" or "I'm amazed that stranger risked his life for me."). In addition, PTG changes how people relate *to others* (i.e. "I truly understand what you're going through because I lost a child to a drunk driver also" or "I don't share your view that 'time heals all wounds.'"). And last, but not least, PTG also alters how trauma survivors see their *future*_(i.e., "I'm not going to put off telling my kids how much they mean to me one more day" or "If I'm going to pursue my dream of visiting the Galapagos Islands, I'd best start planning.")

A competing theory asserts that the most common positive outcome for trauma survivors is increased resilience and improvement in anxiety and depression *provided* they had social support through the ordeal. So, if a person is in a group trauma—say, a train derailment or part of a first responder unit—they are not alone and will likely receive immediate and delayed support from others. By contrast, individual survivors of trauma—such as witnessing a suicide—will fare better if they have help or seek support from others who have gone through the same thing.

Further research has shown that these positive outcomes are more likely in people who: are more extroverted, more optimistic, have spiritual beliefs, are open to new experiences, have resources, are female—because females are more likely to talk about their experiences—and those that develop healthy coping strategies, like staying physically active.

The bottom line is trauma is not ruinous. There is hope.

This isn't to say adverse aspects of trauma will vanish. A theme common to trauma survivors is the lifelong need for boundaries. Their personal space becomes critical. I remain sensitive to perceived invasions of my "borders." An example involved the gym. A staff member cut the lock off my locker and moved my belongings to the lost and found. An error in the gym's spreadsheet listed the locker as vacant. The staff rectified it within an hour, but I felt violated. It irritated me longer than reasonable. Overreactions to common events will occasionally happen.

Besides the need for boundaries, trauma survivors experience flashbacks—a feeling the event is recurring. I accompanied my friends to the movies two years after the trial. Our selection was sold out, but *The Untouchables* was available. We vaguely knew it pertained to Al Capone. My first instinct was to decline but agreed to switch. In one scene, Robert DeNiro, playing Capone, stands to deliver a speech to his men, seated for an elegant dinner. He sarcastically discusses why he loves baseball and teamwork as he grasps a bat and slowly paces behind the seated guests. Without warning, "Capone" clubs the head of a man positioned below him. I became nauseous, my breathing labored. My legs were unsteady, but I made it to the lobby and then the car.

The other night our family watched an episode of the *Sopranos*. Season four, episode nine. I couldn't get through it.

To the PTSD insider, this makes sense. This is to say trauma transforms you *forever*. The invisible scars last a *lifetime*. The lizard brain will awaken and rule at times. It's supposed to. Life does get easier, and some adjustments are necessary, but getting back to baseline is unrealistic. It can't be done. Period.

It is helpful to find meaning from what is appalling. Reestablishing control is key. Setting limits, but welcoming a gradual connection to specific people, can be a positive start. Nourishing your soul and body is essential. Link with something bigger than the immediate situation. Perhaps it is a spiritual connection or deeply satisfying leisure pursuit. For others, it may be a career switch, even with a harsh pay cut and relocation, volunteerism, or reuniting with a long-lost friend. Trauma affects survivors as broadly as their functioning in society, and as narrowly as cells within their body. There is something to appreciate each day if alert to it. Perhaps it is just having the strength to climb a set of stairs or knowing your pet celebrates your return. Take notice of what has *not* been affected by trauma. Return to familiar rituals that brought peace, especially if they involve large muscles. This will "speak to" and help quiet your lizard brain. Prioritize. You know you're on the right path when you cease to be ill as often, humor returns, you experience days, maybe weeks, when upsetting memories are not in your face and sleep becomes more regular. Decisive, realistic actions reduce nightmares, pessimism, insomnia, avoidance, irritability, and fatigue. *You cannot complete this marathon alone.* Genuine offers of help should be considered. Expectations need to be sensible because *the effects of brutality can only be alleviated, never erased.* This is the unvarnished truth as I experienced it. You, or someone close to you, may have been victimized by crime, a horrific accident or war. It is my sincere hope the book you hold will provide hope, empathy and useful strategies.

# FORTY-SIX

# LIGHTS! ACTION! CAMERA!

The setting referred to by inmates as "the canary," was a stark, solitary confinement cell deep inside Marquette Penitentiary, a fossil of a prison. The cement enclosure existed behind a perimeter of old stone rising twenty feet, capped by ten feet tall razor-ribbon wire, electronic detection systems, eight-gun towers, and two chain-link fences. Every inch within the common yard was in the line of sight of those towers. Marquette was for the hardcore, the unrepentant, the inhumane. Most inmates carried shanks. It was more survivable that way. The guards knew but often looked the other way. Fry was a bona fide lifer there, doing time on the installment plan, and most inmates don't mess with lifers. They were the elite. Murder was not out of the question. Did it really matter? Many were already serving two life sentences. What's another?

Within this perilous enclosure, Fry readily

consented to an on-camera interview aired September 24, 1988, on Fox TV with Steve Wilson of *The Reporters*. This was Fry's second tour of Marquette, built in 1889, a refresher of sorts, as he'd been detained a decade prior. He was far from the palm trees and rocky coast of California. The man who boasted he'd never be taken alive, the felon who intended on murdering his aunt, was restrained to a 6x8 near the icy southern shore of Lake Superior where blasts of Arctic winds delivered bitter temperatures even in autumn. Winters were like living on an iceberg. The snow, which blanketed the interior yard, swelled to twelve-foot drifts and didn't fully melt until mid-April. Instead of stretching back and getting high, the convict was surrounded by winds of fifteen below with an average yearly snowfall of 150 inches. John Carl "Lucky" Fry found himself in a setting as cold and unforgiving as his soul. Marquette was an all-male, Level V, maximum-security repository for outcasts. There would be no palm trees or bonfires on the beach. Not that night nor nights to come.

Fry was actually doubly confined. Besides imprisonment, he was silently trapped inside a rapidly failing body, though his symptoms were not yet visible. His past had stealthily caught up. It promised it would. His faded "LBT" tattoo was prophetic. John *was* on borrowed time.

The man from the Tennessee-Kentucky border, the thug who held mock executions for his amusement, arrived at that point where many addicts found themselves. Hepatitis C had corroded his liver, brought on by years of complacency. His eyes and skin had begun to yellow. It would not be long before he lost weight,

411

experienced slowed reaction time, developed tremors, swollen ankles, and nausea. His tongue would thicken, blood vessels in his abdomen would swell and he'd experience intense itching. Spider-like blood vessels would discolor his pale, weathered skin and unfiltered toxins vowed to deliver deadly levels of ammonia to his cynical brain, triggering irritability, lethargy, confusion, and stupor. His death would be slow, prickly, confusing; quite unlike the one he inflicted upon my husband. Fry would then understand that the bottom of the syringe was always empty and unforgiving.

*For the treacherous, it's only a matter of time*
*before the past delivers what they truly deserve…*
---Emily Thorne

Nevertheless, on this day the man beaten long ago with sledgehammer handles in a three-bedroom mobile sat for cameras in a snug purple Los Angeles Rams sweatshirt and handcuffs with a self-satisfied smirk. His rock-hard muscles had softened to dough. Smudgy tattoos covered his thick, handcuffed forearms; the same forearms which sucked the life savings from at least two families. The starchy prison diet inspired a noticeable weight gain and slower pace. His tweed suit worn in court was sidelined long ago, along with his clean-shaven head. He now sported a long, snarly white beard, neglected mustache and bushy eyebrows, reminiscent of an older Walt Whitman. He was forty-two, but could easily pass for sixty-two, if not more.

He faced cameras, lights, reporters, and memories to reminisce about the slaughter of my husband Doc

Miller-Canty. Iron bars were behind him and distant voices echoed. Fry displayed some hypervigilance but was otherwise unperturbed. Speaking softly, slowly, with a slight, Southern accent, he explained himself.

It's a whore's dream come true. That's what...every whore out there's lookin' for. Whether it be, ah, a "sugar-daddy" type situation or one-time thing or whatever, that's what they're lookin' for. I relate it to a Dr. Jekyll and Mr. Hyde situation. He had this very nice life in the suburbs, [sneer] plenty of money [snicker] but wasn't satisfied. She kept records. Like, in the first year, it was about one hundred forty-thousand-dollars. Came in and, you know, he wanted to talk to us. So, we sit down and he, ah, just more-or-less said, "I've fallen in love with this girl. I know you're with her—even though nobody had said anything—and I want to know what it would cost to get her out of your life." Couple days later she mentioned something to him about five grand. And, ah, a few days later he brought the money. I moved my clothes one apartment down the hall... [Al was addicted to] streets, prostitutes, specifically Dawn...that whole street life.

I cut the body up. I'm high. I'm paranoid... Scared. Ah, I know that I got to do *something* 'cause if this body gets found in my house I'm goin' back to prison. Ah [sigh] somewhere the idea came from, ah, to dissect his body and take it out in pieces. [long pause]

I think he fell in love with it [the street life]. Ah, and, I think that caused him a lot of problems. And I don't specifically mean the murder. That had nothin' to do with it. Ah, I think that, within his own, his *own* self. She's a bewitching young girl. [smile]

While Lowell began his book tour, Fry busied himself filing appeals for a new trial arguing he was denied due process and effective counsel. The motion was denied after an evidentiary hearing. He raised the same arguments on direct appeal to the Michigan Court of Appeals. His motion was again denied, in March of 1988. Fry's third attempt was to petition the Michigan Supreme Court with redundant arguments. The court again denied leave to appeal. His fourth and final attempt would be to petition the United States Court of Appeals, Sixth Circuit for the Eastern District of Kentucky, on November 6, 1991. Judges Boggs, Norris and Bertelsman heard the case.

Upon consideration, we conclude this petition was properly denied. At the hearing on the motion for a new trial, Fry's trial counsel testified as to the numerous strategic reasons for not calling the co-defendant to testify... Strategic choices made after a thorough investigation of relevant law and facts for plausible options are virtually unchallengeable. Fry received a fair trial and is not entitled to habeas relief. The motion for counsel is denied and the district court's judgment affirmed.

Later, officials transported this "helluva good man" from his drafty cell in Marquette to his last stop—Jackson State Prison (or "Jacktown" by its tenants). He'd come full circle, back to the first penitentiary where he'd been confined twenty-five wasted years earlier. In the intervening two and a half decades, he left a trail of unsupported children, assault victims, squandered tax dollars, stolen merchandise, counterfeit money, abandoned friends and at least one grave.. He'd turned a wife into a widow and a mother into a mourner. He was like "Mayhem" in the Allstate ads. John Fry's final name was serialized and bureaucratized to #129784. One day in the near future he would get his "back door parole."

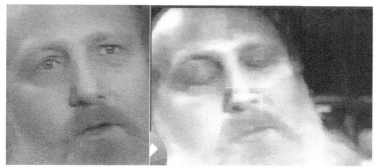

John Fry being interviewed inside Marquette Prison around 1989
(Credit: Fox TV *The Reporters*)

Marquette Prison
Marquette, Michigan

# FORTY-SEVEN

# CROSSROADS

By 1987, Al was interred at Elmwood Cemetery, alongside his father, not far from the imposing Lewis Cass grave marker. Cauffiel's *Masquerade* was gaining traction. Dr. Rutledge had relocated to Florida and had become frail. Dawn graduated to probation and John was still working the system for an appeal. Two long years had passed since the trial. I resisted saying "widow," but was known *only* as that. Many still kept themselves at arm's length, not knowing what to say. If the situation were reversed, I might have done the same.

With the thought of more dreary winters and inevitable press releases for Lowell's book approaching, I wanted to lift the shroud and join the living. This wasn't the endgame I'd imagined. I felt my only alternative was to escape Detroit with my new name. I was thirty-six. Where could this adventure called 'my life' go? The sordid mess left countless invisible footprints in its wake, like fossils from a previous lifetime, but I was no longer content with barriers in front of me, to have others define me, to feel alienated from me.

It was not a painless choice. Detroit was where I'd been born, raised, educated, married, employed and widowed. I'd made lifelong friends, loved its music, Greek Town, Grand Prix races, DIA and my vintage brownstone. I welcomed the fall colors, living in earshot of foghorns on the Detroit River and appreciated the determination of grassroots organizations. It had a grittiness I admired. Its history was rich and varied. The First Congregational Church on E. Forest Avenue played a crucial role in the underground railroad. The bus which Rosa Parks refused to give up her seat on is tucked inside the Henry Ford Museum and she is interred in a beautiful chapel inside Woodlawan Cemetery, close to Aretha Franklin. The Davison Freeway was the first urban freeway in the U.S. along with the Windsor-Detroit Tunnel as the first international underground tunnel for traffic. Vernors, still sold nationwide was the first soda bottled in the country. The 27 massive and once highly controversial frescos dubbed *Diego Rivera's Industry Murals* depicted the automotive industry and assisted by unemployed factory workers in 1932. It surrounds the interior court of the DIA, a building I always admired.

Yet, I'd faded into a mere apparition, not a wholly alive person. I'd been dragged through too much of Detroit's underbelly. It was time to go.

*Your present circumstances don't determine where you can go*

*They merely determine where you start*
        ---Nido Qubein

A wide net was cast to discover my tomorrows. I was again reinventing myself. I interviewed for a faculty position at a modest rural college far west from the glitter and grime and crossed my fingers. It was a substantial pay cut. I'd never taught before, nor did I know anyone there. When the position was offered, I signed on. My belongings were again boxed, goodbyes said to those who kindly, unselfishly accompanied me places I did not want to go, who provided shelter when I did not want to return home, listened when I vented and gave professional counsel in times of indecision. My practice was closed, and office lease terminated. I planned to evaporate. Was this running away, or running toward? In truth, it was a bit of both…

Five weeks later, on an early August morning, the kitchen light was extinguished as I took one last look around my beautiful, vacant townhouse. A hint of an early orange dawn emerged softly through my bedroom windows of what was supposed to be my safe house. It was quiet, fallow and somber. With morning coffee, backpack and suitcase in hand, the door to my life behind me was locked. With a heavy heart, I drove past Elmwood Cemetery, intending to stop but did not. The Corridor was still slumbering, and Chili Pepper was directed to westbound I-94. I'd maneuvered the Edsel Ford Expressway thousands of sun-ups before, but never with the intention of saying farewell to everything, and most everyone, I'd ever known. Doubts lingered. It was, in many ways, another loss, but at least it was my own choice.

The Michigan border was crossed before noon, as I aimed westbound, south of Gary, Indiana, where I experienced my first kiss from a sixteen-year-old boy named Dan on a family vacation decades earlier. It triggered fond memories and a smile. Familiar radio stations crackled and succumbed to the distance. The expanse of Interstate 80 stretched to the horizon as the sun played hide-and-seek behind broken clouds. The urge to second-guess my decision surfaced but what was done was done, right? Each mile behind my taillights detached the ugliness, dead ends, and what-could-have-been.

I pulled off to stretch near I-80 and I-55 and was immediately confronted by afternoon air as sticky as taffy. I glanced east through the smog and din of surging traffic. Had I made the right choice? So many memories, and not all of them bad. A few years ago, it would have been inconceivable to move away. My home was now lost to me.

No one here expressed an interest in my presence. That was reassuring. *I'm a nobody here, and there* I thought, as I looked west, toward my destination. The only way to know what my future could hold was to embrace it. Passing over the wide Mississippi reinforced "the rightness" of my flight plan.

The familiar yielded to the unexplored. Urban transitioned to rural. Sunshine evolved into dusk. Would loneliness and fear do likewise?

> *I'm not afraid to start over.*
> *This time I'm not starting from scratch.*
> *I'm starting from experience.*
> ---adapted from *Amazing Movement*

As miles and hours passed, a trickle of contentment slowly bubbled into feeling hopeful and at peace for the first time in a long time. Accompanied by quiet music in the dark amber vista, both windows were lowered to allow the humid evening to embrace me. I glanced at my suitcases and smiled, knowing I had a gas tank full of freedom. The night air gave me goosebumps. This moment was to be savored. *I felt alive!* The nearly complete sundown was glaring and spearheaded the way like a razor-thin beacon. I was determined to follow. Even the tingling slaps of hair against my face were welcomed. Finally, I was free.

> *Don't stop thinking about tomorrow,*
> *Don't stop. It will soon be here.*
> *It'll be better than before.*
> *Yesterday's gone. Yesterday's gone.*
> --- Fleetwood Mac

Countless miles, pint-size towns, intersections and hours passed until the migration stopped at a darkened, gravel parking lot just over ninety minutes from my destination. As my headlights dimmed, I sat silently, peering into the unknown, the potential, the unexplored. My emotions were mixed and ill-defined. Looking around I cautiously stepped out of Chili Pepper, the vehicle that once carried inmate #129784. This rural corner of the globe smelled different. It sounded different. It unquestionably *looked* different. The air was muggy and cleansed by recent rain. The stars overhead were brilliant without light pollution. The deep blue darkness was unmistakably dotted with faraway galaxies. There were millions of crickets, distant trucks, and a squeaky windmill circling slowly in the heavy air. My first-ever firefly darted overhead. I stretched, yawned, and walked closer to my uncertain future.

The tiny mom and pop motel was straight out of a 1950 movie set with the rusty *A & W Root Beer* sign reading seventy-two degrees near a buzzing, red neon "Vacancy" notice with several moths flitting about. The motel office pulled at my tired back like a magnet and a squeaky screen door led me to an elderly clerk. After a few pleasantries and minimal paperwork, she passed the key with a homemade wooden paddle, recommending dinner next door before they closed. She did not sit behind a wire mesh cage. As far as I knew, rooms were not rented by the half hour. There was no gang graffiti or ghetto grills to mar the never-majestic entrance.

Number six was simple but spotless. An ancient, pink Chenille bedspread dominated the room. Knotty pine paneling, speckled linoleum floors, a clattering tabletop fan, and garish turquoise bathroom tiles completed the obsolete, simple décor.

Gone were skyscrapers, vacant factories, pollution, and airports. Gone was the Corridor, the Fisher Building, the Detroit media, and sirens. But that was the point, *right?*

Dinner was served at the small truck-stop diner, less than half-full, yet brimming with bursts of laughter. The pinball machine in the corner was thankfully quiet at this hour. Some patrons referred to the only waitress, a plump, cheerful, middle-aged woman, by name. She enjoyed their teasing. She addressed me as "Sugar" and joked, "I *knew* you were going to order that!" The light green walls exhibited a haphazard arrangement of framed photos, presumably displaying "locals" playing softball, graduating, winning a rodeo and acting as Santa, thereby binding the community like family. I ate in silence, felt like an eavesdropper and thought about home.

After a long, hot shower, I turned on the television with rabbit ears for reception. There was an unforgettable commercial featuring a cow and bull slowly running toward one another in an open field with dandelions. Symphonic music swelled. As the bovines touched, the sponsor's name appeared, advertising artificial insemination services for cows. My mouth dropped. I'd hoped for a change, but *wow...*

It felt wonderful to be motionless and anonymous and autonomous in this new setting. I still missed "home" but drifted into a dreamless sleep.

The following daybreak, I sluggishly awoke early and deep in the heartland early. I stepped outside the white bungalow to face a wide, watermelon pink horizon with dew-coated soybeans and corn that stretched as far as the eye could see. *Miles* of it. No one was around. It was peaceful and notably unfamiliar. The only sound was the muffled interstate and mobs of crows dive-bombing the ground. A change was definitely afoot. I enjoyed a leisurely cup of coffee at an old, nearby picnic table, watched this new world wake up and wondered what I would have been doing at this hour if I had been home. I ached for my retro townhouse, my close friends, my routine. So much had changed. I felt homeless again but refused to dwell on it.

Faculty were not expected for another day, nor the moving van, but I drove on to my final destination anyway. Many roads were unnamed and unoccupied; nothing like the congested highways back east. Grain elevators and large, white propane tanks resembling gigantic, white Good and Plenty's dotted the flat landscape. John Deere tractors nonchalantly held up what little traffic there was, and the farmer driving them usually waved with a smile when passing, taking no notice of the heavy dirt clogs he deposited.

The college was nestled in a place where vacationers don't trek, where the newspaper had the thickness of a folded napkin and where there was frequent talk about the weather and high school football games past and present. The college's structures were nestled amid mature oaks, which stood firm decades before the buildings saw the light of day. The old white Science Building contained my office and was quickly located. A janitor in bib overalls worked on an outdoor post light and called out in a friendly manner. He glanced at my Michigan license plate, and cheerfully asked, "You the new gal from Detroit?" He let me in without further questions. My new office was downstairs, immediately past a break room. The windows were up toward the ceiling. It had plenty of wood bookshelves and an antique oak desk with matching swivel chair. My name already appeared on the door (in a post-it note), and a welcome message waited on the blotter. A tiny basket held coupons, a list of upcoming county events, homemade candy and a key to my office.

Granted, this setting offered no fancy twenty-four-hour parking garage, marble halls, 50-foot Tiffany chandeliers or brass elevators, but what it lacked in sophistication was offset by unpretentiousness and warmth. Soon my books would be "re-homed" and the Persian rug placed under the desk—the very one my mother wisely prevented me from giving away.

Up a flight of steps then to the right was an empty lecture hall where I was scheduled to teach *Abnormal Psychology, Developmental Psychology* and *Theories of Personality.* I paused behind the podium and glanced up at the unoccupied rows of seats and hanging lights, feeling a little lost and a little found. Years ago, I promised myself to remember what it was like being a college freshman and, should I ever become a professor, strike a balance between constructive criticism and compassion, between lecturing and listening.

Strolling around campus, the few people who passed said hello. A few locals stopped to express anticipation of a productive school year. For a while, I assumed they'd greeted me, the newcomer, but later learned it was just customary to speak to *anyone* and even offer a handshake.

The town square was within walking distance. Around 10:30, I wandered through the bustling, small "central district" under towering oaks that had begun to yellow from August dryness. A drug store with a vintage soda fountain reminded me of the timeworn Sanders "back east." Next stood a no-nonsense feed store and tall, sagging, wooden hardware from some previous century, which didn't remind me of anything. The wooden sign proclaimed they'd "repair any make or model of tractor." Opposite that was a fabric and yarn store. The town square also contained two banks and an insurance company. Most buildings were two-story and appeared to have been built around 1900. Since my car insurance needed updating, I asked a woman working at Allstate if they offered discounts for car alarms, which were not yet standard.

"Gee whiz. Dunno! Never been asked that."

*Really?!*

Locals rarely locked their cars, or houses, and took it personally if someone did. Trust was implicit. One elderly resident, who lived alongside the interstate, said she purposely left her farmhouse unlocked during bitter winter days, "In case someone broke down on the road and needed shelter."

A short drive through a neighboring county concluded at a slight knoll in front of an ornate building with columns, a huge clock, manicured lawn and shiny gold letters proclaiming, "County Court House." This resembled the halls of justice described in John Grisham novels. I stood in front and studied it, then ascended three wide concrete steps. I pulled on the ancient, heavy door. Apparently, this town didn't see the need for metal detectors, hand wands, armed guards, or parking lots. The interior featured gray, polished, granite floors and dark, wood benches. It contained only one large courtroom beyond the open double doors. My feet echoed in the cavernous space with an elevated oak bench framed by flags. The last time I set foot in a courtroom was under different circumstances. That was a different place. In a different time. For a different purpose.

An elderly man in a suit too large for his frail body approached and asked, "No cases today. You a law student?"

"No. Just came a long way to see this for myself."

He smiled broadly, offered a formal handshake, and recited a short history of the structure. He mentioned the more notorious cases argued under the high ceiling. The court held a civil rights trial, a bank robbery (pointing for emphasis) and an arson spree, "where he done burned up two barns and a place of worship." As if that wasn't scary enough, he lowered his voice, leaned in, shook his head and added "and the murder of that little girl. So sad. That was forty-five years ago. I'll never forget her poor mama..."

I stiffened at the narrative.

*I can be changed by what happens to me,*
*but I refuse to be reduced by it.*
--- Maya Angelou

Classes didn't start for two weeks, but faculty meetings would get underway soon. My young, red-headed student assistant introduced herself, gave me an in-depth campus tour and explained her duties.

As expected, my pay was less, but so was the overhead with no office rent, parking fees, Wayne County tax, Detroit property tax, Detroit income tax, an answering service bill, renter's insurance, malpractice insurance nor medical insurance premiums. Car insurance decreased by two thirds. Best of all, my new brick residence cost a fraction of the townhouse back east yet was equivalent in size. It boasted an unobstructed territorial view with a pond of serenading frogs who croaked from dusk to dawn.

Some faculty were curious why someone from a big city would relocate there, but were too polite to ask. Unlike Michigan, this was a Republican-leaning state, but not consistently. Instead of white flight, they spoke of rural flight, especially among better-educated young adults who desired to relocate in urban centers of adjoining counties and states. They could not appreciate the strain of living in a city that drew the attention of the FBI and DEA and where foreign countries issued travel warnings to avoid the location altogether. My adopted community was decidedly Protestant, without religious nor ethnic diversity. The crime rate was flat, not budging in decades. Larceny was the most common offense and usually meant the offender wrote a rubber check or kept a rented movie. And they took this stuff *seriously*. One business owner disclosed the amount of the bounced check and name of the offender on their outdoor sign! Murders were so rare that information about them was about as hard to come by as convictions. Few "notables" called this town their birthplace. Single-parent households were as rare as the elderly living alone. The population held steady at about one-third of the university I attended. Teens aspired to join the FFA (Future Farmers of America) not the BKs, West Side Seven or Earl Flynn's. There wasn't a professional sports team for many miles, nor an airport or trauma center. There was a student-faculty ratio of twelve, however, and the college offered eighty majors, minors and miscellaneous programs.

The day before classes, while finalizing lesson plans and unpacking, a familiar, small paperback surfaced. *Therapeutic Peers: The Story of Project Indianwood* by W. Alan

Canty. The black and white photo on the back cover was signed, *"To Jan-Jan. We make a good team, Al."* I gasped.

"You all right, ma'am? Is it the heat?" interrupted my observant assistant. "Let me get you a cold Coke."

I grasped the familiar publication. It was out of place—an unwelcome, incoming missile from another time. A cauldron of mixed emotions gushed up. This man provided the struggle cup when I wanted to quit college. He bought the car parked outside. Those eyes once glistened when aimed at me. However, he'd never been faithful and, in the end, made decisions that terminated his life and put mine in jeopardy. I slowly put his book up in an inconspicuous slot and tried to forget it. I succeeded—more or less. There was a price for keeping secrets, for dodging the truth.

*Deep down, I knew you were too good to be true*
*But every piece and part of me wanted to believe in you*
*But now it's happily ever never*
*I guess now I know better*
*You were just a lost boy, with your head up in the clouds*
*You were always gonna fly away because you knew you could*
*You never learned there was no such place as Neverland*
— adapted from Kelsea Ballerini, Jessee Lee, Forest Whitehead

My first day of class launched butterflies. Now I stood on the *other* side. The role of clinician was familiar but not assistant professor. Most students were first-generation college students, as I was. Most fathers were farmers and their wives "did the books and orders." Their parents sacrificed abundantly to pay tuition, and the majority of students were determined to become the first college grad ever in their extended family.

My students taught me things, too, such as the number of rows on an ear of corn was always even—usually between eight and twenty-two—while the shriek of a frightened pig measured two decibels more than a jet taking off. One acre of soybeans could yield eighty-thousand crayons. Who knew? One of my students went on to become a fully licensed pediatric psychologist. I still receive a Christmas card from her every year. Moreover, my students were not short on humor, trying to convince me summers were so hot the "corn pops in the field before we pick it." They weren't far from wrong. The month I joined the faculty there was a rash of rearview mirrors letting go of the windshield due to the glue's inability to withstand the heat. By summer's end, hot water came from *both* taps. But winter was just as harsh. The day I visited a pig farm I was grateful the "muck" was frozen solid, and the smell thereby reduced. Engine block heaters were a blessing. Double rainbows after a hard summer thunderstorm were not unusual.

In my new role as psychology faculty. I'm standing with colleagues in front of my office window. Happy memories despite the very hot temperatures that day in those gowns. 1988

Over time, this rural subculture revealed itself to me, though I did not reveal myself to it. Families were self-reliant. Names of extended family were memorized. This led to tighter accountability and less privacy. Most locals avoided activities they didn't want others to know about. Younger generations took care of their elderly. Men took off their hats indoors and cars patiently waited for pedestrians to cross. Pregnancy outside marriage shamed a young woman to flee or marry. Neither appliances nor strangers raised children. Neighbors whispered about problem drinkers and problem marriages and who skipped out on church. Students opened doors for faculty and, if irritated with a decision, they seldom showed it. No homeless men loitered in stairwells, there was no needle exchange program, dedicated police presence nor emergency blue light warning system. The college did not border a red-light district with over 1300 prostitutes.

A year after my relocation I received the sad news that Dr. Rutledge had passed away in May of 1989. I pictured his grieving family and felt so fortunate to have known him. He understood my need to leave Detroit and would have approved of this new setting. Although I was more than six hundred miles from where we last spoke, memories of him came with me.

# FORTY-EIGHT

# RENEWAL

In my forties, after the move and career switch, I decided to adopt. The shock of the events from 1985, coupled with weight loss and irregular heartbeats, initiated premature menopause. Consequently, physicians said I may never be a candidate for natural conception. But first, there was the lingering fear of HIV to deal with. So, in 1992 I ventured into a large city for another blood test and breathed a sigh of relief when it exonerated me. Another restraint from the Cass Corridor mess was shed.

In 1996 I learned of the death of John Fry the previous year. What would his epithet have stated had it been honest?

By persisting through phone calls, paperwork, references and waiting, I was entrusted with two stunning biological sisters, locked in foster care most of their young lives. They, too, had been waiting for their release date. We visited regularly then graduated to overnight. One placed her teddy bear on her bed for safekeeping in her absence. I knew then we were on the right track. Finally, my girls came home "for keeps" with wrinkled, shabby clothes on their delicate backs and one well-worn toy apiece. They slept for days and were delighted I allowed their overhead light to be on all night. We set out to become a family with the formality of adoption on St. Patrick's Day that year. I never doubted they were supposed to be mine. Their biological mother had been murdered when they were barely out of diapers. The assailant was never caught. Justice was not denied nor available to her, merely suspended. Their unmarried father was incarcerated at the time of her homicide, on unrelated charges, and would remain so for the foreseeable future. They, essentially, were orphaned.

My new role gave me purpose. I was revitalized. Not the same as the "me before" but I wouldn't want that. The three of us proved life goes on after a tragedy. A lesson I imparted upon my daughters was how to survive a murder. At this point, they are now beautiful young women, and I have been promoted to grandmother status.

After having been away from Detroit for almost thirteen years I returned to visit friends. On the final day of my trip I proceeded to Al's graveside with my old college friend, Cam, on a soft summer afternoon, the kind where children screamed with delight from playgrounds and innocence and optimism.

Cam respectfully stood at a distance while I absorbed details of the hard, blunt granite as I tried to push the ugliness away. Below my feet were ashes from an incomplete skeleton, one paving brick, answers to my unanswered questions and the source of jarring memories.

Al's modest headstone was near a more substantial, family grave marker that simply said "Canty." The chiseled facts of his life on his salmon-colored marker were as minimal as when he was alive.

It occurred to me years ago that I would outlive him, but never this way nor so soon. Standing atop an emerald green mound with a view of numerous tombstones and verdant maples, a reassuring, soft breeze brushed my face. I pushed away two lime green leaves concealing the "W" on his marker and tidied up margins of grass that intruded over the boundaries. Eventually, anger and disbelief swelled to the surface, though I wanted to buckle it down. *Why, Al? Why did you throw us away?"* As in life, silence was my answer. There is always a mystery at the core of murder. Murder and infidelity made no sense, and those closest to it shoulder the brunt of the absurdity.

Harder questions were directed toward his name, brushed in sunlight and disgrace. *Did you love me? Were you ever faithful? Was I a mere well from which you drew your self-esteem?* Grief and disgust dueled within me. I stood motionless as if an answer was forthcoming. *Did you know you were going to die when you returned the last morning to tell me you loved me?* His chiseled letters remained mute. *Did you feel pain in your last moments? It haunts me to think you saw it coming. Did you intend for him to execute you? Only you know.* The rustling of leaves and a distant plane answered obliquely. I slowly stood. What now? What's left to do?

Though it was nameless then, I was experiencing what I now know as "conflicted" or "ambivalent" grief. This was a response to a death that brought sadness mixed with relief because it signaled a cessation of life, of pain, of endangerment. There was no going back, no hope for an apology or explanation for the mystery. Some things could not be fixed—only carried.

It is socially taboo to admit such relief aloud—which intensified my mourning and isolation—and I banished it to society's "whisper corner." Instead of someone saying, "I'm sorry for your loss," I wish someone, *anyone,* would've said, "I'm sorry how he treated you, this must so difficult."

His mother had visited his grave over the years and wondered how it all came to pass. She undoubtedly missed him each day and was glad for the years they shared. She had held to her blackmail theory. In the end, no one knew him. *Not even his mother.*

Over time, his headstone became a tourist destination of sorts, a place for true crime fans to pause. In life, he set in motion his own death. In death, his secret life became an open book.

*Death is the last scene of the last act.*

---Joyce Carol Oates

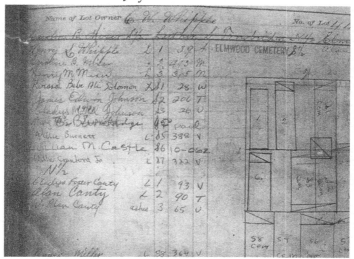

Official Elmwood Cemetery record of Al's burial plot

# FORTY-NINE

# RESUSCITATION

Years later, I married a man who is my equal, who does not need admiration nor pranks to feel whole. I found the same happiness as my parents after all. My husband is a (retired) U.S. Army Lieutenant Colonel. He adopted my daughters and stood by me during the tough teen years. He is an avid fly angler and bellows at the television during football season. He refers to himself as a "knuckle dragger" on occasion, but his tastes in reading belie this. A recent check of his Kindle shows *Forgotten China WWII 1937-1945*, *Three-Volume Biography of Churchill* and *The Ghost of Cannae*.

As our children grew up, we moved again and now live on acreage dense with trees soaring eighty feet high. I finally found my safe place to land. This modest, reliable man shares my love of dogs and exudes a steadiness that grounds me. He is good-natured about the slobber and shedding from our St. Bernards. He is a homebody and prefers reading, riding his lawnmower, following politics and tying flies. He knows the superficial facts of my life in Detroit, but it has never been a focus whatsoever. The topic triggers protective irritation.

Another dimension to my healing involved a return to photography. A good image can stop time, preserve moments indefinitely and reveal things unnoticed. But an outstanding one can transport the viewer to unseen worlds. It is a form of storytelling and a satisfying way to nourish the soul.

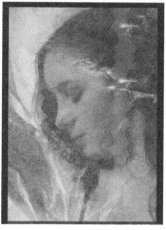

Portrait of a young woman

A boy in Guatemala

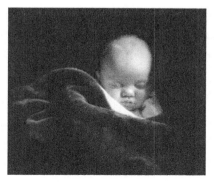

My little granddaughter

A little boy in India          A double frozen waterfall in Iceland

I am fond of photographing indigenous people around the world, framed by passageways of ancient cities or dense vegetation and creating fine art portraits. I spent time with workers in the Andhra Pradesh region of India who didn't possess safe drinking water nor reliable electricity. My photography beckoned me to the Winter Palace in St. Petersburg in the former USSR. I trekked frozen waterfalls in Iceland, explored damp ruins in the San Francisco Abbey, Guatemala, strolled under a thick canopy in the Pacific rainforest, slept in a tent in Kenya overlooking the Rift Valley where I battled Army ants, walked on the Great Wall of China, spent time with the Hopi during their annual Rain Dance atop the Third Mesa under a blazing sun and hiked to Horseshoe Bend at the edge of the massive Grand Canyon, laying down slightly over the edge to take a photograph of the Colorado River some 3,200 feet below me.

In his 2013 retirement, Sapala was quoted as saying that the Fry-Spens murder case was the "most twisted" proceeding he ever witnessed. Likewise, Prosecuting Attorney Agacinski regarded this trial as his "most noteworthy case." Apparently, the trio left lasting impressions wherever they went. What a salacious legacy…

In May of 2014, while recovering from surgery, I ventured back to Detroit again to meet with Mark Bando, retired from DPD, and revisit places where Al and I had a life — and death — together. In so doing, we turned off Woodward onto Temple heading for the notorious bordello. However, instead of finding a narrow 1880 brick building, we witnessed a wrecking ball swing in a flawless arc, crashing into the back of the burned-out hotel. *Contact!* A plume of red brick dust showered the area and cranes moved in to assure it was reduced to a heap of broken bricks and tangled metal, erasing a disreputable landmark that began with such promise.

As I rounded the corner I saw the machinery move in to reduce the Temple Hotel to a pile of rubble.

Most nights I sleep soundly. There is no fear in answering the door, no mystery about finances. Our drapes are left open, and friends freely come and go and enrich our life. Our house hums with music, art projects, snoring from our Gentle Giants, the busy feet of my tiny granddaughter and animated discussions on a variety of subjects. I'm outside every chance I get to tend my garden, or work in my greenhouse, trying to replicate the beauty I saw in Antigua, Guatemala. My camera is always at the ready. It turns out this journey delivered me to a much more preferable place, and my life has changed in ways I could not have imagined, with far greater understanding about how life "works."

My friend, Matt, was absolutely right. Life *is* an adventure. I hope yours is an astonishing one.

*We will be known forever by the tracks we leave*
--- Lakota Nation

Took this photo flying back from Detroit

# APPENDIX
# WHERE ARE THEY NOW?

- <u>Jay Nolan</u>, Defense Counsel for John Fry, moved to Grosse Isle, Michigan and passed away in 1998.

- Prosecuting <u>Attorney Robert Agacinski</u> spent twenty-seven years in the Wayne County Prosecutor's Office, before appointment to lead investigator for Michigan's Attorney Grievance Commission in 2000. In May of 2014 he was fired. Agacinski initiated a lawsuit alleging wrongful termination against Michigan Supreme Court Chief Justice Robert Young. In May of 2016 Agacinsky's lawsuit was dismissed.

- <u>Detroit Police Officer John Woodington</u> died of a massive heart attack in November of 2008.

- <u>Medical Examiner Marilee Frazer</u> died of kidney failure in 2004 at the age of fifty, after obtaining a law degree.

- <u>Detroit Police Officer William "Tony" Brantley</u> is retired from police work and lives in Northwest Detroit.

- <u>Detroit Police Officer Bernard Brantley</u> left the Detroit Police Department in 1995 and is now a Commission Investigator with the Board of Police for the City of Lansing, Michigan.

- <u>Donnie Carlton</u> was incarcerated for manslaughter on April 6, 1987 and sentenced to a minimum of ten years. He moved to Virginia upon release, then Pennsylvania.

• Detroit Police Officer Mark Bando retired from the Detroit Police Department in 1999 after twenty-five years of service. He has written eight books on World War II and other military conflicts and is involved with his ninth manuscript. He lost his only son on June 12, 2016 in the deadliest mass shooting in U.S. history in Orlando. He still resides in Michigan.

• Detroit Police Detective Landeros ran unsuccessfully for public office in Michigan. She experienced a serious injury twenty-three years ago and lived with her daughter until the time of her death on December 22, 2019. I flew back to Detroit to attend her funeral in January of 2020.

• Commander Gil Hill retired from police work in 1989 and became president of the Detroit City Council in 1991. In 1994 he appeared once more as Inspector Todd in *Beverly Hills Cop III*. Hill ran unsuccessfully for Mayor of Detroit against Kwame Kilpatrick in 2001. He passed away on March 5, 2016, from pneumonia at the age of eighty-four at Mt. Sinai Hospital. Sadly, Gill Hill died under a cloud of suspicion of bribery and obstruction of justice spearheaded by the FBI.

• Ray Danford, Sr. passed away on Valentine's Day, 2012.

• Gladys Canty died of heart failure on March 11, 1995, at St. John's Hospital in Detroit age of eighty-seven. Her funeral took place in the same facility as her only son. She was laid to rest between her husband and son.

-    <u>My father</u> died during the preparation of this manuscript from sudden heart failure weeks short of his eighty-ninth birthday. He was supportive of my efforts to write this book. He was the gold standard of men. I miss you terribly, Dad.

-    <u>My mother</u> passed away in March of 2017 from complications of a stroke. She contributed to this manuscript through her own words. She was a success in every way and rose above despicable circumstances in her childhood. I admire and love you, Mom. You will always be missed. I think of you whenever I see birds in my garden, as you always loved them.

-    <u>Frank McMaster's</u> whereabouts are unknown.

-    <u>Aaron L. Rutledge</u>, Ph.D. moved to Florida in 1988 and died of leukemia on May 23, 1989. He was seventy, with so much left to contribute.

-    <u>John "Lucky" Carl Fry</u> died in Jackson Prison on September 15, 1995 (the same year as Mrs. Canty) of Hepatitis C after serving a portion of his life sentence. As Lt. Doug Topolski, DPD, Retired, said, "He was paroled to the hereafter." Fry was forty-nine.

-    <u>Dawn</u> <u>Marie Spens</u> is alive and well and in her fifties. Spens met all conditions of her probation—and *then* some. She earned a degree in accounting and a career path in finance. She works for an international automotive supplier and lives in southeast Michigan. Her appearance no longer hints at her sordid past. She has married twice. For the sake of her husband and children, I choose not to disclose additional facts.

Tragically, the young, missing woman from Dearborn, Michigan, Brenna Machus, was laid to rest after the discovery of her body in an open field near a noisy freeway in a suburb of Detroit in July of 2013. She was tossed aside as if she were garbage, as if she was unwanted and faceless. She was a delicate twenty-year-old who loved soccer, music, the color pink, animals and her family. Her traumatized parents were summoned to identify her at the dreaded medical examiner building. They also attended the first-degree murder trial at the Frank Murphy Hall of Justice where her attacker was found guilty and sentenced to mandatory life in prison without parole on December 11. He had the same fate on the same date in the same place that awaited John Fry twenty-eight years earlier. Or so it seemed. Brenna's attacker spent his days filing petitions to reverse his sentence. Unlike Fry, it paid off. In 2016 his conviction was overturned on a technicality, despite physical evidence linking him to the abduction/murder.

# EPILOGUE

I did not know, until the late afternoon of April 9, 2014, that life had set me up for a one-two punch. That day I stumbled and broke my right arm while climbing a steep hill for a photograph. The ground was so soft and the distance so near, the fall should not have even left a bruise. Within twenty-four hours a titanium rod replaced my disintegrated humorous, and a secondary fracture was identified in my spine. A diagnosis of cancer was documented. There is treatment, but no cure. I underwent the usual trilogy of slash-burn-poison with the addition of an autologous stem cell transplant. I think of my illness as a junkyard dog: caged, but always trying to escape. It's now a waiting game.

Cancer has taught me to face mortality. It's not exactly in my face, so near I cannot see anything else, but it does offer vivid depth perception. While this illness has been a distraction, an invisible weight and caused anxious hours, financial loss and sleepless nights for my family, it has not silenced hope nor erased treasured memories.

Once again I have been lucky to be surrounded with experts to guide me. Cancer affirmed my longstanding belief of the importance of taking advantage of every day and letting go of things impossible to change. Being grateful is a powerful tool, and so is a connection with others. I live in the present because no one is promised tomorrow.